Executive's Guide to
Web Services

T0324973

Executive's Guide to
Web Services

ERIC A. MARKS
MARK J. WERRELL

WILEY

John Wiley & Sons, Inc.

For general information on our other products and services, or technical support,
please contact our Customer Care Department within the United States at 800-
762-2974, outside the United States at 317-572-3993 or fax 317-572-4002.

Wiley also publishes its books in a variety of electronic formats. Some content that
appears in print may not be available in electronic books.

For more information about Wiley products, visit our Web site at www.wiley.com.

Library of Congress Cataloging-in-Publication Data:
Marks, Eric A.
    Executive's guide to web services / Eric A. Marks, Mark Werrell.
        p. cm.
Includes index.
    ISBN 0-471-26652-3
    1.   Business enterprises—Computer networks—Management. 2.
Information technology—Management. 3. Internet programming. 4.   World
Wide Web. I. Werrell, Mark. II. Title.
    HD30.37.M3643 2003
    658'.054678—dc21

                                                    2003001693

10   9   8   7   6   5   4   3   2   1

For my mother, Marie I. Marks. Thank you for everything.

—Eric A. Marks

For my wife, Jadwiga, and my mother and father, Vicky and Mike.

Your love and support make all things possible.

—Mark J. Werrell

contents

preface

"The irony is that most disruptions create a net growth in the economy. By nature, disruptive innovations start new markets and attract new customers."

—Clark Gilbert & Joseph L. Bower,
"Disruptive Change," *Harvard Business Review,* May 2002

WHO DARES WINS

The phrase *"Who Dares Wins"* is the motto of the Special Air Services (SAS), a unit of the British Army—very similar, in many respects, to the U.S. Navy Seals. In the context of Web services, those business leaders *who dare* to be early adopters, those that take the initial plunge, will undoubtedly be the first to truly leverage the strategic and competitive advantages that Web services can deliver—in other words, those that *win*!

Web services are rapidly evolving from an over-hyped vision of *just-in-time* system integration to a set of standards and technologies that can be used to solve real-world business problems today. The challenge for most of us is how to distinguish the hype from the reality, to identify the real opportunities for the application of Web services, and to create an achievable plan that can rapidly deliver business value. In the *Executive's Guide to Web Services,* we have sought to remove the hype surrounding Web services, to navigate a path through the maze of standards and acronyms and to identify real opportunities to leverage Web services for business value and competitive advantage, both today and in the coming months and years.

Today, the reality is that the adoption and use of Web services is not an option, but rather a necessity. Web services are fundamentally changing the way in which information technology is used, both within the enterprise and across organizational boundaries. They are the foundation from which the World Wide Web is evolving, propelling us into an era in which the Internet is truly *the* de facto platform over which businesses operate. A decision to ignore or shun the business potential of Web services will likely imperil an organization's market position, and even its viability, as market fundamentals begin to shift.

INTENDED AUDIENCE

The *Executive's Guide to Web Services* targets a diverse group of potential readers. This book *is not* meant to be a technical reference, and therefore does not explain the details of programming Web services. It *is*, however, a business book that provides a Web services primer, focusing on the application of Web services for the creation of business value and competitive advantage. The primary readers of this book will likely fall into the following categories:

- *"C-Level" and Senior Executives*—Those executives and business leaders who need to understand the strategic implications of Web services and how they might be used to create business value, lower cost structures, enable entry into new markets, and allow access to new customers and suppliers.
- *Business and IT Managers*—Those business and IT managers with divisional or Line of Business (LOB) responsibility who need to understand how Web services can be used to drive greater operational efficiency and identify new sources of competitive advantage.
- *Business and IT Practitioners*—Those business and IT professionals who will be asked to design, build, and implement Web services solutions and need to determine if, where, and when to use Web services to deliver the right solutions in support of the business strategy.

This book is essential reading for all executives, managers, and practitioners who want or need to gain an understanding of how this nascent technology will imminently change the global competitive landscape—providing all the information that business leaders need to keep up to speed with this rapidly emerging technology.

CHAPTER OUTLINE AND USAGE

To enable both technical and non-technical executives to truly understand Web services and appreciate their full potential, we begin the book by introducing first principles—laying the foundation upon which to build a deep knowledge and understanding of the opportunities for use of Web services, as well as their real-world application. Thus, the majority of readers will find it beneficial to read this book in chapter order, gaining additional perspectives and understanding as each chapter incrementally builds upon previously covered topics. Those readers who have a solid understanding of the Web services fundamentals might choose to read specific chapters or sections of greatest interest, adding new and previously unexplored perspectives to their current portfolio of understanding and knowledge.

The following outline introduces each chapter and discusses its specific focus, as well as the key topics covered:

- *Chapter 1, "A Day in the Life of a CIO"*—Chapter 1 begins by looking at a hypothetical Fortune 500 organization, following the dialogue between the CEO and CIO as they discuss the organization's current business objectives and jointly explore the potential for use of Web services. The dialogue focuses on the strategic goals of the organization and scenarios for which Web services might be considered as an enabling technology. Subsequent sections explore the business environment and Information Technology (IT) challenges that most organizations have experienced over the past 10 years, providing a backdrop for the use of Web services and their anticipated adoption over the next 3–5 years.

  At its core, this chapter seeks to illustrate that IT in general, and Web services specifically, need to be considered as a strategic asset—an asset that must be leveraged to obtain accurate and timely management information, an asset through which organizations must seek to gain and sustain competitive advantage in their chosen markets. The truth of today's business landscape is that the availability of timely and accurate information is no longer a luxury, a *nice to have,* but rather a *must have* requirement for effective business leadership and management.

- *Chapter 2, "Standards, Concepts, and Terminology"*—This chapter begins by illustrating a real-life example of how Web services are being used today. We examine how Dunn & Bradstreet (D&B) are using Web services and highlight potential benefits and competitive advantage that they might seek to gain. Subsequent sections take the reader step-by-step through the maze of Web services standards, concepts, and terminology.

The Web services standards framework is introduced and used to group the plethora of standards into the categories of *enabling, evolving,* and *emerging.* Each category is examined in detail as the concepts and initial considerations for implementation of Web services are explained.

- *Chapter 3, "Web Services Adoption"*—Chapter 3 details the Web services adoption model, describing the four phases through which adoption will likely progress over the next 3–5 years. We propose that organizations will initially use Web services for internal *integration,* then progress onto *collaboration* and *innovation,* and finally *dominance* as market leaders extend their competitive advantage over rivals. Each phase of the adoption model explores the business landscape and the planning considerations and proposes a plan of action to ensure that you are not left behind by the impending Web services tsunami.

- *Chapter 4, "Strategic Implications of Web Services"*—This chapter discusses the implications of Web services for corporate strategy, business models, and value chains. We suggest that business and IT executives need to collaborate more effectively to incorporate the use of Web services into every aspect of business planning, to infuse Web services into the business model and the value chain. Further, we propose that it is only through the effective alignment of both the business and the IT value chains, that it will be possible to determine how costs can be reduced, how new customers can be reached, and how partners and suppliers can be tied into the value chain to optimize the creation of business value.

- *Chapter 5, "Vertical Market Implications of Web Services"*—In Chapter 5 we examine the implications of Web services from a vertical market perspective. The vertical market in which an organization competes will, to some extent, determine how Web services might be leveraged to achieve internal efficiencies and enhance its ability to interact with suppliers, customers, and trading partners. The manufacturing and financial services verticals are examined in detail with specific attention given to a selection of industries including computer and electronics, automotive, pharmaceutical, and banking, to name a few.

- *Chapter 6, "Where to Begin?"*—This chapter seeks to separate Web services hype from reality and to provide a realistic and pragmatic foundation upon which to evaluate an organization's ability to implement Web services. We detail three steps for the initial implementation of Web services: "Start Preparing," "Select a Pilot," and "Incremental Adoption." These steps will help business and IT executives to better understand where to begin implementing Web services and what pitfalls to avoid.

▨ *Chapter 7, "Architecting for Competitive Advantage"*—In Chapter 7 we present the case for the use of Service-Oriented Architecture (SOA) principles and Web services standards as the lynch-pin for reinvigorating an organization's enterprise architecture. We suggest that an enterprise architecture implemented in this manner can be leveraged to enable greater business flexibility and agility—achieved, in part, through more effective reuse of application and system infrastructure, and more rapid deployment of the systems required to support changes in business direction and strategy.

Beyond the implementation of an SOA we compare and contrast the virtues of Microsoft's .NET and Java 2 Enterprise Edition (J2EE)—the two primary vehicles for implementation of Web services. Many organizations will likely have a heterogeneous environment in which both .NET and J2EE are used. In this section we highlight the rationale for use of either .NET or J2EE, but also discuss the potential for their interoperability enabled through the use of Web services standards.

▨ *Chapter 8, "The Web Services Vendor Landscape"*—In Chapter 8 we map elements of an organization's systems architecture to seven vendor categories. Each category is reviewed in detail to determine the categories and vendors that will likely gain ground as the use of Web services continues to spread. This chapter represents a point-in-time overview of software vendors, summarizing market positioning and capabilities of BEA Systems, IBM's "Services On Demand," Microsoft's ".Net," Oracle's "Oracle Dynamic Services," and Sun Microsystems' "Sun ONE," among others.

▨ *Chapter 9, "The End is Only the Beginning"*—This, the final chapter, provides a retrospective summary of the key topics covered in the book, as well as final thoughts to consider as you embark upon your Web services voyage.

This chapter closes with an epilogue, "One Year Later," in which we revisit the hypothetical Fortune 500 organization introduced in Chapter 1. The dialogue between the CEO and CIO is rejoined as they review the progress that has been made over the past year and discuss the benefits gained through the use of Web services.

During the creation of this book we have continually sought to bring a business driven perspective to the subject of Web services. Our hope is that you will find this to be a valuable guide as you begin to explore the business opportunities that Web services will enable, and that the *Executive's Guide to Web Services* will be a useful addition to your reference library.

CHAPTER 1

A Day in the Life of a CIO

"The last thing one knows—is what to put first."

Blaise Pascal

"While we ponder when to begin, it becomes too late to do."

Quintillan

It is Monday morning . . . Bob Dunston, a Fortune 500 Chief Executive Officer (CEO), is pondering alternative strategies to spur growth for the next five years. He knows that organic growth from ongoing operations can be improved through a number of programs focused on increasing operational efficiency and productivity. Specifically, it will be critical to reduce cycle times in manufacturing, lower inventory levels, improve supply chain visibility, and enhance customer satisfaction and loyalty. Dunston hopes that he can achieve these goals without the need to invest in another huge enterprise application project. "The ERP project was tough," he says to himself. "I'll retire before I do that again!" Of course, his Information Technology (IT) organization is now consumed with the early phases of an enterprise wide Customer Relationship Management (CRM) project, defining the organization's CRM strategy and performing preliminary vendor evaluations.

The current Research and Development (R&D) pipeline of new products is a bit thin, and until a strategic initiative revamping R&D takes hold, the company will need to pursue a Merger and Acquisition (M&A) strategy. Realizing the M&A challenges that most companies face, he knows that any acquired company must integrate into the parent organization quickly and efficiently to achieve the synergies of the acquisition. With a desire to leave the acquired company's R&D and manufacturing operations intact, Dunston knows that it is critical to initially seek financial integration, followed by

1

absorption of the remaining business operations such as information technology, human resources, and other centrally leveraged functions. How can he complete this goal quickly and inexpensively while helping to achieve the intent of his M&A strategy? He ponders this, then he recalls a lunchtime conversation with his Chief Information Officer (CIO), who had explained the potential of some rapidly emerging technologies and standards to help improve their supply chain visibility and reduce inventory, as well as enabling other business initiatives, such as M&A integration and procurement processes. He picks up the phone and punches the CIO's extension, muttering to himself, "Let's see if Sedgewick can help with these problems."

Bill Sedgewick scans his calendar for the week, paying particular attention to the pending close of the quarter. He knows that the company's results, although solid, have slowed for the past four quarters. While he is doing the best he can to support the business units with reliable IT solutions, Sedgewick knows that there is untapped potential in the IT organization to drive better business results. When he arrived at the company three years ago, they hadn't had a CIO for two years. In fact, the previous vice president of IT, who worked for the CFO, was an operations guy who formerly ran the data centers. With the rapid pace of IT change and explosive growth of the Internet, his capabilities had been clearly challenged and the business lost faith in the IT function. The CEO hired Sedgewick to fix that situation, and although Bob Dunston was an old-school manager, he was prepared to listen to new ideas.

The phone rings. Sedgewick answers, pressing the speakerphone button. "Hi, Bob. What's up?"

"Bill, what's your day looking like? I'd like to continue that discussion we were having at lunch the other day about—what were they?—Web services; yes, that was it, right? Web services? I've been kicking some ideas around, and I wanted to get your perspective."

He hears Sedgewick shuffling papers and tapping on his keyboard, the staccato clicking of his keys pouring through the phone line like machine gun bursts. "Bob, I'm slammed this morning, but can we catch up later this afternoon, say around four? Does that work?"

"Yes, Bill, that's fine. It's no big deal, but I wanted to finish that discussion in light of some new ideas I've been mulling over. I'll update you at four, okay?" Dunston says.

"Great, see you then, Bob." Sedgewick hangs up the phone and sits back in his chair, wondering to himself, "Hmmm, what's he up to now?"

Later that day, Sedgewick knocks on Dunston's office door. "Hi, Bob. Are you ready?"

"Bill, yes, come on in. How goes the battle today?" Dunston clears his desk as Sedgewick settles into one of the four chairs surrounding the polished table positioned across the office from the CEO's modest, yet contemporary desk.

"Well, you know, we're fighting the good fight. So, what's up?"

Dunston picks up a legal pad, a pen, and his half-full bottled water and eases into a seat across from Sedgewick. "Bill, I want to get back to that Web services discussion we were having the other day. I want to see if there's a fit for some of your ideas on Web services to some of the strategies and business initiatives I think we'll have to embark on over the next two years. Now, you know I've talked about using a few strategic acquisitions to beef up our R&D and product pipeline, right?"

"Yes, Bob, and I've got a team working on an integration strategy that will allow us to very quickly absorb acquisition targets, first for financial reporting purposes, and then complete integration of all order entry, product and customer master data, fulfillment and logistics processes, as well as other key business processes and functions, too."

Sedgewick's face lights up as he explains this point. He is clearly excited about implementing corporate strategy using his information management organization, processes, and capabilities. "We'll have a draft strategy document to show you early next week."

Dunston nods vigorously, clearly eager to hear this information from Sedgewick. "Good, I like that. We're already evaluating M&A targets based on a rigorous profiling methodology, and we should have a short list ready by the end of the month. I want you involved in the due diligence process as we get that short list pulled together."

"In addition, though, you know we're under continued pressure to drive productivity and improve operating margins. I'm concerned with our core businesses—their organic growth is slowing and margins are deteriorating, so I'm looking at a number of programs to reverse these trends. Inventory management could be improved. Reducing cycle time in manufacturing is important. Ultimately, I'd like to shift a large percentage of our business to a make-to-order model, much like Dell's, versus our current inventory-intensive make-to-stock model."

As Sedgewick rapidly scribbles notes, Dunston continues. "Take inventory management, for example. We need better visibility across our entire supply chain to effectively manage inventory. That means tapping into a bunch of different systems in order to expose inventory information—components and stock, work-in-process, and finished goods—at every point in our supply chain. If we can't see it, we can't measure it and reduce it. I'd like to get your help to make that program happen. You need to talk with John about this, but let him know we've talked and you're to help drive this initiative." Sedgewick nodded. John Bentley was the Chief Operating Officer (COO) responsible for manufacturing, R&D, and overall operations for the company. Bentley was fairly receptive to new ideas if they could drive the metrics of the business, so Sedgewick was confident about defining and implementing the processes and systems to help better manage the company's inventory.

"Anyway, I wanted to pick up our discussion from lunch last week to see if there might be a way to use your ideas about Web services to help implement these initiatives. You were pretty bullish on the whole Web services thing, so let's continue with that for a bit." Dunston leaned back in his chair and looked expectantly at Sedgewick, waiting for him to begin.

Sedgewick decides to recap their previous discussion and then apply it to these newly articulated business strategies.

"Bob, you remember how I described what Web services are, right? The definition I like best is one I've synthesized from all the trade rags I've been reading. Here's my definition of Web services. Web services are 'loosely coupled, self-describing services that are accessed programmatically across a distributed network and exchange data [or information with one another] using vendor, platform and language-neutral protocols.' They are software modules or applications that are designed to be run across Intranets or the Internet using the underlying protocols that the World Wide Web is based upon today."

Dunston leans in with interest. "So, give me an example, Sedgewick."

"Well," Sedgewick replies, "think of when you said you wanted to see inventory information—let's say work-in-process inventory. In order to do that, you would need information from multiple locations from multiple Manufacturing Execution Systems (MES) and multiple Enterprise Resources Planning (ERP) systems, right?"

"Yes, and it's a pain in the neck to do that, right?" Dunston half asks and half states.

"It is and it isn't," replies Sedgewick. "These days, you would typically use tools such as Enterprise Application Integration (EAI) that specialize in tying disparate systems together. There are a bunch of products that do this today, and they vary in what they do and how they do it. They can be expensive, and require adapters or interfaces to tie into back-end systems and extract information in the manner in which it is desired. It depends on the business need that drives the use of the tool."

Sedgewick continues, "Now, let's suppose you want to get inventory information from the manufacturing execution systems and ERP systems in three different plants in three different geographies to update an inventory management portal." Sedgewick stands up and walks to the whiteboard, unwrapping a Snickers bar while he uncaps a dry erase marker. He draws a blue box to represent headquarters and three additional blue boxes to represent the international manufacturing sites. "We have a portal running here at headquarters, and we are populating the portal with real-time inventory updates from the plants. That means we have to gather information from the ERP system at each plant. SAP in this plant, JD Edwards for this plant, and Oracle Applications for this plant. It's a pretty typical scenario for many organizations."

Sedgewick pauses, exchanging the blue marker for a red marker. He draws red lines from each of the blue plant boxes, connecting them to the headquarters box. "Now," Sedgewick continues, assuming the instructional tone of a college professor, "updating the headquarters inventory management portal can take place in a number of ways. For example, there could be a real-time connection from the portal application, over our internal network, tapping directly into each ERP system. Beyond that, we could add logic to push information from the ERP systems, only processing updates if there has been a change, versus pulling all the inventory information and updating the portal application regardless of whether it has changed or not."

"Solving this problem with EAI software is pretty typical, and it works. The only problem is that these point-to-point interfaces can be cumbersome to maintain, and EAI software can be expensive to purchase, install, and maintain."

Dunston's face wrinkles as the word "expensive" enters the conversation, but he doesn't say anything. Sedgewick, noting the change of expression, quickly responds. "That's why Web services are such an exciting and timely technology, Bob."

"Theoretically, Web services can eliminate the integration problem that we would use EAI software for, and it's ideally suited to loosely coupled interfaces between applications or business processes, much like the inventory portal problem we are discussing." Sedgwick walks to the whiteboard again. "You see, these red lines represent the connections we would build using the EAI software, and these processes would remain in place to pull inventory data from the targeted ERP systems on a periodic basis, either polling them or being updated as inventory information changes. EAI implementations are fine, but they have some limitations. There are platform and version issues to contend with, such as HP's Unix, IBM's Unix, and Sun's Unix versus Microsoft Windows NT, all versus Linux—the OpenSource version of Unix. Then, you have the application software itself and the task of making sure that the versions of software are the same, or at least can be accessed using the same EAI software and adapters. And, in many cases, the ERP software has been customized such that it really isn't the standard functionality the vendor originally offered. Web services offer a better way to make applications interoperate using Internet protocols and emerging Web services standards."

Exchanging the red marker for a green one, Sedgewick draws small green boxes inside each of the blue boxes on the board. "Now, with a Web services approach to this problem, we would build small, modular applications that perform simple computing tasks—for example, retrieving inventory updates from ERP systems." Pointing to the little green boxes, Sedgewick continues. "Each of these little applications are Web services, written in Java or C/C++—it really doesn't matter. In addition to the main application functionality, which is simply to get inventory records from the ERP system or database, they have some eXtensible Markup Language (XML) code added to them."

At the mention of these acronyms, Dunston's face brightens because he has read about XML and Web services in the *Harvard Business Review*, so at least he understands some of it. Dunston quipped, "You mean, expensive markup language, don't you?"

"Yeah, right," chuckles Sedgewick as he proceeds. "The XML code that I am referring to does two simple things: It has a SOAP protocol layer, which is Simple Object Access Protocol. The SOAP protocol is a messaging standard to format messages between Web services consumers and producers. SOAP specifies the message envelope, the header, and the message body—all in XML. This is how a consumer or user of a Web service and the producer of a Web service communicate via Internet protocols, typically HTTP."

Dunston furiously scribbles notes as Sedgewick describes these primary Web services standards for messaging. Sedgewick watches Dunston's facial expression as he continues, making sure that there is no confusion or boredom in his eyes. "The other piece of XML code that is added is known as Web Services Description Language (WSDL). This XML-based standard describes how a Web service is accessed and what its inputs and outputs are. WSDL provides the interface to the Web service so it can be used programmatically by other Web services without ever needing human intervention."

"What this all means," says Sedgewick, "is that these software components are designed to work together, over the Internet, or in this specific case over our corporate intranet, to gather inventory information from three different systems and aggregate it in the inventory portal. Using Web services in this way can help us integrate legacy information systems by exposing important business information using standards such as XML, SOAP, and WSDL—as opposed to often expensive EAI tools and proprietary and inflexible integration techniques."

"Will our integration expenses go down with Web services?" Dunston asks. His inquiry draws a quick grin from Sedgewick.

"It's conceivable that over time, the effort and expense associated with internal systems integration will be reduced significantly as Web services are used to expose information from proprietary business systems for use by other business applications. Web services could reduce or eliminate the need for EAI tools because Web services are based on standard Internet protocols and XML. As more and more Web services are made available, initially within organizations and eventually publicly via shared Universal Description, Discovery, and Integration (UDDI) registries, the need for specialized integration software will decline."

Dunston leans back in his chair and folds his hands behind his head. "Okay, Bill, you've explained what Web services are—at a high level, I'm assuming—and you've said they can reduce the amount we spend integrating systems together within the organization. I understand that. But I can't imagine that's where all the benefits of Web services will be realized. There has to be more to it than that."

Sedgewick, almost anticipating this question, jumps back up to the whiteboard—again with a marker in hand. "You're right, Bob—there is."

"We've talked about doing some acquisitions to fill the R&D pipeline, right?"

Dunston nods, answering, "Yes, that's right."

"So think about the inventory update example I started with. You have these small, distributed applications that we can assemble together, via Web services standards and Internet protocols, to retrieve inventory information from proprietary ERP systems running on distinct hardware and operating systems. This entire process is running over our intranet."

"Okay, so say we buy a company. What's the first thing we have to do?"

"Integrate the financials," Dunston quickly replies. He had orchestrated multiple acquisitions during his career and knew the playbook by heart. "Integrate financials first, then rationalize and consolidate product families and customers into a single view of the business."

"Right," replies Sedgewick. "And one potential way to do that is to use Web services to tap into the acquired organization's financial reporting systems to aggregate their financials and report them back to us here at corporate."

Dunston nods vigorously. "But wouldn't that mean using Web services across the internet? Aren't there security issues still?"

Sedgewick responds with marker in hand, "Well, from an IT perspective, one of the first things we'd do is dismantle the acquired firm's firewall and bring them onto our private network as soon as the deal closes. So, really this is similar to the internal integration example. Nonetheless, it offers significant benefit in quickly integrating an acquired company into the operations of a parent company, regardless of the IT infrastructure or the application portfolio choices of the acquired firm."

"The interesting and perhaps most elegant part of this approach is repurposing of the Web services used for the M&A integration for other acquisitions and internal integration needs. That's a real benefit of Web services—the ability to reuse services because they are open, standards-based and flexible as opposed to being rigid, monolithic software applications with proprietary interfaces."

Sedgewick, looking pleased with himself, sits down across from Dunston and finally puts the marker down on the table as Dunston finished writing a few more notes in his legal pad. "So, based on our discussion, what would you suggest we do to get started here? Are there some things we should begin doing right away, as well as planning for the future?"

Sedgewick promptly replies. "First, I'd like to get some of my core team educated about Web services, and I also suggest we arrange a briefing for all of the executive team as well. That will be important so we're all speaking the same language about Web services and their potential. Next, we can begin prioritizing the list of business and technology initiatives you're considering for next year and see where we can drive their completion faster with Web services and realize the business benefits more quickly."

Dunston tilts his head back and looks up at the ceiling. "What about the M&A integration issue? I'd like to begin working on that process as well—perhaps putting some kind of a specification or architecture together describing how we can use Web services to shorten the integration time of an acquisition." Sedgewick nodded his agreement.

"Okay, we'll put together a briefing describing how we might streamline the systems integration component of the M&A process, what we would need to begin developing a Web services framework to achieve it, and when it can be tested and ready. We can fine-tune it once we begin the due diligence process."

Satisfied, Dunston finished taking notes. "Good. Let's fast-track the executive briefing and get your team trained, and I'll have a standing agenda item every two weeks at our staff meetings to discuss how these Web services initiatives are progressing. Let me know what resources you need."

The meeting ended, and Sedgewick exited Dunston's office—bidding him goodbye as he walked out. Both executives are thinking the same thought as they part: "Web services are going to have a significant impact on the way we do business! We'd better make sure that we're ready to take the Web services initiative before our competitors do."

Both Dunston and Sedgewick are correct. Web services will have a significant impact on the way they do business in the coming years. Arising from the dust of the dot-com boom and bust, Web services are perhaps what the Internet should have been originally. While we are still studying the business lessons of the first Internet wave, one thing is clear: Technology does not stand still, even though business conditions might be difficult. Once the technological genie escapes from the bottle, the possibilities that are unleashed are endless.

Web services will change the way that organizations locate, research, assemble, test, and deploy software to solve business problems, as well as how they tackle new market opportunities. Web services will have a profound impact on the way in which software companies build, sell, and deliver software to their customers. Web services will enable the traditional IT organization to truly evolve into a strategic business asset, no longer relegated to the status of a support organization. The corporate computing model will change, and the management skills required to navigate these changes will be as much business and strategy as they are technology.

A BRIEF RECAP: THE PAST 10 YEARS

During the dot-com bust of the past two years, something amazing occurred. While the business world watched dot-com after dot-com fold, and the luster of e-Business and the Internet steadily dulled, the technology visionaries were hard at work. The business world was under attack on a number of fronts, including the economic slump, the technology hangover from e-Business spending, and rapidly changing business conditions. Add the economic recession and the financial scrutiny caused by Enron's stunning collapse, as well as the failures of venerable organizations such as K-Mart and Global Crossing, and you have the makings of trouble.

The business issues facing organizations over the past few years have been considerable. Between year 2000 preparations, then the tremendous investment in e-Business followed by the economic slump of the past two years, organizations have faced travail upon travail. Of course, the world of IT has also been pressed. Organizations have invested millions in ERP platforms, CRM solutions, and e-Business initiatives. They have implemented the supporting applications and infrastructure to drive their businesses via the Web, such as content management, enterprise portals, data warehousing, and analytics solutions. Organizations have spent hundreds of millions of dollars on complex IT solutions—solutions that often resulted in application silos that are massively inflexible and extremely difficult and costly to implement. Many organizations spent tens of millions of dollars and several years installing ERP solutions, only to find that by the time they were through, their business had changed—both internally as well as externally. The monolithic application footprint and rigid architectures of ERP solutions have created a host of copycat organizations that have implemented the same solutions in the same industries. This resulted in lost competitive advantage and uniqueness of business models. It resulted in an inability to change business processes as well as information systems to meet emerging needs. ERP implementations resulted in a business architecture based on internal operations versus interactions with customers and suppliers. The difficulty of integrating ERP-centric backbones with other organizations' ERP backbones persists and has created a substantial market for Business to Business (B2B) integration tools such as Enterprise Application Integration (EAI), messaging software, and other middleware solutions.

The Internet exposed this problem even more as organizations attempted to link their businesses and systems in support of new initiatives such as collaboration, partner relationship management, product life cycle management, and other emerging business needs. Business strategies such as M&As drove a need to rapidly integrate an acquired organization's business processes and IT systems. Issues such as master data management, managing customer and product information, and eliminating redundant systems have plagued businesses in M&A mode. Productivity gains were sought through initiatives such as employee self-service and enterprise portals, which made it easier to access relevant information by role and needs. B2B collaboration has to date been inhibited by expensive integration efforts, inflexible enterprise business applications, and the inability to extend and/or augment existing business applications to accomplish new business functions as business needs change.

The Enterprise Application Phenomenon

The enterprise application phenomenon is the culmination of the client-server era of computing. Client-server computing based on the three-tier, then the n-tier architecture, completely revolutionized computing as it was known in the early 1990s. Client-server computing models broke the paradigm of large centralized mainframes serving masses of dumb terminals based on the dramatic rise of the Personal Computer (PC) in corporate and home computing. Client-server computing hailed the introduction of the distributed computing model, where applications could be built and deployed more efficiently and targeted to distinct business audiences, departments, and end users, as opposed to being driven by internal IT organizations that were the traditional buyers of computer applications. The client-server architecture created new "markets" for software vendors to sell to by virtue of the increasing development of departmental and functional applications that solved targeted business problems, yet interacted with other functional applications or modules from the same vendors. SAP R/3 arguably represents the pinnacle of client-server success. This ERP solution is the industry's leading business computing platform, followed by offerings from Oracle, PeopleSoft, and a host of others. SAP's dominance in the ERP arena can be explained by a number of factors, but one surely is that it was among the first business application suites to be built on a client-server architecture. When SAP R/2, the mainframe version, was replaced by its R/3 client-server release, SAP took off and never looked back. SAP rolled over all the competitors in the ERP space and established itself as a major force. The Big 5 consulting firms were profiting handsomely from SAP implementation services, and analyst organizations were raking in fees for research, vendor selection, and analysis. The SAP ecosystem was rich with revenue opportunities that supported or complemented the SAP ERP solution. PeopleSoft, which was also known for its client-server architecture in the human resources arena, attempted to challenge SAP by acquiring other vendors and rapidly expanding its application footprint to additional functions and departments of the business enterprise. SAP had an advantage in functional breadth, however, and the battle was won before it began.

The point of this story is that client-server computing brought with it a number of changes in the way that applications were developed, sold, and implemented by software vendors and consumed by corporate users. The client-server architecture created a wave of change across the entire information technology value chain, threatening the incumbents and embracing new entrants who had a new way, a better way, for computing to be performed. The PC was clearly one of the drivers of the client-server wave, as well as the desire to break the traditional highly centralized mainframe computing model. The client-server computing paradigm for the first time invited end users into the corporate computing dialog, and extended the reach of business software from the IT department to all business departments. Client-server computing, based on the widespread penetration of PCs into homes around the world, enabled users to do more with technology.

Today, Web services are about to create a new wave of change. This new engine of change is relatively simple: The catalyst for Web services is agreement. At its foundation is agreement on the adoption of three fundamental standards for communicating between computer systems: TCP/IP, HTTP, and XML. TCP/IP, or Transmission Control Protocol/Internet Protocol, Hypertext Transport Protocol, and Extensible Markup Language are the pervasive standards for computing that emerged from the Internet revolution. The Internet capped the client-server era of computing by making computing pervasive to all users, in organizations, and in homes. The Internet extended the reach of computing into virtually all aspects of the human experience, from CEOs of multinational conglomerates to home users e-mailing vacation pictures to relatives. Much as the Internet broke the communication and information bottleneck for information consumers of the client-server computing model, Web services will break the communication and information bottleneck for business enterprises.

Web services will take B2B communication to new levels. The Internet enabled personal collaboration via e-mail and instant messaging tools; Web services will enable corporate collaboration via loosely coupled applications across organizational boundaries. Web services will enable much more than information exchange between organizations based on dedicated interfaces at the system level. Web services will enable businesses to interoperate at the business process level in dynamic and emergent ways as new processes arise in response to changing business conditions and changing corporate priorities.

Rise of the Wintel Duopoly

While client-server computing rode the PC-driven Wintel (Microsoft Windows operating system and Intel microprocessor) wave, the Internet began exposing this architectural paradigm's weaknesses. Web browsers removed application-specific user interfaces as the method of choice for navigating applications and content, and the rapid adoption of the Web meant that desktop computing wasn't really what users wanted. PCs were not used as computing devices; they were used as communication devices. As mobile computing has increased in popularity, and as the inherent difficulties in business-to-business integration have been realized, a new paradigm of computing is being hailed as the solution. Web services are here.

The inevitable saturation of homes with PCs, combined with the rapid rise of wireless devices, has huge implications for Microsoft and for Intel. First, slowing license revenue from Windows and related desktop software is forcing Microsoft into new ways of revenue and profit creation, such as set top boxes and gaming devices. Microsoft's core business of desktop operating systems and desktop software will be increasingly threatened as computing devices move away from the desk and become increasingly mobile. Slowing sales of perpetual software licenses has Microsoft concocting new ways to drive revenue growth, and one of those ways spells the end to these licensing arrangements. Some see a future in which software is sold as services through subscription fees. Microsoft is already considering a rent-for-use model for Microsoft Office, much like subscribing to cellular service and cable television. ERP vendors might consider licensing modules on a metered, per-click basis as opposed to licensing on a per seat basis. Some speculate that Web services will help to revive the flagging Application Service Provider (ASP) market and perhaps make business applications more affordable for all organizations, especially those in the mid-market that can not expend the millions of dollars required for a typical ERP implementation.

Web services are perceived by some skeptics as an attempt by Microsoft and other large enterprise software platform vendors to halt eroding license revenues by providing software as services. This action will help stave off declining revenue from slowing PC sales and the shift from desktop computing toward mobile computing. Others see IBM's Web services thrust as a way for it to maintain hardware and services revenue by positioning itself as the software and platform vendor of choice, much as Sun Microsystems was perceived as the Internet platform of choice.

While there might be some truth in these ulterior motives by some platform vendors, Web services are farther reaching than that—and the benefits are far too compelling to ignore. The fact that all major software vendors have embraced the standards of Web services, and are racing to develop tools and solutions to facilitate the adoption of Web services, shows how the move toward Web services is beyond the span of control of any single software vendor.

BUSINESS VALUE FROM WEB SERVICES

Web services will drive new levels of collaboration between companies in existing value chains as well as enable new relationships with trading partners in emerging value chains. This situation will occur because of the friction-reducing promise of Web services, making it easier to perform B2B integration at the business process level. The last several years have witnessed the rise of middleware solutions to solve the problems of tying business systems together, to perform transactions and information exchange across organizational boundaries. Enterprise Application Integration (EAI) tools emerged, messaging-oriented middleware took hold, and a host of similar solutions addressed the need to make application portfolios work together within the organization and across organizational boundaries. Middleware solutions, and now Web services, present the opportunity to solve a number of broad business and technology issues, including the following:

- Reintroduce the business flexibility that Enterprise Resources Planning (ERP) and other large, enterprise applications removed through rigid business process definition and proprietary application interfaces.
- End the debate about IT alignment by allowing the idea of Just-In-Time (JIT), or the implementation of new applications as the business needs them without the implementation and integration lag that accompanies large, enterprise software implementations.
- Extend CRM, ERP, and other large, monolithic software applications to add new business functions or capabilities in response to changing business needs.
- Provide connections to other trading partners for collaborative processes such as forecasting and supply chain planning, transaction management, and others.
- Help organizations manage change given their existing reliance on large, legacy systems and change-resistant business processes.

* Revolutionize the corporate computing model for software-producing companies, for software-consuming companies, for hardware and infrastructure companies, and for services companies.

Specifically, Web services promise to deliver the following high-level benefits to organizations:

* Support application integration internally and externally, across the firewall.
* Provide easier B2B collaboration between business partners.
* Transition software deployment models from big-bang, high-footprint implementations to just-in-time applications that are appropriate to the business challenge being addressed. This is the beginning of the idea of Just-in-Time Information Technology based on Web services. Software rental models and grid computing are simply specific subsets of the idea of JIT IT.
* Reduce costs of software procurement, deployment, and integration.
* Increase business and technology agility by deploying loosely coupled business applications versus monolithic enterprise applications.

Why Was the Internet Not Sufficient?

One question about the Internet is why it was not robust enough for true B2B collaboration, as well as for complex processes that span multiple Web sites or multiple organizations for Web transactions. The Internet rapidly evolved for B2B transactions, yet it fell short for complex collaboration between organizations due to the following issues:

* Lack of standards for B2B integration and B2B automation
* Manual searching of Web content by browsers versus registry-based applications that find one another and auto-invoke (this result is a future but possible scenario)
* Emerging standards such as XML have already become fragmented, diminishing their ability to create consensus among industry solution providers and consumers
* Internally-focused application procurement and deployment models

Of all these, the most difficult to overcome is probably the internal IT architectural models of organizations. Internally focused application procurement and deployment models have to date dominated the IT architecture of organizations, in contrast to collaboration-centric application models. Most IT architectures of today's corporations are based on a single-company view of their own internal operations. That is not necessarily bad or wrong. It merely means that an organization's investment in its IT architecture—its infrastructure, transaction systems, and application portfolio—has been focused on internal operations and efficiencies, not on interacting with trading partners and customers. In various industry value chains, for example, the application portfolio of the dominant firm in the value chain exerts a strong influence on how its trading partners interact, both with the dominant company as well as among the trading partners. This dominant application influence often forces trading partners to embrace the nuances of that architecture and the interfaces to the ERP applications. In an SAP-centric extended enterprise, trading partners will have to interface to SAP to exchange forecasts, purchase orders, and other B2B transactions.

However, in today's business world, collaboration with trading partners is fast becoming the rule, not the exception. Companies understand that significant benefits can be realized through better cooperation and information sharing with their customers and suppliers. Their existing application portfolios, however, are not built for collaboration across the firewall with outside agencies. Web services offer a way to bridge the gap and overcome the legacy of internally-focused IT architectures and application portfolios.

Business Process Collaboration

Web services will enable business collaboration at the process level. Process-level collaboration requires new software architected for collaboration across corporate firewalls. Web services will be the foundation for creating these new applications. Business Process Collaboration (BPC), augmented by electronic means over the Internet, has wide-reaching implications for the ways in which business will be performed. Many organizations have not had the discipline or desire to focus on business processes as a legitimate pursuit, largely as a result of the ongoing backlash against the business process re-engineering phenomenon of the 1980s. However, as the word "collaboration" has entered the mainstream dialog of business and IT professionals, the sharp edge of re-engineering has been dulled. Collaboration as a discipline is on the rise as the Internet continues to thread its way into organizations around the world.

We can simply define collaboration as cooperation to achieve a particular goal or goals. Collaboration involves teaming, sometimes with competitors, to achieve a higher, shared purpose. This is sometimes called co-opetition, which refers to the periodic vacillation between competing with organizations and cooperating with organizations based on market dynamics, competitive pressures, or other business forces. Collaboration has been around in various forms for many years, including incipient technology implementations such as Electronic Data Interchange (EDI), point-to-point interfaces between application systems, and other means. What is different is that the Internet has opened the door for organizations to exchange information electronically over a set of agreed-upon standards, collectively known as the Internet standards of TCP/IP, HTTP, and XML. The Internet altered the cost structure of collaboration for organizations because of the global acceptance of these technology standards. EDI has been around for years, for the most part implemented by large corporations that could afford to install the technology for inter-organization purchasing processes, forecast sharing, payment and reconciliation of shipments, and more. The Web has changed the cost equation for exchanging business information between firms, which means the price of entry is now much lower. A rich variety of new solutions are embracing collaboration, or c-commerce as some analysts have dubbed it. Early implementations of collaboration demonstrated the potential—yet they also illuminated the shortcomings of existing Web technologies and standards to support this rapidly emerging space. But the act of collaborating with another organization, not to mention many organizations, requires new ways of connecting businesses together. Collaboration is far more than the static exchange of e-mail or spreadsheets. It is interactive. It is live, or real time (or should be as required by the business process being driven by collaboration). Business process collaboration necessitates more than limited information exchange.

The brutal shakeout of dot-coms, further complicated by the economic recession, proved that despite all the glamour of e-Business and technology, there was an obvious problem. The business environment had not really changed for most businesses, and the rules of survival had not changed either. Business models were still stagnant, fixed, and unchanging. IT architectures are still ERP-centric, prone to inflexibility, and very difficult to customize and extend to support emerging business needs. These application strategies lock an organization into a fixed way of conducting internal operations according to the business model of the software vendors. Implementing a typical ERP application requires the adoption of a view of internal operations that substantially complies with that of the software vendor and its other customers. This situation removes opportunities for unique competitive advantage through business process execution and operational excellence.

ERP-centric architectures are based on the architectural philosophy of internal operations efficiency. Building a single view of internal operations based around a centralized database of the organization allows visibility of financial metrics, inventory levels, customer information, orders, and more, all in real-time. This capability is powerful, despite some of the issues that attend these implementations. These issues include, but are not limited to, the following:

* Rigid architectures freeze corporate operations into a fixed, inflexible model
* Complex architecture means changing one module often necessitates changes in many other modules

▪ Large software footprint and module inflexibility result in long, expensive implementation cycles that, when completed, are already outdated

▪ Internal orientation and architecture of ERP systems limits the ability to engage in collaboration with outside trading partners. This situation is primarily due to proprietary application interfaces and business process inflexibility forced onto a business by the ERP architecture

Streamlining internal operations and allowing financial management of an organization's operations was a significant benefit of ERP systems. However, times have changed for all firms. Inward-focused systems and business processes can only deliver limited value in a world dominated by a desire, and more importantly a mandate, to work with other trading partners to accomplish business success. The rapid rise of the Internet exposed the inadequacy of ERP and other enterprise systems to rapidly accommodate new business processes. As new business needs continued to grow, the increased need for agility and new business functionality has outstripped the ERP capabilities of today.

There has been a dramatic shift from the internal focus of ERP systems to collaboration with outside trading partners. This shift from internal operations to collaborative interaction with external trading partners has challenged the business processes and the IT application portfolio of most organizations. The shift to the front for CRM and other e-Business applications has placed an unprecedented demand on IT systems, and the need to securely share internal, potentially sensitive, information will continue to increase. However, as these inter-enterprise collaboration requirements continued to grow, the technology supporting collaboration proliferated. Enterprise application integration and other collaboration products emerged as the next hot space. EAI continues to be an important area, and will serve as one of the critical pathways to Web services because these tools are designed for connecting systems and enterprises across the firewalls.

As you will see from the Web services adoption model—introduced in the following section—pragmatic uses of Web services will carry us for the foreseeable future. As the standards and technology progress, more sophisticated Web services capabilities will emerge.

WEB SERVICES ADOPTION MODEL

Web services, like the Internet during the mid-1990s, will be adopted in phases based on what a company hopes to achieve and how it desires to operate within its chosen markets. It is important to note that there are significant differences that distinguish the adoption of Web services when compared to the rise of the Internet. Firstly, there is widespread agreement on the basic standards of Web services. All major platform providers, software vendors, and professional services organizations are embracing Web services standards. Secondly, Web services hold great promise for the realistic support of complex B2B transactions and processes that span organizational and business boundaries. Web services will be able to fulfill these capabilities primarily due to the broad support within the software industry for the acceptance of Web services standards.

Web services will be adopted in four distinct phases. These phases are based on how Web services will be implemented within organizations, within industries, and across the global business landscape. They are based on how businesses evolve and absorb new capabilities rather than on the use of technology for technology's sake. Web services will initially deliver business value through enablement of information integration and collaboration, followed by increased innovation as new uses of Web services are devised. Finally, the effective use of Web services to enable superior business execution will lead to the separation of market leaders and first movers from the rest of the pack.

The four phases of Web services adoption are:

1. Integration
2. Collaboration
3. Innovation
4. Domination

These four phases of change capture how organizations will enter into the world of Web services, conservatively at first with internal integration projects, and then expanding into inter-organization, cross-firewall implementations with trusted partners, followed by further-reaching implementations with a network of trading partners. As cycles of learning are executed by the first movers, they will begin a wave of rapid innovation with Web services, developing new, industry-shaping and market-making distributed business solutions. These solutions will have the potential to completely reshape the competitive landscape of an industry. As innovation continues, and competitive advantage is extended through faster execution of industry-leading capabilities and strategic execution, these Web services thought leaders will eventually dominate their respective industries. They will demonstrate first-mover advantage. They will be the leading edge organizations that understand the information imperative of competition today—that information-based business models are critical to winning in today's global economy.

Figure 1.1 depicts the evolution of Web services according to the Web Services adoption model.

Integration

•Experimentation with Web services with small, internal integration projects

•SOAP-enablement of legacy applications and ERP, CRM systems

•Fast cycles of learning reach the limits of early Web Services, immature standards, and unprepared IT architectures

•Increase in shared information across the business

Collaboration

•Experimentation with WS outside firewalls

•Increasing interaction with trading partners & customers

•Close trading partners implement Web services to drive shared value

•"External" trading partners begin sharing information to drive industry value chain benefits

Innovation

•Lessons from integration and collaboration applied to new processes and business models

•New distributed WS processes and applications drive business change

•Dramatic business results are achieved as WS are applied in new ways, driving new value propositions

Domination

•First movers begin to assert their dominance over respective markets and industries

•Industry dominance achieved by innovating new business models as well as out-executing competitors

•Web services leaders win through rapid innovation and cycles of learning

•Web services mastery creates new company and industry structures as boundaries are redefined

FIGURE 1.1   Phases of Web services adoption.

Phase 1: Integration

The first phase of Web services adoption will begin with internal system integration projects. The need for internal integration derives from the myriad of information silos created by proprietary enterprise applications implemented to support activities such as financial management (general ledger, accounts payable, accounts receivable), costing systems, order management, procurement, and production scheduling. These enterprise applications are typically large, client-server implementations built with an internal, organization-facing view of the world, and oriented toward internal efficiency and controls.

In their initial deployments of Web services, organizations will write services that expose the functionality locked within enterprise applications and legacy systems, enabling that functionality to be leveraged by other applications or business processes. The integration phase of Web services adoption will prepare organizations for the next phase, collaboration. The lessons learned from applying Web services internally to systems integration and enterprise application integration problems will be leveraged for the benefit of external trading partners in the collaboration phase of Web services adoption.

Phase 2: Collaboration

The collaboration phase of Web services adoption will drive process and operational improvements in many business areas, provided that the integration hurdles can be overcome and that the tools and technologies are mature enough to enable true collaborative behavior. Maturation in the collaboration phase of Web services adoption will prepare organizations for the next phase, innovation. This phase of Web services adoption will spur a new wave of rapid business change, which will largely shape the next wave of Internet expansion worldwide.

Phase 3: Innovation

During the innovation phase of Web services adoption, organizations will devise completely new ways of doing business based around Web services. These firms will leverage what has been learned from internal integration projects and from collaboration projects with outside customers, partners, and suppliers. These organizations will be able to turn these lessons into new business processes and new sources of competitive advantage. They will use Web services as an innovation platform to drive new levels of business performance along multiple dimensions of their value chains.

The innovation phase will spur a wave of new ideas for how business processes can be distributed, organized, and executed across corporate and industry boundaries. With Web services, the notion of industry convergence has a higher probability of realization because of the widespread agreement that it is the right way to conduct business. The innovation phase of Web services adoption will eliminate major roadblocks to the widespread use of Web services to drive new business process innovation and, ultimately, dramatic levels of business execution and performance.

Phase 4: Domination

The domination phase of Web services adoption will be the culmination of the previous three phases: integration, collaboration, and innovation. The domination phase is where the winners are separated from the also-rans, based on their ability to drive superior business value through the use of Web services in Distributed Business Process Execution (DBPE).

The domination phase will be based on superior performance in business as well as in the use of and innovation in Web services. Dominance will be established by a few organizations in each industry that realized the potential of Web services, both in changing internally the ways in which organizations can operate and outperform their competition using their information technology capabilities.

This introduction to the Web services adoption model shows a very real high-level scenario for how Web services will be deployed by corporations. Chapter 3 explores Web servcies adoption in greater detail.

SUMMARY

Web services are on the rise for many reasons. Some of these reasons are good for businesses, some are good for consumers, some are opportunities for entrepreneurs to create new business paradigms. It is not our intent to over-hype Web services with reckless exuberance. Nor is it our intent to underplay just how this rapidly emerging set of business ideas and technologies might impact our daily lives. We seek the middle ground while striking a compelling tone.

The value chain of information technology promises to shift radically with the emergence of Web services. The emergence of Web services has already created many new companies hoping to tap into this new paradigm, and there will be many more. By the time readers have digested Chapter 8 of this book, "The Web Services Vendor Landscape," which is a brief vendor survey, some of those companies will either have been acquired or will have gone out of business. Welcome to the Darwinian world of emerging technology.

Web services will impact the business world in new, unexpected ways. But before you, as a business executive or IT professional, make up your mind about Web services too quickly, remember one thing: Business benefit will carry the day for Web services, not technology alone. Read on, and think *business value!*

CHAPTER 2

Standards, Concepts, and Terminology

"There is always an incentive for one company to try to move standards, to change standards and leave other companies inoperable, but there's a tremendous incentive for the (World Wide Web) community as a whole to prevent that."

Tim Berners-Lee, *World Wide Web Journal*, Summer 1996

If you have ever seen the film "The Wizard of Oz," you probably remember the line, "Pay no attention to that man behind the curtain!" when Dorothy eventually makes it to the wizard's castle. With all the hype surrounding Web services over recent months, it is easy to feel like the software industry is collectivity asking us to, "Pay no attention to that *reality* behind the *hype!*" It is as though we are expected to blindly believe that Web services are the best thing since sliced bread and the panacea for all computer system ills. Obviously that is not the case.

This chapter takes a close look at what really constitutes a Web service, describes how Web services are defined, and untangles the maze of standards, concepts, and terminology that blurs the actual capabilities that Web services may deliver. The goal of this chapter is to arm the reader with the basic concepts behind Web services and to provide a solid foundation and reference text for later chapters. The Web services arena is plagued by an amazing number of mind-bending and tongue-twisting acronyms that can be very intimidating. Upon completing this chapter, the readers will have an arsenal of acronyms and be able to talk Web services like a pro.

REAL-LIFE WEB SERVICES

Before diving into acronyms and definitions, let us explore a real-life example of how the concepts behind Web services are already being leveraged by Dunn and Bradstreet (D&B) today. D&B provides a range of services to an extensive client base; D&B is best known for its credit-rating services. D&B's credit-rating services are typically used to determine whether a new customer (or perhaps a partner) has a solid financial background and a reliable history of on-time bill payment.

D&B has offered direct system integration to its services for some time, historically using Electronic Data Interchange (EDI). Using EDI, the effort and cost associated with direct integration has been relatively high, often requiring custom integration and testing before a connection can be established. The costs associated with this type of integration are typically very high, and only larger organizations have made the investment required to complete EDI integration. This forced the small and mid-size organizations to rely on e-mail and the telephone as the primary vehicle for requesting credit information from D&B.

In May 2001, D&B introduced the D&B Global Access Toolkit. The toolkit provides D&B clients with the ability to easily integrate real-time credit information into existing applications and decision support systems. The toolkit leverages Web services standards to significantly reduce the cost and effort required to integrate with D&B's services when compared to earlier custom integration efforts.

Strategically, through the implementation of the Global Access Toolkit, D&B has been able to do the following:

- *Open New Market Opportunities*—Lower integration and operating costs allow D&B to offer services at new price points while still maintaining attractive per-transaction profit margins. The combination of lower services costs and simplified service integration will inevitably be appealing to small and mid-level clients that otherwise might not have considered using D&B's services.
- *Create "Stickier" Client Relationships*—By providing the Global Access Toolkit, D&B has significantly reduced the cost for clients to directly connect to its services. Typically, clients that are directly connected to a service are far less likely to swap providers than those who do not have this type of connectivity. In effect, directly linking a client to a service creates a "stickier" relationship. Even improving client retention by a few percentage points can significantly increase revenue and profitability.

▪ *Improve Customer Satisfaction*—By providing real-time credit-rating services, eliminating the turnaround time associated with responding to a phone call or replying to an e-mail, D&B can offer superior service to its clients—enabling them to make critical, time-sensitive business decisions based on reliable, up-to-date information.

This example shows how Web services capabilities are beginning to be used. Consider for a moment whether there are any opportunities in your organization where Web services might be used to create a "stickier" relationship with your customers or partners? Or, perhaps there are opportunities to reduce costs by using Web services, to offer products and services to small and mid-size clients that were not previously economically viable? Hold those thoughts. We will explore them further in later chapters.

WEB SERVICES DEFINED

We all understand the need to continually seek opportunities to improve operational efficiencies, perhaps through better communications or through closer collaboration with partners and suppliers. These pressures, combined with the emergence of open standards, have created an environment in which Web services are poised to become the platform of choice for future application integration projects. Web services deliver the basic building blocks that enable the World Wide Web to evolve to a new level. The Web will no longer be the sole domain of the solitary "Web surfer" flitting from Web page to Web page. Increasingly, we will see the Web being leveraged as a key business tool where computer systems will exchange information with each other via Web services. Early adopters are already are using Web services to reduce the cost of internal system integration. Moreover, a few leading-edge organizations are already taking the first tentative steps toward implementing Web services that operate across the Web, as with the example of D&B's Global Access Toolkit.

Looking beyond the early adoption of Web services for integration and collaboration, it is likely that Web services will have a significant influence on the way in which computer systems are developed and deployed. Similar to the paradigm shift of the early 1990s with the move from monolithic mainframe systems to client-server systems, today we see the start of a new paradigm shift from client-server and distributed systems to service-oriented systems, implemented using Web services. As illustrated in Figure 2.1, the migration from the monolithic systems of the 1970s, through client-server and distributed systems toward service-oriented systems, has progressively seen the following trends:

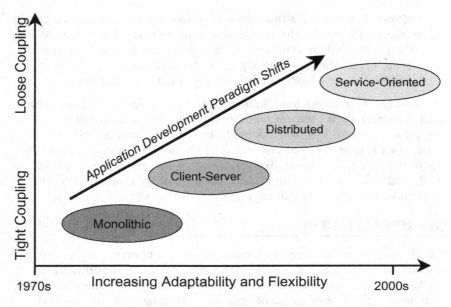

FIGURE 2.1 Shift to service orientation.

- *A Migration to Loosely Coupled Systems*—The mainframe systems of the 1970s were implemented as large blocks of functionality that ran on a single mainframe computer. In contrast, service-oriented systems are implemented as discrete business services that are loosely coupled to other services running of a mix of hardware and software platforms across the organization.
- *Greater Adaptability and Flexibility*—Early mainframe systems used paper tape and punch cards to store data and programs. The use of mainframe processing time was strictly managed and allocated in sequential blocks or batches. In contrast, service-oriented systems (implemented as discrete business services) are interconnected across an organization's computer network, where it is possible to locate and reuse services registered with a central registry or "yellow pages" of services.

Unlike previous architectural paradigms, the move to Web services will not necessitate a "rip 'n' replace" approach. Rather, Web services will encapsulate existing systems and expose functionality as reusable services using Web services standards.

Service-oriented system development, and more specifically Web services, leverage five key principles that, when considered together, define and differentiate Web services from previous application implementation paradigms. The five key principles maintain that Web services are:

1. *Loosely Coupled*—One of the key advantages of Web services is that loosely coupled systems are more flexible and more easily reconfigured—enabling components of a system to be replaced or exchanged with relative ease.

2. *Self-Describing*—The Web Services Description Language (WSDL) is an XML document that describes a Web service's inputs and outputs in a structured manner. The WSDL document enables other software to determine how to invoke the service and determine what results the service will return.

3. *Accessed Programmatically*—Web services do not have a Graphical User Interface (GUI) because they are not designed to be accessed directly through human interaction. Instead, they are invoked by and exchange data with other software applications programmatically using the Simple Object Access Protocol (SOAP).This programmatic access enables a Web service to be incorporated into other software applications, Web sites, or even other Web services.

4. *Network Distributed*—Web services are accessed using Internet protocols and data formats such as TCP/IP, HTTP, and XML. Using these existing protocols and data formats, Web services comply with current company security measures and policies (for example, corporate firewalls). This feature makes it possible for Web services to be deployed and accessed across corporate intranets or the Internet.

5. *Exchange Data Using Vendor, Platform and Language-Neutral Protocols*—This capability is perhaps the most important and compelling aspect of Web services. The ability for a Web service to exchange data in a vendor, platform and language-neutral format is facilitated through broad industry agreement on open standards.

These five defining principles can be combined into a succinct definition of a Web service:

> *"Web Services are loosely coupled, self-describing services that are accessed programmatically across a distributed network, and exchange data using vendor, platform, and language-neutral protocols."*

Fundamentally, the key principles of Web services are enabled by agreement on standards across a broad group of hardware and software organizations. The following sections examine the standards that form the foundation upon which Web services are implemented and discuss why the continued agreement on standards is so important to the realization of business benefit from Web services.

ADOPTION OF STANDARDS

Reflecting about one's experiences over the past few years, an executive might be asking the question, "Why should I invest in Web services, especially when my prior investment in e-Business didn't provide the returns that the software vendors and consultants promised?" That executive might also ask, "Aren't Web services just hype created by the software and services industries to generate additional revenues?" This skepticism is understandable.

In considering these questions, executives should understand the critical difference between previous IT trends and what we are seeing today with the development of Web services. Today, there is a previously unseen level of agreement and collaboration on the development of a core set of standards for system interoperability using Web services. This unprecedented level of collaboration, from the likes of IBM, Microsoft, and BEA—in developing standards to enable and extend Web services— represents an early sign that the software industry is entering a phase of maturation (a phase in which more consistent standards for interoperability will likely become the norm).

When considering this concept, think back to the 1970s with the emergence of the home video recorder. In 1975, Sony introduced the first home video recorder using its Betamax standard, while one year later JVC released the first VHS home video recorder. During the following years, Betamax and VHS fought for market acceptance and dominance. By 1988, the VHS standard held 99% of market share, while Sony held the remaining 1% with Betamax. The economics were no longer viable for Sony, and in late 1988 they dropped the Betamax standard and produced their first VHS video recorder. Today, each manufacturer uses proprietary technologies to implement their range of VHS video recorders, but standards broadly ensure that a tape recorded on one VHS recorder will play on other VHS recorders.

Similar to the way in which proprietary technology is used to build a video recorder, proprietary software can be used to develop a Web service. Again, much as the proprietary technology used to build a VHS recorder is hidden from the user through the use of standards (In this case the standard VHS cassette and the recorded VHS signal), the inner workings of a Web service are also hidden through the use of standards. In this way, it is possible for an organization developing Web services using Microsoft .Net (pronounced "dot net") to interoperate with an organization implementing Web services using Java or other implementation languages. Web services standards provide a level of abstraction that "mask" the underlying programming language, allowing systems to be implemented using a combination of services developed in different programming languages.

Not only do Web services standards make it possible to hide the specifics of the programming language in which a service is developed, but they also make it possible to hide the specifics of the hardware on which the service is implemented—and even the physical location from which the service is being provided.

STANDARDS FRAMEWORK

As discussed, Web services are implemented by using a collection of standards. These standards, when considered together, form what is widely referred to as the "Web services stack." Figure 2.2 illustrates the seven distinct layers of the Web services stack, which should be read from bottom to top.

The Web services stack can be thought of as a set of layered building blocks, each layer supported and enabled by the preceding layers. As illustrated, we have grouped the layers of the stack into three distinct levels— each level indicates a level of maturity for the layers it contains. The three levels are: enabling standards, evolving standards, and emerging standards. These levels represent a framework that can be used to evaluate the maturity of Web services standards today, and can also be used to monitor how Web services standards progress over the medium to long term. Figure 2.3

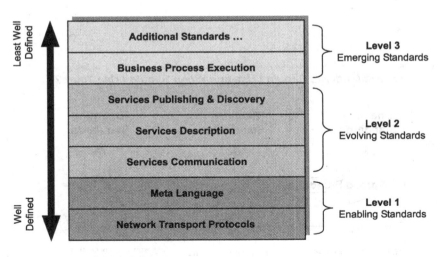

FIGURE 2.2 Web services stack.

illustrates the maturity of Web services standards, from the enabling standards at one end of the spectrum to the emerging standards at the other.

Four characteristics should be considered when evaluating a standard to determine its relative position as enabling, evolving, or emerging. These are described below.

1. *Industry Support*—The number of key industry players that support the standards (for example, IBM, Microsoft, BEA, Sun Microsystems, and so on). Where many key players support a specific standard and there is little infighting and discord, it is likely that a standard will gain acceptance.

2. *Standards Governance*—Accepted governance by a recognized standards organization active in the Web services space. The two key organizations defining Web services standards are the World Wide Web Consortium (W3C) and Organization for the Advancement of Structured Information Standards (OASIS).

3. *Update Frequency*—The frequency at which new versions of a standard are published. Typically, high update frequency indicates an immature standard that is being enhanced to fill gaps in its capabilities.

4. *Competing Standards*—The existence and active promotion of competing standards. If competing standards exist and are being independently promoted by key industry players, it is likely that acceptance

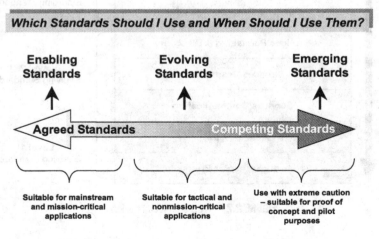

FIGURE 2.3   Spectrum of enabling to emerging standards.

of a single standard will be inhibited. This very situation is occurring around the standards in the "Business Process Execution & Management" layer of the Web services stack, where Sun Microsystems is promoting the Business Process Management (BPM) standard, Microsoft, IBM, and BEA systems are promoting the Business Process Execution Language for Web Services (BPEL4WS) and the Business Process Management Initiative organization (BPMI.org) is promoting the Business Process Modeling Language (BPML).

Figure 2.4 illustrates how the four characteristics are applied to determine at which level a standard should be placed.

As firms begin implementing Web services, it is critical that they consider the maturity of the standards they will be using. Standards in the enabling level are well understood and are widely used in mission-critical systems. Conversely, standards in the emerging level are fluid, with the existence of competing standards, and are used for tactical, nonmission-critical applications.

Given the rapid pace at which Web services standards are introduced, along with the unprecedented level of collaboration between key industry players such as IBM, Microsoft, BEA, and Sun in moving from proprietary technologies to jointly developed standards, it is advisable to regularly revisit the standards framework. As you do, consider the following dynamics:

- *Adding Standards*—Are there any emerging standards that should be added to the radar screen?
- *Progressing Standards*—Have the existing standards gained greater acceptance, and do they need to be considered for progress from the emerging to evolving level or evolving to enabling level?

Characteristic	Level 1 - Enabling	Level 2 - Evolving	Level 3 - Emerging
Support of Key Industry Players	All	3 or More	1 or More
Governance by a Single Standards Organization	Yes	Yes	No
Frequency of New Versions	> 6 Months	< 6 Months	< 4 Months
Existence of Competing Standards	No	Yes	Yes

FIGURE 2.4 Enabling, evolving, and emerging standards.

* *Retiring Standards*—Looking at the emerging level, have any existing standards been superceded or merged? For example, have Sun, Microsoft, IBM, and BEA systems agreed on a single specification for standards in the Business Process Execution & Management level?

By regularly updating the standards within this framework, firms can better decide which to incorporate into mainstream projects and which are better left to experimentation and "skunk works" initiatives.

Extreme caution should be exercised when considering the use of emerging standards for mainstream or mission-critical projects. The very real possibility exists that standards in this level will either fade away or be subsumed by competing standards. This situation would likely leave organizations in the unenviable position of incurring the cost, time, and effort to migrate systems to an alternate evolving or enabling standards in the near future. As Dana Gardner of the Aberdeen Group put it:

> *"I don't think it's too soon to step into the waters, but I think it's important to realize that these standards are fresh, not fully cooked and there are needs for more standards. [You have to be careful] not to get too far into the technology. Web services are something you should try out and use in pilots [pilot programs] inside the firewall. But when it comes to mission critical activities, particularly those outside the corporate boundaries, [it's not ideal]. It's too soon to look beyond the firewall except if it's something that couldn't make or break your business."[1]*

WEB SERVICES STACK

This section takes a detailed look at the three levels of the Web services stack. At each level, current Web services are explained and appropriate examples are provided. Figure 2.5 again illustrates the layers of the stack but now identifies the key standards associated with each layer.

Level 1: Enabling Standards

The enabling standards level contains two layers: the network transport protocols and meta-language. The layers within the enabling standards level contain well-defined and accepted standards and protocols that are widely used to support mission-critical business applications and capabilities today.

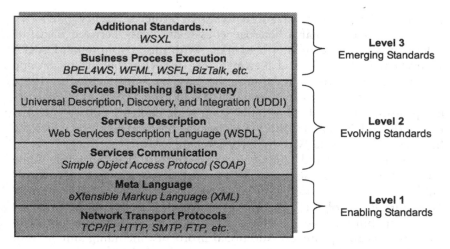

FIGURE 2.5 Standards of Web services stack.

Network Transport Protocols Layer The network transport protocol layer is well defined and understood, using pervasive standards and protocols that form the foundation of today's World Wide Web. Taking a closer look at this layer, we discover that it contains three sublayers, as illustrated in Figure 2.6.

The first two sublayers, Transmission Control Protocol (TCP) and Internet Protocol (IP), are typically grouped together and jointly referred to as the TCP/IP network layer. These sublayers originated from an initiative

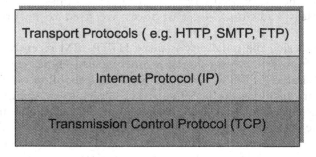

FIGURE 2.6 Internet protocol stack.

started at the Defense Advanced Research Projects Agency (DARPA). DARPA wanted to enable heterogeneous connectivity between disparate defense department computer networks. With this goal in mind, DARPA awarded Bolt, Beranek, and Newman, Inc. (BBN) a contract to develop ARPANET. From the initial four-node network implemented in 1969, ARPANET continued to grow and in 1982 adopted TCP/IP as its underlying protocol. TCP/IP later was included with Berkeley Software Distribution (BSD) UNIX and subsequently became the foundation on which the Internet and the World Wide Web (WWW) are based.

Above the TCP and IP layers is the Transport Protocol layer. While the concept of Web services is designed to be transport protocol-independent, the predominant protocol used today is the Hypertext Transport Protocol (HTTP). The ubiquity of HTTP, coupled with its innate capability to navigate firewalls, makes it the most common Web services transport protocol. Additional protocols, including Simple Mail Transfer Protocol (SMTP), File Transfer Protocol (FTP), and even TCP can be can used, but from a practical perspective few implementations support these protocols.

When considering the implementation of Web services, it is critical to understand that HTTP is not a reliable transport protocol. To appreciate this concept, think of HTTP as providing similar functionality to a basic pager. When sending someone a page, there is no guarantee that the message will be delivered to the recipient (for example, they might have their pager turned off or be out of range). The critical point to appreciate is that a basic pager is not two-way and cannot reply with a confirmation that the message was received. Similarly, HTTP does not guarantee receipt of a message, and it is possible that a message could get lost if part of a network goes down or if other network issues occur. Right now, this lack of reliability precludes the use of Web services over HTTP for mission-critical applications unless additional logic or tools are used to ensure reliable messaging.

In considering the reliability issue of HTTP, IBM recently published a proposal for a reliable messaging protocol called Hypertext Transport Protocol Reliable (HTTPR). HTTPR builds its reliability on HTTP 1.1 and therefore includes the benefits of HTTP, while ensuring that messages are delivered to their destinations unimpeded. Reliable messaging will become an important aspect of Web services and will undoubtedly appear in some form in the near future, although it is questionable whether the network layer is the most appropriate position for its implementation.

Meta Language Layer   The Meta Language layer is enabled with the eXtensible Markup Language (XML) as a means to describe structured data. A metalanguage is a language that can be used to describe other languages, enabling the creation of specific markup languages for specialized purposes. For example, XML could be used to define the grammar for HTML, the language used to display graphical pages on the Web. XML is enabling a new generation of Internet-based data manipulation applications and is undisputedly the universal language for data exchange over the Web.

XML's key strength is its capability to significantly reduce the complexities associated with the exchange of data between computer systems. It often takes a considerable amount of time, cost, and effort to enable data transfer between organizations or even between departments of the same organization. This is typically caused by a lack of standardization on how data is represented as well as the array of proprietary tools and mechanisms for extracting and transmitting data. XML provides a standard means of describing data while also providing the data context required to interpret the data if manipulation is necessary.

For example, a firm could choose to define an XML document describing a purchase order. The main element of this document might be "purchaseOrder" and would typically contain the subelements "shipTo," "billTo," "comment," and "items." Each of these subelements might themselves contain a number of subelements that enable a purchase order to be fully described. A sample XML document showing a specific instance of a purchase order is shown in Figure 2.7.

The power of XML is that information is represented as a structured document making it possible for the data to be interpreted and manipulated by a range of systems without manual intervention. As long as all parties that need to use the purchase order agree on the document structure, it is possible for the document to be shared across multiple systems or even multiple organizations. For example, the purchase order document illustrated in Figure 2.7 could be used to update order information in an order tracking system, a billing system, or an inventory management system. If these systems can not directly interpret the purchase order document in its native form, then the XML document structure makes it relatively easy to process the document and translate it into an alternative format.

XML is a key enabling component of Web services. It is the language in which Web services communicate as well as the language used as the foundation for other layers of the Web services stack (for example, SOAP and WSDL). As is so often the case, however, a technology's strength can also be its weaknesses. In the case of XML, the very flexibility that has been a cornerstone to its adoption can also present a very real challenge.

```
<purchaseOrder orderDate="1999-10-20">
   <shipTo country="US">
      <name>Alice Smith</name>
      <street>123 Maple Street</street>
      <city>Mill Valley</city>
      <state>CA</state>
      <zip>90952</zip>
   </shipTo>
   <billTo country="US">
      <name>Robert Smith</name>
      <street>8 Oak Avenue</street>
      <city>Old Town</city>
      <state>PA</state>
      <zip>95819</zip>
   </billTo>
   <comment>Hurry, my lawn is going wild!</comment>
   <items>
      <item partNum="872-AA">
         <productName>Lawnmower</productName>
         <quantity>1</quantity>
         <USPrice>148.95</USPrice>
         <comment>Confirm this is electric</comment>
      </item>
      <item partNum="926-AA">
         <productName>Baby Monitor</productName>
         <quantity>1</quantity>
         <USPrice>39.98</USPrice>
         <shipDate>1999-05-21</shipDate>
      </item>
   </items>
</purchaseOrder>
```

FIGURE 2.7   XML purchase order document.

Need for Data Definition Standards XML and Web services simplify the complexities of system integration and system interoperability through the use of technologies and standards to transport, route, discover, and connect services together. XML and Web services do not resolve the challenges of aligning data definitions, jargon, and vocabularies within and across organizations, however. For example, if one organization refers to an inventory item as a part number represented as "partNum," while another refers to it as a stock keeping unit, or "sku," both organizations might mean the same thing, but a computer system typically cannot resolve this discrepancy. When this type of naming discrepancy occurs, human intervention is required to analyze the meaning or semantics of the data. As the following quotes illustrate, this situation is a real challenge and potential inhibitor to deployment of Web services.

> "... *data definitions usually vary from company to company—or even within a single company . . . that's the bigger problem than being technically able to pass data from one system to the other.*"[2]

> "*In the context of the extended enterprise, common business semantics are critical to successfully interfacing business processes.*"[3]

Currently, the only way to deal with this challenge is to agree beforehand on naming conventions and data schemes. As organizations leverage XML and begin implementing Web services, it is absolutely critical that they develop consistent data-naming conventions within the organization. Companies should first look to leverage data definition standards that might already have been developed within their industry, and where industry standards do not exist, they should act now to start the process of defining their own standards.

In an effort to tackle these data definition issues, many industry groups have already started the process of defining the standards required to enable cross-organization data exchange. Figures 2.8a, 2.8b, and 2.8c identify a number of the most visible organizations that are actively involved in creating XML data definition standards.

Organization	Description
Financial Information eXchange (FIX) Organization	The Financial Information eXchange (FIX) protocol is a messaging standard developed specifically for the real-time electronic exchange of securities transactions. FIX is a public-domain specification owned and maintained by FIX Protocol, Ltd. The mission of the organization is to:
	Improve the global trading process by defining, managing, and promoting an open protocol for real-time, electronic communication between industry participants, while complementing industry standards.
	For additional information on the FIX standards go to fixprotocol.org.
IFX Forum	The Interactive Financial eXchange (IFX) is a financial messaging protocol, built by the financial services industry and technology leaders. The goals of IFX are:
	1. *To use real business use cases and develop content that is meaningful and useful to the financial services industry.*
	2. *To create a strong, flexible, open architecture that will support extending the protocol in an efficient, interoperable manner.*
	For additional information on the IFX forum go to ifxforum.org.
fpML	FpML (Financial products Markup Language) is the financial services industry-standard protocol for complex financial products. FpML plan to describe all categories of privately negotiated derivatives using FpML. Version 1.0 of FpML covers interest rate swaps and Forward Rate Agreements (FRAs).
	For additional information on the fpML standard go to fpml.org.
FinXML Consortium	FinXML™ is an XML-based framework developed to support a single universal standard for data interchange within the Capital Markets. FinXML acts as a common standard for cross application information exchange, allowing a financial institution or other organization to communicate the details of highly structured financial transactions in electronic form. As such, FinXML can be used as the basis for straight-through processing (STP) and risk management within a financial institution as well as conducting e-Commerce over the Internet.
	For additional information on the FinXML standard go to FinXML.org.
Financial Services Technology Consortium (FSTC)	The Financial Services Technology Consortium (FSTC) is a consortium of leading North American-based financial institutions, technology vendors, independent research organizations, and government agencies.
	FSTC is working to enable the Bank Internet Payment System (BIPS), which is an open specification for enabling spontaneous payment instructions to be initiated over open public networks using a standard interface to existing bank payments systems.
	For additional information on the FSTC or the BIPS standards go to fstc.org.
ACORD	ACORD is a nonprofit insurance association whose mission is to facilitate the development and use of standards for the insurance and related financial services industries.
	The ACORD Property & Casualty XML and ACORD XMLife standards are widely used in the Property and Casualty and Life insurance sectors.
	For additional information on ACORD standards go to accord.org.

FIGURE 2.8a   Financial services data definition standards.

Organization	Description
Health Level 7	Health Level Seven's domain within the healthcare industry is clinical and administrative data, their mission is: *To provide standards for the exchange, management and integration of data that support clinical patient care and the management, delivery and evaluation of healthcare services. Specifically, to create flexible, cost-effective approaches, standards, guidelines, methodologies, and related services for interoperability between healthcare information systems.* For additional information on the HL7 standard go to hl7.org.
Centers for Medicare & Medicaid Services (CMS)—HIPAA	The Centers for Medicare & Medicaid Services are responsible for national adherence to the Health Insurance Portability & Accountability Act (HIPAA) of 1996. HIPAA calls for: 1. *Standardization of electronic patient health, administrative and financial data.* 2. *Unique health identifiers for individuals, employers, health plans and health care providers.* 3. *Security standards protecting the confidentiality and integrity of "individually identifiable health information," past, present or future.* For additional information on the HIPAA standard go to cms.hhs.gov; further information can be found at hipaadvisory.com.

FIGURE 2.8b   Healthcare data definition standards.

Organization	Description
ebXML	ebXML (Electronic Business using eXtensible Markup Language) is an organization co-sponsored by UN/CEFACT and OASIS. With ebXML the goal is to create a modular suite of specifications that enables enterprises of any size and in any geographical location to conduct business over the Internet. Using ebXML, the hope is that companies will be able to use a standard method to exchange business messages, conduct trading relationships, communicate data in common terms and define and register business processes. ebXML's mission is: *To provide an open XML-based infrastructure enabling the global use of electronic business information in an interoperable, secure and consistent manner by all parties.* For additional information on ebXML standards go to ebXML.org.

FIGURE 2.8c   Additional data definition standards.

In the context of this book, it is only possible to scratch the surface of XML data definition standards. For those interested in learning more about XML and XML data standards, there are several excellent sources additional information, a few of which we include here:

> *Oasis-Open.org*—The Organization for the Advancement of Structured Information Standards (OASIS) produces worldwide standards for security, Web services, XML conformance, business transactions, electronic publishing, topic maps, and interoperability within and between marketplaces.
>
> *XML.org*—XML.org's mission is to accelerate the global utilization and adoption of XML by providing an open and nonprofit industry portal that brings together all members of the XML community, including technologists, developers, and business people.
>
> *RosettaNet.org*—RosettaNet.org is a nonprofit consortium of more than 400 of the world's leading IT, Electronic Components (EC), Semiconductor Manufacturing (SM), and Solution Provider (SP) companies working to create, implement, and promote open e-Business process standards.

In cases where consistent data definition standards are not being used, the need to translate an XML document from one format to another becomes unavoidable. This situation is where the translation capabilities of the eXtensible Stylesheet Language Transformations (XSLT) become a necessity. XSLT provides a transformation language for transmuting a XML document into an alternate format. Alternate formats could be another XML document with a different set of data definitions, a simple text document, or perhaps an HTML page.

Level 2: Evolving Standards

The evolving standards level contains slayers for SOAP, WSDL, and UDDI. Collectively, these layers form the core standards for deployment of Web services. Figure 2.9 illustrates the role that each layer plays in the execution of a Web service, and their relationship to the requestor, broker, and provider network.

This figure shows that the service provider preregisters their service(s) with the service broker, the service is registered in a UDDI repository, and the service is described using WSDL. Subsequently, a service requestor initiates a search for a service by contacting the service broker and searching the registry for services that meet specific search criteria. The broker returns a list of services along with details of the associated provider for each service meeting the search criteria. The requestor binds (creates a communications link) with a selected provider using the SOAP messaging standard. Also using SOAP, the requestor sends a service request and receives the result set of the executed service.

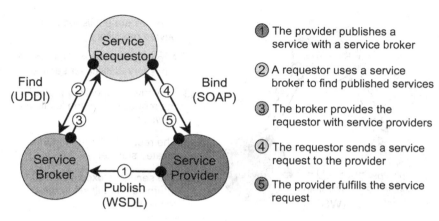

FIGURE 2.9 Web services: publish, find, and bind.

Figure 2.9 illustrates how the large industry players (such as Microsoft, IBM, Sun, and so on) envision Web services working, but this is not necessarily representative of how Web services are initially being implemented. The original vision of Web services, as illustrated in Figure 2.9, was for large public repositories of services to be published on the Internet by service brokers, to which companies would subscribe and search for services to incorporate into their own applications. In this model, the requestor, broker, and provider are all independent entities dispersed across the Internet. Today's reality is a far more conservative environment, as illustrated in Figure 2.10.

This figure illustrates a number of key points. First, where services are being published today, they are typically published to a private UDDI repository behind a corporate firewall. Second, the repository itself is an optional element of the model. In many cases, Web services are being developed for private consumption and are not being described or published. This model significantly reduces the envisioned flexibility of the Web services model, but does provide an adequate entry point, that can later be extended to include both private service repositories and public service brokers.

The evolving standards level provides a good degree of stability and is the basis upon that which the current mix of Web services development and deployment tools are based. The current set of Web service development tools, available from the likes of IBM, BEA, and Microsoft, provide a solid framework with which companies can start to implement real-world Web services.

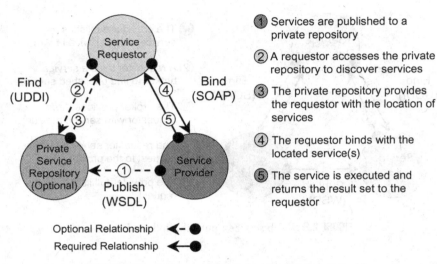

FIGURE 2.10   Web services: optional publish and find.

Services Communication Layer   The services communication layer uses SOAP as a lightweight protocol for exchange of information in a decentralized, distributed computing environment. SOAP is an XML-based protocol that allows communication between multiple computer architectures, languages, and operating systems.

In the past, many attempts have been made to develop a common communications protocol that could be used for systems integration, but none of them have achieved the widespread adoption required to be truly successful. One of the most compelling considerations for the use of SOAP is that it has already been implemented on more than 70 hardware and software platforms. This widespread adoption of SOAP is primarily due to its lightweight nature and its relatively low complexity when compared to precursors such as the Distributed Computing Environment (DCE) or the Common Object Request Broker Architecture (COBRA).

The first SOAP specification was released as Version 1.0 in late 1999 as a result of collaboration between Microsoft, UserLand Software and DevelopMentor. The original specification was submitted to the Internet Engineering Task Force (IETF), at which time Microsoft made the following announcements:

> *"The key enabler for Microsoft's vision of integrated, programmable Web services is XML. Through the exchange of XML messages, services can easily describe their capabilities and allow any*

other service, application or device on the Internet to easily invoke those capabilities. To help realize that vision, Microsoft today is submitting to the Internet Engineering Task Force (IETF) an Internet draft specification for the Simple Object Access Protocol (SOAP), an XML-based mechanism that bridges different object models over the Internet and provides an open mechanism for Web services to communicate with one another."

"To help developers build Web services and link heterogeneous components over the Internet, Microsoft worked with industry experts to create the Simple Object Access Protocol. SOAP provides an open, extensible way for applications to communicate using XML-based messages over the Web, regardless of what operating system, object model or language particular applications may use. SOAP facilitates universal communication by defining a simple, extensible message format in standard XML and thereby providing a way to send that XML message over HTTP. Microsoft is soliciting industry feedback on version 0.9 of the SOAP specification."[4]

The original SOAP specification was subsequently revised with input from IBM and Lotus and submitted to the W3C as SOAP version 1.1 on April 18, 2000. The W3C published the submitted specification as a W3C Note. The W3C has now adopted the SOAP specification and integrated ongoing work for future releases into the XML Protocol working group. The specification for SOAP version 1.2 is currently an in-progress working draft at the W3C.

To help appreciate how SOAP might be leveraged, imagine that an organization has implemented a Just-In-Time (JIT) inventory and order management initiative, and it is pondering how Web services could be used to improve the order management process, perhaps automating the process of placing orders with key suppliers:

Your firm has implemented a number of new Web services that allow your top suppliers to track your inventory levels, and you've provided them with documentation that details how to interface with the SOAP services. The documentation you've provided lets the suppliers know where your services are located, what parameters they require, and what data will be returned. Using this information, your suppliers manually implement the code to interface with your services.

This description is exactly the model outlined in Figure 2.10, where your firm is the service provider and your suppliers are the service consumers. Your suppliers (the service consumers) inter-

face, or in Web services terms "bind," with your inventory man-
agement service to allow them to automatically view your inven-
tory levels.

In a nonstandards-based environment without Web services, it is very
likely that this type of integration would only be accomplished through the
investment of a significant amount of time and effort developing custom
integration between your systems and your suppliers' systems. Custom
integration would require that all parties agree on proprietary file formats
and data exchange mechanisms for which custom interfaces would be
developed.

Services Description Layer   The services description layer is where WSDL—
often pronounced "whiz-dull"—is used as a common XML framework for
describing a Web service. A WSDL document describes a set of messages in
terms of what they contain and how they are exchanged. In addition to
describing the message contents, WSDL defines where the Web service is
available and what communication protocol is used to talk to the service.
In other words, the WSDL file defines all the information required to
invoke a Web service.

Over the past few years Microsoft, IBM and others have proposed
service description languages for component-based Web applications
including: Service Description Language (SDL), Service Contract Language
(SCL), and Web Interface Definition Language (WIDL). These early proposals have been superceded by WSDL, which now has broad support and
widespread industry adoption. The vast majority of Web services development toolkits and component application servers have built-in support for
creating and manipulating WSDL documents.

The WSDL standard was jointly developed by Ariba, IBM, and Microsoft, debuting on September 25, 2000, with the release of WSDL version 1.0.
The original specification was subsequently revised with input from a number of organizations including BEA, HP and SAP. The revised specification
was submitted to W3C as WSDL version 1.1 on March 15, 2001. As with
SOAP, the W3C initially published the WSDL specification as a W3C Note,
and now has an in-progress working draft of WSDL version 1.2.

The real value of WSDL is in providing the potential to automate the
connection to and consumption of Web services. Building on the JIT inventory management example from the prior section, it is possible to use
WSDL to remove the need for suppliers to manually develop the code to
bind with the inventory management Web services.

In the SOAP example from the previous section, it was necessary
to document your company's services and for the suppliers to use
that document to determine how to use your services. Wouldn't

it be great if there was some way in which your suppliers could automatically determine how to communicate with your services? This is exactly how WSDL can be used. A WSDL document describes all the information that a supplier needs to use your services. In fact, with the appropriate systems in place, the suppliers could completely automate the process of interfacing with your organization's services.

Use of WSDL documents mean that it's no longer necessary to go through the time-consuming process of manually documenting the SOAP interface requirements, the WSDL document provides this information in a form that can be interpreted by other systems. Once the suppliers' systems interpret the WSDL documents, they can establish a binding with the inventory management services— allowing direct system-to-system communications.

By removing the manual process of hand coding the interfaces, it is possible to significantly reduce the time and cost needed to develop a systems interface, allowing connectivity to a far larger number of suppliers than was previously feasible.

Service Publishing and Discovery Layer   The UDDI specification defines a data structure standard for describing organizational entities (businesses, not for profit organizations, and so on) and the services they provide using XML. UDDI provides high-level business information that complements the information contained in a WSDL document. Information within a UDDI registry is conceptually divided into three distinct elements—white, yellow, and green pages:

- *White Pages*—Contains general contact information about the entity. An entry would contain a business name, address, and contact information such as phone, facsimile, and e-mail.
- *Yellow Pages*—Contains classification information about the types and location of the services the entity offers. Examples might be Standard Industrial Classification (SIC) codes or the North American Industry Classification System (NAICS) categories.
- *Green Pages*—Contains information about how to invoke the offered services and might reference a WSDL specification for the service.

Figure 2.11 illustrates the three distinct page sets represented in a UDDI registry.

The UDDI version 1.0 specification was first published in September 2000 by Ariba, IBM, Microsoft and 33 other companies. Since September 2000, the UDDI specification has had several updates—most recently with the release of UDDI version 3.0 on July 19, 2002. With the release of

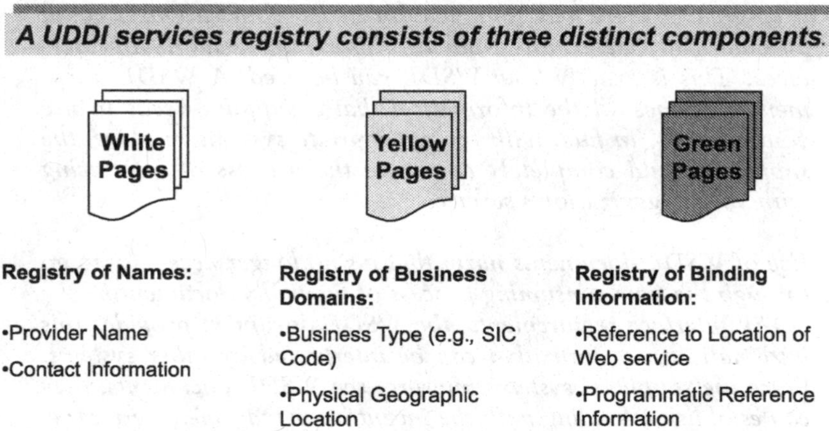

> ## A UDDI services registry consists of three distinct components.

White Pages

Yellow Pages

Green Pages

Registry of Names:

•Provider Name

•Contact Information

Registry of Business Domains:

•Business Type (e.g., SIC Code)

•Physical Geographic Location

Registry of Binding Information:

•Reference to Location of Web service

•Programmatic Reference Information

FIGURE 2.11   Elements of the UDDI registry.

UDDI version 3.0, the UDDI standards body, UDDI.org, has now merged with OASIS.

The UDDI specification has gained significant momentum, in no small part due to the backing of Microsoft and IBM, but has not achieved the same level of acceptance enjoyed by SOAP or WSDL. This lackluster acceptance is primarily because the functionality of UDDI registries precedes the real-world need for their adoption. UDDI adoption has been inhibited by the following factors:

* UDDI was originally envisioned as the basis for public internet service registries, but the majority of Web services are being developed today for intra-enterprise consumption and do not leverage public service registries.
* Participation in public registries has been low, which undermines any compelling reason to consume services from public registries. In fact, many of the early services being registered publicly provide little more than a proof of concept for UDDI capabilities.
* Progress toward fully securing Web services is moving rapidly, but the lack of a fully implemented security model for public services will continue to impede public registry usage.

Fundamentally, the addition of dynamic discovery and integration with services from a UDDI registry adds a level of complexity to Web services for which there is not yet a compelling need. Recent revisions to the UDDI specification provide broader support for implementation of private intra-enterprise service registries, which will likely gain greater acceptance in the short-term.

Further building upon our inventory management example, let us assume that an organization places orders with a closed network of preferred suppliers. Under certain conditions, it might be desirable to leverage an open network of suppliers where a firm can dynamically determine which suppliers it wants to partner with. The company may want to place orders with suppliers based on specific requirements or parameters such as unit price, payment terms, time for delivery, and so on. These parameters may fluctuate over time based on the business pressures that an organization is experiencing, and the firm's closed network of suppliers may not have the flexibility it is seeking.

In this case, it is necessary to search for suppliers that met the firm's prioritized parameters. To achieve this goal, a yellow pages directory of all businesses that expose Web services is needed. Like a typical yellow pages directory, UDDI provides a database of businesses that is searchable by business name, type of business, geographical location, and so on:

Again using the inventory management example, from the previous section, a UDDI services registry could be leveraged to further extend your purchasing capabilities. In the previous examples your firm used a push model, where suppliers can determine your inventory levels and automate shipments when inventory levels get low. In this example, your firm will use a pull model, where your company uses a services UDDI registry to find suppliers that meet your purchasing needs.

You have received a special order from an important client and need to locate parts that are not available from our existing suppliers. Similar to the way in which a yellow pages directory could be used to manually locate a supplier, you will use a UDDI registry to locate suppliers that meet your specific search requirements. In this case, you are going to locate suppliers that:

- *Fall within a specific Standard Industrial Classification (SIC) code.*
- *Are within 100 miles of our production facility.*
- *Publish Web services that enable us to determine product type and availability based on our specific need.*

Using the search criteria, the UDDI registry will return information regarding contacts, links, technical data and specifications, allowing you to evaluate which services best meet the requirements. Once you have identified the services that you want to bind with,

you will then determine the call interface and semantics for the ser-
vice and automatically configure your own software to connect
with the service. Having connected with the service, you can then
search for the product you need, perhaps also determining the
availability of on-hand stock, unit price, shipping terms, and so on.

This process could automatically be completed with a number of
suppliers to determine which supplier best met your specific
requirements. Once the best match has been found, an order can
be placed and shipment of the product can be initiated.

UDDI is not strictly necessary to enable Web services, but as the number of available services grows, organizations will need somewhere to reg-
ister their services so they can be found easily and consumed. This will lead
to the implementation of private intra-enterprise UDDI registries.

From a longer-term perspective, it is possible to envision an environment in which systems may be assembled from a collection of Web services
provided over the Web—similar to way in which D&B is providing its
credit-checking services. In this future, when a business changes the way in
which it executes a transaction or process, the appropriate service(s) and
process flow(s) will be modified and the changes will ripple throughout the
organization's IT systems.

Level 3: Emerging Standards

The emerging standards level has the least well-defined capabilities. This
level represents proposed standards that are promoted by individual vendors, have not yet gained broader endorsement or acceptance in the wider
Web services community, and have not been adopted as open standards for
development by key standards bodies such as the W3C and OASIS.

The Web services space is moving at a tremendous pace. Therefore, it
is important for companies to carefully watch the emerging standards,
monitoring which gain greater acceptance and which will perhaps move
from an emerging to an evolving status. As illustrated in Figure 2.12, the
Web services stack has been extended from the version introduced in
Figure 2.2, adding vertical layers that traverse the stack. These new layers
provide capabilities that will be required as organizations continue to build
out their Web services portfolio.

Business Process Execution   Using the evolving standards of SOAP, WSDL,
and UDDI, it is possible for applications to find each other and interact following a loosely coupled, platform-independent model. To realize the full
potential of Web services as an integration platform, however, a standard

The Web services stack is further extended with emerging standards that traverse the stack, adding much needed capabilities across all levels

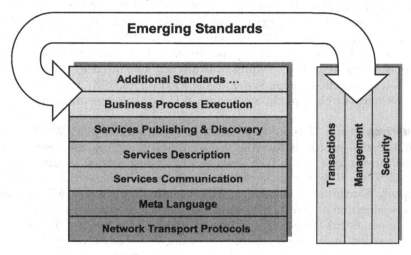

FIGURE 2.12 Extended Web service stack.

business process integration model is required, enabling complex interactions between business processes and Web services.

A number of Business Process Management (BPM) or workflow languages have been proposed by vendors, including the Web Service Flow Language (WSFL), XLang, Web Services Choreography Interface (WSCI), Web Flow Markup Language (WFML), Business Process Markup Language (BPML), and so on. In fact, there have been so many proposed process management standards that it has been difficult to know where to look.

A key obstacle to the emergence of a clear leading standard in this area has been Microsoft and IBM's independent offerings of XLang and WSFL, respectively. Recently this standoff was resolved with the announcement by Microsoft, IBM, and BEA Systems that they have joined forces to propose the Business Process Execution Language for Web Service (BPEL4WS).

BPEL4WS is designed to ensure that individual business processes can understand one another in a Web services environment. It is a hybrid of WSFL and XLang, combining the capabilities of both into a single cohesive BPM language. Using BPEL4WS it is possible to define a new Web service that is composed of existing services, with the resulting Web service being described by its own WSDL document. The resulting composition, or process, defines how each individual service is combined to enable the execution of an end-to-end business process.

It appears likely that BPEL4WS will be adopted as a broad industry standard for BPM with Web services, but as yet BPEL4WS has not been submitted to a standards organization for independent governance. At this time, it is clear that BPEL4WS has superseded the WSFL and XLang specifications, and possibly the BPML specification. It will be interesting to see what happens with WSCI, which was already submitted to the W3C by Sun Microsystems. Perhaps Sun will join forces with IBM, Microsoft, and BEA systems, or perhaps choose to push WSCI as an opposing standard.

Transactions   Core Web services standards (specifically SOAP, WSDL, and UDDI) define protocols for Web services interoperability. Increasingly, as organizations look to use Web services for business process execution and workflow, it will be necessary to link large numbers of services into loosely coupled, distributed applications. The resulting applications will require the coordination of complex transactions between participant services.

Transactional consistency will be a fundamental requirement for building reliable service-based applications. Specifically, it will be necessary to ensure all the participants in an application or service achieve a mutually agreed upon outcome based on the success or failure of a transaction. Traditionally, transactions have held properties collectively referred to as ACID (Atomic, Consistant, Isolated, and Durable):[5]

- *Atomic*—An atomic transaction is all-or-nothing. Either everything is successfully updated or nothing is updated.
- *Consistent*—A consistent transaction is one that leaves data in a consistent state. The resulting data records should not contradict each other.
- *Isolated*—An isolated transaction is one that cannot be viewed by another transaction before it is committed. A transaction should not be able to view the transitional state of another transaction.
- *Durable*—Once a transaction successfully completes, the changes survive failure. Changes due to a transaction should be reliably stored and should be recoverable in case of system failure.

Web services will require the ability to coordinate transactions and implement ACID transaction processing, as well as the ability to coordinate the results from multiple services in a more flexible manner. This flexibility will require more relaxed forms of transactions—those that do not strictly abide to the ACID properties—such as collaboration, workflow, real-time processing, and so on. The emerging WS-Coordination and WS-Transaction specifications, announced by IBM, Microsoft and BEA systems on August 9, 2002, provide a framework for enabling strict ACID transaction management as well as the flexibility required to support more relaxed transaction requirements.

Management As organizations build out their Web services capabilities, there will be an explosion in the volume of Web services. A rapidly increasing portfolio of services will require software to catalog, track, manage, and monitor service availability. The emerging Web services managed space will play an important role in answering the following questions:

- What Web services are available, and what do they do? Can they be reused?
- Who is authorized to use various Web services?
- What is the performance load on the servers that are running Web services? Are Web services running optimally?
- Are consumers of Web services receiving response times within acceptable Quality of Service (QoS) limits?

Web services managment tools are emerging to help organizations answer these questions and more, including performance management, quality of service, logging and auditing, and so on. Answers to all of these questions will become increasingly important as Web services are initially deployed for integration, followed by collaboration initiatives.

Web services management needs have received less exposure than other Web services requirements, such as security and business process execution As such there is currently a lack of standardization, leaving the Web services management space open to proprietary solutions. Proprietary Web services management solutions from startups such as Amberpoint, Infravio, Confluent Software, and Talking Blocks are emerging. These organizations provide a range of Web services management tools that will support Web services, management capabilities, including the following:

- *Availability*—Tracking which services are online or offline
- *Management*—Load balancing of services across multiple machines and platforms
- *Visibility*—Clear visibility of who is using what services and when
- *Exceptions Management*—Management of both business and technical exceptions
- *Quality of Service (QoS)*—Ensuring that both QoS and service-level agreements are being met
- *Metering and Billing*—In a pay-per-use environment, ensuring that services are metered and billing information is tracked
- *Security*—Ensuring that access to services is secure and that service usage is authenticated

As organizations continue their Web services buildout, management tools will rapidly become necessary for effective tracking and management of a growing portfolio of services.

Security   It is relatively easy to secure a private network with trusted partners, suppliers, and customers using Virtual Private Network (VPN) capabilities. But as the need to use services outside of private networks increases, it will be necessary to consider emerging Web services security standards.

> *". . . there is a need for securing XML documents and messages in addition to transport layer security . . . without a reliable and flexible security solution, Web services will die its own death," said Sudhir Agarwal of Verizon.*[6]

Web security experts identifiy three types of security threats that must be guarded against when implementing Web services outside of the corporate firewall:

1. *Exposed Systems*—Web services can leave open security holes, allowing hackers to gain access to private corporate information and internal corporate systems. As Web services leverage HTTP, make sure that the corporate firewall is configured to protect internal networks.
2. *Exposed Information*—As consumers begin to use Web services, unencrypted information transmitted over the Web can be "stolen" from internet traffic. Stolen information, for example a credit card number, could be used to complete fraudulent tractions. This type of security threat can be eliminated relatively easily using existing Web-based encryption and security standards such as Secure Socket Layer (SSL).
3. *Spoofed Transactions and Services*—Fake Web service transactions may be used to commit cyber theft. For example, services may be published from nontrustworthy sources, taking personal or financial information and appearing to complete a transaction, but actually capturing financial information (for example, credit card or bank account details) for later fraudulent use.

To fully secure Web services it is likely that a combination of existing security technologies will be leveraged, such as SSL, combined with emerging Web services security standards such as XML Key Management System (XKMS), Security Assertion Mark-up Language (SAML), and XML Signature.

In April 2002, IBM, Microsoft, and BEA systems submitted the WS-Security proposed standard to OASIS. WS-Security provides a flexible framework that can be used as the basis for the construction of a wide variety of security models, including Public Key Infrastructure, Kerberos, and SSL. Specifically, WS-Security provides support for multiple security tokens, multiple trust domains, multiple signature formats, and multiple encryption technologies.

WS-Security is a building block that will likely be used in conjunction with other Web service extensions and higher-level application-specific protocols to accommodate a wide variety of security models and encryption technologies.

Additional Standards The Web services space is moving at a tremendous pace, and it seems that every day there are new emerging standards proposed by one of the key players. One such example is the Web Services Experience Language (WSXL). WSXL version 2 was announced by IBM on April 10, 2002. IBM outlined the focus and intent of WSXL standards as follows:

> *". . . [WSXL] is a Web services centric component model for interactive Web applications, that is, for applications that provide a user experience across the Internet. WSXL is designed to achieve two main goals: enable businesses to deliver interactive Web applications through multiple distribution channels and enable new services or applications to be created by leveraging other interactive applications across the Web."*

> *"To accomplish these goals, all WSXL component services implement a set of base operations for lifecycle management, accepting user input, and producing presentation markup. More sophisticated WSXL component services may be specialized to represent data, presentation, and control. WSXL also introduces a new description language to guide the adaptation of user experience to new distribution channels."*

> *"User experiences that are implemented using WSXL can be delivered to end users through a diversity of distribution channels—for example, directly to a browser, indirectly through a portal, or by embedding into a third-party interactive Web application. In addition, WSXL user experiences can easily be modified, adapted, aggregated, coordinated, synchronized or integrated, often by simple declarative means. New applications can be created by seamlessly combining WSXL applications and adapting them to new uses, to ultimately leverage a worldwide pallet of WSXL component services."*[7]

WSXL can be thought of as putting a face to Web services. All the other technologies and standards discussed in this chapter operate behind the scenes providing the foundation for a Web services architecture, but WSXL makes it possible to integrate Web services more easily into interactive user environments such as portals.

As with all of the standards discussed in the emerging standards section, it is to early to tell if WSXL will find broad support and the required governance of a standards organization, but the ability to integrate Web services into rich interactive environments will inevitably be an essential requirement as Web services continue to gain momentum.

STANDARDS GOVERNANCE AND INTEROPERABILITY

As highlighted throughout this chapter, the agreement on Web services standards has been a key contribution to the rapid evolution and adoption of Web services. Looking back to the early releases of XML and SOAP, the W3C has played a pivotal role in governance of Web services standards, but since late 2001, OASIS has played an increasingly visible role in the Web services standards space. Perhaps we are beginning to see a shift in the balance of power around Web services standards? If so, what does this mean for organizations that are using Web services today and in the near future?

W3C and OASIS

Reviewing the Web services standards discussed in this chapter, referenced the W3C and OASIS on numerous occasions. These two standards organizations are very much at the epicenter of the evolving and emerging Web services standards. As yet there has not been a clear demarcation line drawn between the roles and responsibilities of these two organizations, but there could well be an impending struggle for dominance and ownership of Web services standards on the horizon.

Some key differences exist between the approaches that the W3C and OASIS have taken toward defining and publishing standards that will undoubtedly influence how IBM, Microsoft, BEA systems, and Sun Microsystems, among others choose to work with these standards organizations going forward. Figure 2.13 highlights fundamental differences between the W3C and OASIS.

Of the three evolving standards at the core of Web services (specifically SOAP, WSDL, and UDDI), two are governed by the W3C and one by OASIS. As the boundaries of Web services capabilities are pushed, it is

	Time to Market	Intellectual Property
W3C	The W3C has large working groups that agree on specifications and standards before they are published. This approach has often meant that W3C specifications take a long time to appear. This has at times appeared to frustrate member organizations that might be focused on the commercial viability of using W3C standards in their products.	The W3C explicitly excludes the adoption and governance of any technology or specification for which an intellectual property claim, patents or trade marks exists. As such, organizations are free to use W3C standards and specifications without the need to pay third-party royalties.
OASIS	OASIS has smaller working groups that appear to drive the definition and publishing of specifications more rapidly than the W3C. This has been viewed as advantageous by software vendors, as they are able to more rapidly leverage OASIS standards in their products for commercial return.	OASIS does not exclude the adoption and governance of technologies or specifications for which an intellectual property claim, patents or trade marks exists. However, any such claim must be clearly stated and justified when a specification is submitted to OASIS. This policy is advantageous for organizations that may wish to receive royalties for use of submitted technology or specifications.

FIGURE 2.13   W3C and OASIS approach to governance.

unclear if emerging standards will be submitted to the W3C or to OASIS. Given observations regarding time to market and intellectual property, it is possible that OASIS will be favored by the likes of Microsoft, IBM, BEA Systems, and so on—but only time will tell where the demarcation line will fall between the W3C and OASIS.

Web Service Interoperability

Recently a new standards organization has appeared on the Web services scene. The Web Services Interoperability (WS-I) organization was jointly launched by IBM, Microsoft, BEA Systems, Fujitsu, Hewlett-Packard, Intel, Oracle, and 46 other vendors on February 6, 2002.

The WS-I was formed to help organizations working with Web services to establish which version of Web services standards to work with. The goal is to ensure that Web services developed on different platforms, using different development tools, will interoperate seamlessly. With this goal in mind, the WS-I's charter is as follows:

> *". . . promote Web services interoperability across platforms, operating systems, and programming languages. The organization works across the industry and standards organizations to respond to customer needs by providing guidance, best practices, and resources for developing Web services solutions."*[8]

The promise of greater interoperability is central to the mainstream adoption of Web services, but the plethora of standards and the availability of tools that implement various versions of these standards may potentially to impede this goal. For example, a firm may have developed services using tools that create a WSDL version 1.1 services description, while another system is looking for service descriptions conforming to WSDL version 1.0. As WSDL version 1.1 implements an extended instruction set it is quite possible that the services on these systems will not interoperate as intended.

To tackle this type of interoperability challenge the WS-I has introduced the concept of Web services profiles. The WS-I defines a profile as:

> *". . . a named group of Web services specifications at specific version levels, along with conventions about how they work together."* [9]

Further, the WS-I has stated that it will:

> *". . . develop a core collection of profiles that support interoperability for general purpose Web services functionality."* [10]

To date the WS-I has defined a single profile, this being the basic Web services profile. Figure 2.14 illustrates the four standards and the associated versions that together form the basic profile.

The WS-I is actively working to define Web services profiles that will be used to ensure interoperability of rapidly developing Web services standards.

WS-Basic Profile	Universal Description Discovery and Interoperability (UDDI) Version 2.0 ***Under OASIS Governance***
	Web Service Description Language (WSDL) Version 1.1 ***Under W3C Governance***
	Simple Object Access Protocol (SOAP) Version 1.1 ***Under W3C Governance***
	eXtensible Markup Language (XML) Schema Version 1.0 ***Under W3C Governance***

FIGURE 2.14   WS-Basic Web services standards.

Additional profiles will be published as new standards gain acceptance and existing standards are updated to newer versions. WS-I members may self-certify that their software conforms to a specific profile, and it is initially expected that self-certification will be further policed by other WS-I members. It is yet to be determined how effective self-certification will be.

SUMMARY

Conceptually Web services are relatively straightforward. However, the maze of arcane terms and acronyms that surround Web services can at times create an impenetrable barrier. In this chapter we have sought to break that barrier down, brick by brick, by defining what Web services are, by introducing the enabling concepts behind Web services, and by demystifying the standards and terminology surrounding Web services. Furthermore, our goal has been to give the reader a solid Web services primer and create a Web services foundation for subsequent chapters.

Our hope is that readers now feel more comfortable with the Web services standards, concepts and terminology, and better appreciate some of the business implications of Web services, and where to leverage Web services in your organization. Subsequent chapters take a deep look at the "How's?", "Where's?" and "When's?" of Web service implementation from a business perspective, starting with Chapter 3, "Web Services Adoption."

ENDNOTES

[1] www.internetnews.com, March 13, 2002, "Web Services Moving Beyond the Hype" by Thor Olavsrud.

[2] www.cio.com, *CIO Magazine*, January 15, 2002, "Costly, Painful and Worth It" by Derek Slater.

[3] Gartner Research, February 28, 2002, "Enterprise Integration: A Key Driver for Web Services Adoption" by Debanish Sinha.

[4] www.microsoft.com, Microsoft Press Release, September 13, 1999, "Windows DNA 2000 Provides Pervasive XML Support For Next-Generation Web Development."

[5] www.ibm.com, IBM, August 2002, "Transactions in the World of Web Services, Part 1" by Tom Freund and Tony Storey.

[6] www.infoworld.com, *InfoWorld*, October 14, 2002, "Netegrity Minding the Web Services Security Store" by Brian Fonseca.

[7] www.ibm.com, IBM, April 10, 2002, "(WSXL) Web Service Experience Language Version 2."

[8] www.ws-i.org, October 3, 2002, "WS-I Overview," Version 1.4.

[9] Ibid.

[10] Ibid.

CHAPTER 3

Web Services Adoption

"In preparing for battle, I have always found that plans are useless but planning is indispensable."

Dwight D. Eisenhower (1890–1969)

"Far better to dare mighty things, to win glorious triumphs, even though checkered by failure, than to take rank with those poor spirits who neither enjoy much nor suffer much, because they live in the gray twilight that knows not victory, nor defeat."

Theodore Roosevelt (1858–1919)

The implementation of Web services as part of an overarching business strategy will be critical to both the effective use of the technology as well as the success of the business. Chapter 1, "A Day in the Life of a CIO," outlined the Web services adoption model that profiles four macro phases in which Web services will be incorporated into the fabric of all organizations. This chapter takes a detailed look at the phases of the adoption model and discusses practical actions that every organization should consider as their use of Web services evolves and expands.

ADOPTION MODEL

The Web services adoption model identifies four phases of Web services adopton: integration, collaboration, innovation, and domination. Each phase builds on the previous phases as organizations gain the requisite skills and experience and as standards gain acceptance and the maturity to enable the transition to the next phase. Figure 3.1 illustrates the time frames that are expected for each phase of the Web services adoption model.

PHASE ONE: INTEGRATION

Phase one represents the early adoption of Web services through "skunk works," Proof-Of-Concept (POC), and pilot projects. During this phase, organizations will leverage Web services to develop a standard integration framework within the security boundaries of their firewall. Basic integration Web services will be implemented primarily leveraging XML and SOAP, but WSDL may also be used for early collaboration initiatives with trusted partners. Some early adopters have already committed significant financial and human resources to Web services implementations, while many more cautious organizations are just beginning to examine their potential. We believe that Web services will be leveraged as a mainstream integration tool during 2003 and early 2004 as the benefits of using Web services for integration become more apparent and compelling.

Business Landscape

The current technologies and approaches being applied to application integration are failing to achieve their business objectives. To date, integration solutions have been too complex, too difficult, too expensive, and too rigid to meet the constant changes of today's dynamic business environment. The majority of Fortune 500 IT organizations list system integration as their number one challenge, and systems integration failures can be traced to nearly every aborted industry exchange and value chain integration project. Below is a recent example of how challenging and costly systems integration initiatives can be:

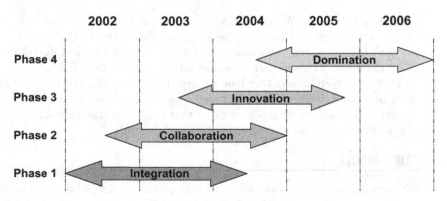

FIGURE 3.1 Web services adoption phases.

"Nike reportedly spent $400 million to overhaul its supply chain infrastructure, installing ERP, CRM and SCM—the full complement of analyst-blessed integrated enterprise software. So what happened? In the third quarter of last year, the Beaverton, Oregon-based sneaker maker saw profits drop by $48 million, year over year, thanks in part to a major inventory glitch (it overproduced some shoe models and underproduced others). Nike blamed one piece of its integration puzzle—its demand and supply chain management software—for the mix-up. ("This is what I get for our $400 million?" CEO Phil Knight famously asked, referring to the total cost of the integration project.) And what CIO reading the Nike tale didn't feel an uncomfortable mix of emotions: relief that he wasn't responsible for such a public and pricey screw-up, and worry that his own integration project could fail in just as spectacular a fashion."[1]

Such challenges are not uncommon when integrating large, complex enterprise applications. The ongoing challenges of systems integration are a significant burden and arguably a distraction from the more strategic tasks of improving operation efficiencies and tracking too-rapid changes in the marketplace. As illustrated in Figure 3.2, Forrester Research estimates the average 2001 spending on internal systems integration to be $3.5 million, breaking down to 27% on software, 30% on professional services, and 42% on internal integration staff. Beyond the integration of internal systems alone, Forrester estimates that total system integration costs, including B2B integration for collaboration, are at $6.3 million in 2001 and will grow to $6.4 million in 2003.[2]

The need to focus so much effort on integration mainly derives from the heterogeneous application architectures that have evolved within the vast majority of organizations over the past 10 years. Many organizations have implemented Enterprise Resource Planning (ERP), Customer Relationship Management (CRM), and Supply Chain Management (SCM) systems. While they are valuable management tools, enterprise applications frequently become information silos in which key business information is locked. Today, these enterprise applications are typically large client-server systems implemented by using proprietary software and providing proprietary data integration tools. Beyond the enterprise applications, organizations typically have an abundance of custom applications and smaller departmental or niche package applications, all of which need to be

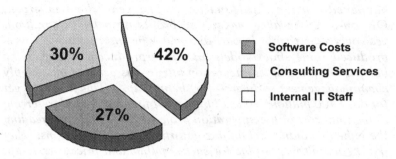

FIGURE 3.2   The cost of internal application integration.

integrated to provide a coherent view of the business operations and to reduce the need for duplicate data entry (which itself is error-prone and often leads to confusing and conflicting information).

The challenge of integrating these disparate information silos has been met with a mixed bag of system and data integration approaches, including:

* *Ad-Hoc Custom Integration*—Many application integration projects are implemented using a custom development approach on an ad-hoc, as needed basis. This approach, and technology used to implement the interface, might be proprietary to the systems being integrated, might adhere to an enterprise architecture, or more likely will be based on the skills of the individuals implementing the interface.
* *Data Warehouse and Data Marts*—Data is often extracted from operational systems and stored in data warehouses and data marts in an effort to provide a consolidated and consistent view of operational metrics for reporting and analysis. Depending on sources from which data is gathered, a data warehouse might reflect a near real-time perspective, but it more often reflects a weekly or monthly snapshot.
* *Enterprise Application Integration (EAI)*—In an effort to integrate the silos created by enterprise applications, EAI capabilities have been implemented. EAI makes it possible for data entered into one enterprise system to be replicated across other core systems. For

example, a customer setup in an order processing system will automatically be created in the call center systems as well as all other core systems. You can think of EAI tools as enterprise middleware used to tie key enterprise systems together into the semblance of a cohesive whole.

Regardless of the approach used, the results of these system integration efforts are often typified by:

* *Significant Investment of Time and Money*—Integration projects, either as a single custom interface or as a large enterprise data warehouse or EAI initiative, represent a large percentage of current IT budgets. This huge investment reduces the funds available for other projects that may provide longer-term strategic value to the organization.
* *Poor Data Quality*—Through a lack of data definition standards and master data sources, it is extremely difficult to consolidate data from multiple sources without highlighting data errors and inconsistencies. This often leads to the need for individuals to identify the source of these inconsistencies and further contributes to limited operational visibility.
* *Limited Operational Visibility*—Current approaches to system integration struggle to provide the real-time operational visibility that executives require to effectively run their business. Too often, when faced with a critical business decision, the majority of time is spent trying to gather the right information rather than analyzing the data. In this scenario, executives are often left with too little information and not enough time to make the right decisions.
* *Lack of Flexibility*—Current systems integration techniques often result in tightly coupled interfaces between systems. The impact of this tight coupling is often manifested as significantly reduced organizational flexibility. As we witnessed with the advent of e-Business requirements, the internally focused applications and supporting systems lacked the flexibility required to enable e-Business processes. Organizations struggling to integrate e-Commerce web sites with back-office fulfilment systems in many cases resorted to manual internal processes. It certainly was not uncommon for orders submitted via a Web site to be manually rekeyed into back-office order management systems. The e-Business imperative exposed a deeper, more elemental problem for many organizations: lack of flexibility in the business processes underlying the enterprise and e-Business applications.

The advent of Web services promises to provide the tools required to tackle these issues while providing an architectural approach that leverages current application portfolio investments. These issues will not be resolved overnight, but early POC and pilot projects are a first step in the right direction. For some time, early adopters have been leveraging XML to develop Web services. Initially, two types of services are being developed: virtual services and custom services.

- *Virtual Web Services*—Most organizations will find that they have already implemented core business functionality several times, and that this functionality is replicated across a variety of business systems in the organization. Given that much of the functionality targeted for implementation as Web services already exists, why reinvent the wheel? Using Web services standards, a company can encapsulate functionality embedded in existing systems and expose that functionality as Web services.

  The key advantage of this approach is that firms are leveraging existing assets and investments as well as jump-starting the creation of Web services registries. As they begin to encapsulate existing systems, they will be able to rapidly build out their Web services toolkit, and minimize the need to custom develop new services from scratch. When possible, and when it makes sense, look at existing systems for the creation of virtual Web services before custom developing a new Web service from scratch.

  The vast majority of enterprise application vendors are already working feverishly to expose functionality from their systems as virtual Web services. And when it makes sense to upgrade enterprise applications, firms will be able to add new virtual services made available from each enterprise application. One important consideration here is that it might be more cost- and time-efficient for organizations to create a few focused virtual services of their own, where the availability or complexity of an enterprise application upgrade is an issue.

- *Custom Web Services*—Pilot applications are being developed from scratch as custom Web services. Initially, these projects are using Web services to tackle nonmission-critical applications, supplementing the creation of a service portfolio being developed from existing applications.

These services might be implemented in a three-tier model, as illustrated in Figure 3.3. As shown, the familiar presentation tier and data storage tiers are maintained, but rather than the middle tier being composed of a single unit of functionality, it is now composed of a number of Web services. These might be new custom services (identified with a "C") developed for a specific requirement, or virtual services (identified with a "V") where functionality from an existing enterprise application or custom applications is exposed as a service. It is important to appreciate that,

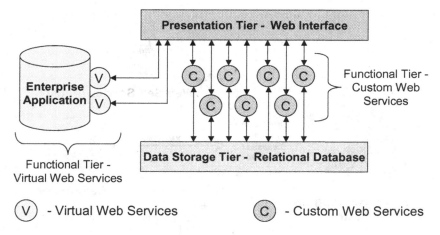

FIGURE 3.3 Implementation of virtual and custom services.

unlike previous models used to develop the functional tier, once a service has been implemented it is relatively easy to reuse for multiple applications. Figure 3.4 illustrates this principle for a simple order status service.

This figure illustrates an example in which a virtual order entry Web service has been created by encapsulating the order entry functionality already available from the ERP system using Web services-based standards (specifically, XML and SOAP). As illustrated, the new order entry service is reused by the online purchasing system, the call center system, and the shipping systems. In this scenario the order entry service could provide the ability to enter a new order, maintain an order, or even check the order status.

Since the order entry service now resides between the ERP system and the other systems that use the order entry Web service, it provides a level of abstraction from the underlying ERP system. If, in the future, it is necessary to update or replace the ERP system, the order entry Web service can be used to separate the Web self-service, call center, and shipping systems from the implementation detail of the new ERP system. In effect the systems using the order entry service are abstracted from the implementation details of the ERP systems.

These early projects are a first step in a much longer multistep process that will ultimately see the migration of internal systems from multiple proprietary application interfaces and architectures to Service Oriented Architectures (SOA) based on open standards. Chapter 7, "Architecting for

FIGURE 3.4   Re-use of functional tier from ERP system.

Competitive Advantage," takes a closer look at SOAs as well as the broader architectural considerations for SOAs and Web services.

Planning Considerations   In determining why internal integration should be the starting point for Web services implementation, consider the following thoughts:

- *Cost Avoidance*—The implementation of an Enterprise Application Integration (EAI) system is often an expensive and time-consuming process, with EAI software licenses costing between $500 thousand to $1 million, and the implementation costs for a single EAI system often running in excess of $3 million.

  "Enterprise Application Integration (EAI) is a journey, not a destination. Higher business value can be realized as increasingly complex business processes are automated, standardized, reused, and shared. Yet EAI costs can also be substantial from a financial standpoint and in terms of the organizational disruptions that are often involved."[3]

Even though EAI software can handle many of the integration problems between enterprise systems, EAI solutions are typically built using proprietary technology. This means that the data that was freed from enterprise systems may now be locked in the proprietary scheme of the EAI application. Web services promise to enable the next wave of EAI solutions using XML as an open, standards-based communication layer, breaking the proprietary nature of EAI tool sets and allowing open standards to be used as the basis for application integration.

The vast majority of enterprise application vendors have either already implemented Web services interfaces to their application suites, or are currently in the process of implementing these changes.

* *Skills Acquisition*—The deployment of Web services for internal pilot integration projects provides a low-risk training environment in which the IT organization can begin learning the concepts behind Web services and the real capabilities of Web service development tools. Skills acquisition during this phase should primarily focus on XML, SOAP, and WSDL.

* *Evolving Standards*—The standards that will be at the core of Web services collaboration are either toward the outer bounds of the evolving tier of standards (for example, service publishing and discovery using UDDI repositories) or are still within the emerging tier of standards (such as business process execution using BPEL4WS tools). These standards are still experiencing a significant degree of flux and as yet are not recommended for mission-critical uses. For further information, refer to Chapter 2, "Standards, Concepts, and Terminology." This rapidly evolving landscape creates a moving target for the development of broad-based collaborative Web services.

* *Robust Security*—By using Web services for internal integration, all activity occurs behind the corporate firewall. This means that the same security that protects all other existing core systems remains intact, and security software and policies are unaffected. Web services security standards remain an open issue. While it is possible to operate Web services with trusted partners over a Virtual Private Network (VPN), which may be a consideration for a closed network of trading partners, this type of security will not support the use of services accessed from public directories over the Web.

Internal integration will be facilitated using XML and SOAP to unlock information stored in application silos, from ERP backbones to CRM systems. Freeing up this information will significantly reduce the cost of systems implementation, allowing organizations to maintain a consistent view of business operations and metrics across the enterprise in support of real-time executive information systems and portal solutions for employees, customers, and suppliers.

Plan of Action

In order for the integration phase to be successful, the following steps are recommended:

1. Schedule executive briefings and initiate discussions regarding the strategic value of Web services for your organization.
2. Develop a broad-based Web services education and training program covering the high-level concepts and terminology. Completion of this training should be mandatory for management and executive roles.
3. Complete an inventory of the application portfolio and determine when each software vendor plans to rollout Web service-enabled versions of their applications. This will help firms decide when and where it makes sense to consider creating virtual services for reuse versus waiting for software vendors to add Web services interfaces to their packages.
4. Investigate industry-specific data definition standards and ensure your firm consistently uses those that apply to your organization. Where industry data standards do not exist, develop internal standards that can be used consistently across your organization.
5. Identify areas where the availability of real-time business intelligence will provide strategic business value to your executives. For example, availability of real-time channel inventory and Point of Sales (POS) data for the largest customers, cross-referenced with your own manufacturing schedules, might make it possible to better balance manufacturing capacity with anticipated demand. With enough forward visibility into your own, customer, partner, and supplier data, it becomes far more possible to manage proactively rather than reactively. Implement Web service-enabled, real-time executive dashboards, and collaborate with partners, suppliers, and customers to pool operating data, improving visibility into business network inefficiencies, and create opportunities to reduce operating costs.
6. Pilot Web services in areas where EAI tools might have been considered. This will result in immediate cost avoidance as integration problems are solved with open, standards-based technology.
7. While implementing early pilot projects, ensure both business and IT personnel are tasked with the identification and prioritization of both tactical and strategic opportunities in which Web services can be further leveraged. This is the ideal time to start prioritization of your firm's internal Web services build-out.
8. Begin identification of critical business processes and functions that can benefit from Web services as your firm moves into the collaboration phase.

9. Continue to monitor emerging standards to determine when standards such as *business process execution* (for example, BPEL4WS) transition from the emerging to the evolving tier. This will indicate that the collaboration phase will imminently become a mainstream focus for many organizations.

The experience gained during the integration phase of the Web services adoption model will lay the foundation for the collaboration phase, both from a business and technical perspective.

PHASE TWO: COLLABORATION

Phase two is the collaboration phase, in which Web services standards are used to enable closer real-time collaboration with partners, customers, and suppliers. Early collaboration will leverage the same standards (specifically, XML, SOAP, and WSDL) and techniques used during the integration phase, but as experience and confidence in Web services increase, organizations will begin to implement extended business processes that go beyond the limits of the organizational boundaries. These extended business processes will leverage both internally developed Web services, as well as exposing services to trusted partners and suppliers over the Web. These extended business processes will necessitate the use of standards that are currently on the outer fringes of the evolving tier and in the emerging tier of the Web services stack (for example, UDDI and BPEL4WS). Figure 3.5 builds on our example of the virtual order entry service discussed in the previous section, and leverages the Provider, Broker, and Consumer model introduced in Chapter 2.

In this example, the model has been extended to incorporate additional aspects of Web services that support collaboration activities. Here the virtual order entry service has been described using WSDL and published in a private UDDI services registry. From the services registry it is possible to search and find the order entry service. Once the service has been found, it is then possible to bind with it for communication and execution. In this example the service registry might purely be leveraged as an internal services repository, but it may also be extended to allow access by authorized partners, suppliers, and customers. A customer may choose to integrate access to the order entry service into their own systems, allowing automation of the order entry process and giving them real-time visibility of the order status. The ability to deliver this type of functionality will likely reduce costs, as well as improve customer satisfaction and retention. Providing this level of service may also differentiate a firm from its competitors.

Collaboration is defined as the act or process of working with others. Collaboration in the business sense is the active partnering with allies, and even competitors, for the mutual benefit of all participants. Collaboration

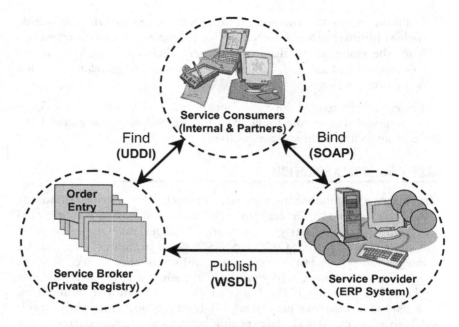

FIGURE 3.5 Leverage the provider, broker, and consumer model.

was viewed as one of the Holy Grails of the Internet boom as more and more organizations adopted B2B models by joining trade exchanges or creating their own private B2B exchanges. However, as many B2B exchanges and other collaboration efforts failed, the reasons for their demise became clear: The challenges and cost of integration for collaboration were too high for most organizations to bear.

We anticipate that a few early adopters will have entered the collaboration phase by early 2003, while others will wait for greater stability with emerging standards in the business process management and execution layer, which will likely occur in mid to late 2003.

Business Landscape

The collaboration phase of Web services adoption is characterized by the following traits:

- The opportunity to achieve significantly reduced per transaction costs with business partners, suppliers, and customers by using Web services to reduce the level of human intervention in collaborative business processes.
- Building on reduced transaction costs, it may be possible to offer new products or services targeted toward a lower price point, allowing entry into new markets and creating new revenue streams.

- Attain closer collaboration with external trading partners, where real-time information enabled through the use of Web services will help identify and achieve new sources of business benefits.
- Larger organizations will reduce their operating risks through better information management and by pushing risk out along the extended value chain to their vendors, suppliers, and partners.

Collaboration using extended business processes can be applied to many aspects of a business value chain, including:

- *Product Development*—New product development collaboration can dramatically shorten the time to market for new products as organizations share design and simulation data with critical suppliers for key components and modules of manufactured products. Faster time to market, combined with a reduction in industry R&D through shared design processes, will drive dramatic gains in efficiency and productivity for the manufacturing industries.
- *Procurement and Strategic Sourcing*—The use of Web services to share production schedules and projected purchasing needs in near real-time with suppliers can drive tremendous savings in an organization's procurement spend. Forecasts for long and short lead-time commodities will become more accurate through increased sharing of information and real-time analysis. This use of Web services is already visible in the computer manufacturing industry, where the shelf-life and obsolescence of components is a constant challenge.
- *Inventory Management*—Inventory levels can be reduced within an organization as well as across an industry supply chain as organizations work together to share customer information and aggregate market demand. This is especially important in industries where rapid product obsolescence erodes the value of inventory, and therefore minimizing inventory levels is critical for maintaining razor-thin profit margins. Collaborating on demand signals from the sell side of the supply chain (such as, end-customers, retailers, distributors, contract manufacturers) as well as the buy side of the supply chain (such as contract manufacturers and suppliers, manufacturers) can dramatically shorten lead times and reduce the amount of inventory required to keep up with market demand.
- *Supply Chain Management (SCM)*—Supply chain management can be improved with collaborative processes within a manufacturing organization as well as in services industries. Managing order fulfillment, order to cash processes, logistics processes, inbound and outbound inventory processes, customer service processes—all of which can be considered part of the macro-level view of a supply chain for an

organization. And these are not just manufacturing issues. Insurance companies also have supply chains in the form of quoting insurance policies, sending paper or electronic quotes, integrating agents and brokers in the distribution channel, mailing actual paper policies and invoices to customers, and more. These are inbound and outbound shipping and order fulfilment issues that are common to almost any industry, and therefore collaboration techniques can be used to improve the management of information as well as physical objects to and from customers and suppliers. All industries have pro-curement processes for direct and indirect materials. All industries have outbound processes that service customers and trading partners.

■ *Logistics Collaboration*—Collaboration can provide great benefits in inbound, outbound, and reverse logistics processes. Original Equipment Manufacturers (OEMs) can use collaboration processes to manage outsourced shipping and receiving processes, and to provide visibility to third-party logistics providers (3PLs).

Planning Considerations

As discussed, collaboration can drive process and operational improvements in many business areas, provided that the integration hurdles can be overcome and that the tools and technologies are mature enough to enable true collaborative behavior.

Web services can facilitate increased collaboration among businesses along the dimensions described above, since in many cases they fit the generic criteria for successfully deploying Web services: processes that are recurring, dynamic, and disconnected.[4] Web services provide the right blend of standards-based technology and cost-benefit to allow organizations to realize the real business benefits of collaboration.

Initially, as collaboration processes are implemented, they will be targeted toward close trading partners or internal divisions of large multinationals and conglomerates:

> "*Companies experimenting with Web services over the Internet are doing so only with established business partners. For now.*"[5]

As experience is gained through increasing the scope and reach of collaboration for a variety of business processes, organizations will have the confidence to extend collaboration to trading partners outside of their normal partner channels. As the reach of collaboration is extended through Web services, increased benefits will accrue through interaction with more partners and by implementation across additional business functions.

As Web services standards and technology mature, particularly security standards, Web services collaboration will be extended to reach a growing number of trading partners. As this network or ecosystem of connected partners, suppliers, and customers continues to grow, organizations will increasingly derive greater business benefit through, for example, reduced inventories, improved cash flow, and greater customer satisfaction. Collaboration will inevitably be a significant driver behind the adoption of Web services technology, and will lead to more creative uses of Web services, along with their increased penetration into all areas of business operations, internally as well as across a networked value chain.

Plan of Action

Collaboration using Web services will require that every organization take specific actions in order to take advantage of their collaboration opportunities. These actions include:

1. Continue education and communication programs to ensure that both business and technical personnel are aware of the direction in which the organization is moving and how the deployment of Web services will impact them.
2. Start working with key trusted partners to ensure that they are willing to participate in pilot collaboration projects and that they are developing the technical capabilities to support the implementation of Web services.
3. Identify candidate business processes that can be extended across corporate firewalls using Web services. Initially focus on processes that can be automated with close trading partners who are willing to pilot programs for mutual benefit. Use the lessons learned from these initial forays to tackle high-cost, high-value process that can yield the greatest returns.
4. Consider where collaborative processes can improve business fitness metrics such as time to market, operating efficiency, cycle times, inventory costs, cash flow, and customer satisfaction.
5. Monitor Web services standards, specifically looking to the adoption of service registries (specifically, UDDI) for service publication and discovery, as well as business process execution (for example, BPEL4WS) standards.
6. Secure Identity Management (SIM) will play an important role in the collaborative use of Web services. Look to OASIS and the Liberty Alliance to see how the technologies that enable services registries and identity management will possibly converge.
7. During the early stages of the collaboration phase, it is not necessary to wait for Web services security to be fully ironed out. Virtual Private

Networks (VPNs) can be established with trusted partners to provide bulletproof security. Investigate the deployment of a VPN, but track the progress of Web services security standards such as WS-Security and XML Key Management Service (XKMS).

Maturation in the collaboration phase of the Web services adoption model will prepare organizations for the innovation phase of the Web services adoption model. The innovation phase will spur a new wave of rapid business change, which will largely shape the next wave of Internet expansion for organizations worldwide.

PHASE THREE: INNOVATION

During the innovation phase of the Web services adoption model, organizations will devise new ways of doing business enabled through the use of Web services. The innovation phase will require use of the full complement of Web services standards, spanning the spectrum of the identified enabling, evolving, and emerging standards. Specifically, standards and capabilities that support Web services security, management, asynchronous transactions, and process orchestration will become increasingly important. During this phase organizations will leverage what has been learned from internal integration projects and from collaboration projects with customers, partners, and suppliers. These organizations will rely on their experience and knowledge base to develop new business opportunities and sources of competitive advantage. These organizations will use Web services as an innovation platform to drive new levels of business performance, or fundamentally change the dynamics of the markets they operate in.

Two key categories of organizations will emerge as the leaders during the innovation phase:

1. *Early Adopters*—Those organizations that were early adopters during the integration and collaboration phase will be among the first to truly grasp the innovation potential of Web services.
2. *New Entrants*—Any disruptive technology creates the potential for significant shifts in market dynamics, and the emergence of Web services will be no exception. Consider how Dell Computer forever changed the landscape of the personal computer (PC) market place by mastering the direct channel sales model. In just over fifteen years Dell was able to evolve from a garage business to the number one PC manufacturer in the world.

Expect to see the first signs of truly innovative Web services usage in late 2003, to early 2004. Usage of Web services to drive innovation will continue to disrupt markets for several years as new opportunities to drive competitive advantage or change market dynamics are discovered.

Business Landscape

The innovation phase of Web services adoption will be characterized by the following traits:

- Organizations will apply the lessons learned from the integration and collaboration phases of Web services adoption to new processes and business models, redefining how organizations work with partners, suppliers, and customers.
- Publishing and discovery of services using UDDI registries will be widely utilized as organizations begin exposing and extending their internal processes using Web services standards.
- Organizations will transition from purely Web service consumers to also being Web service providers. Those organizations that recognize the value of their IT intellectual property, based on core competencies in IT, will be able to create new revenue streams by publishing their IT assets as Web services for others to consume. This in effect will change the IT department from a cost center to a profit center.
- Distributed Web services will be leveraged in extended business processes, driving business change in unanticipated directions as first movers experiment with Web services to drive new sources of competitive advantage.
- New business value will be created as value chains are expanded beyond traditional industry segments and boundaries.

Web services innovators will be forward-thinking organizations that see the big picture of how this technology will fundamentally change business dynamics. Innovators will seek new ways to drive business value and develop new revenue streams through the application of Web services technology. These organizations will redefine how business processes will be conducted across the boundaries of the traditional four walls of the organization. They will know how to expose very specific operational elements of their enterprise and dynamically link them to the corresponding processes of partners, suppliers, and customers.

For example, Wachovia Corporation and Thomson Financial extended their business processes using Web services by leveraging Grand Central as a services broker:

> *Wachovia Corp.'s Securities Equity Capital Markets division, in Charlotte, North Carolina, uses Grand Central's Web Services Network to share market data with Thomson Financial, which provides data and analysis services to the financial industry. Wachovia's intranet connects to the Grand Central network using SOAP, and Thomson connects to Grand Central using Microsoft's ASP.NET. Previously, the companies were exchanging these reports via FTP; the failure rate was 2 to 4 percent.*

Though the Wachovia IT team considered tackling the development themselves, Gwen Moertel, head of IT for the Securities Equity Capital Markets group, ultimately decided there were just too many hurdles. One of the biggest was getting a sign-off from numerous internal groups. "I would have had to go to our FTP guys, to our security guys, and to our database guys—just getting the approval would have taken months—so outsourcing made sense for us," she says.[6]

Such operations are bound by workflow processes and Web services technologies into distributed information-based processes, reaching new levels of efficiency, collaboration, adaptability, and flexibility.

Planning Considerations

During the innovation phase Web services will truly become a disruptive influence for many organizations and markets. Initially, most disruptive technologies cause chaos, and the disruption created by Web services will be no exception. Thinking back to the introduction of the first microprocessor by Intel in 1971,[7] IBM and the other mainframe manufacturers showed no interest in, and saw no market potential for, small PCs.

The development of the 4004 and later the 8008 microprocessor chip created the opportunity for innovators such as Apple, Tandy, and Commodore to capture an early lead in the emerging PC market. By the time IBM entered the PC market, it faced stiff competition from organizations that had already been selling PCs for a number of years.

The point is that even though large established organizations such as IBM have the people and capabilities, they sometimes lack the organizational flexibility and vision to embrace disruptive technologies. This allows those unencumbered by predefined operating plans, corporate mandates, and rigid reporting structures to grasp the innovation opportunities.

As the number and pace of disruptive ideas continues to increase, it is increasingly important that organizations develop and nurture the ability to think "Out of the Box." As James C. Collins and Jerry I. Porras discuss in their book *Built to Last*,[8] it is critical to preserve the core, but continually stimulate progress. From the perspective of stimulating progress Collins and Porras suggest three organizational characteristics that can play a significant role in an organizations ability to adapt and innovate:

- *Try a Lot of Stuff and Keep What Works*—It is critical that organizations create an environment in which it is okay to experiment, to learn what does not work, and perhaps be surprised by what does.
- *Good Enough Never Is*—Everyone in every part of the organization should push the accepted boundaries, striving for never-ending improvement in all aspects of the organization.

* *Big Hairy Audacious Goals (BHAG)*—A BHAG (pronounced b-hag) represents a project or goal that goes to the roots of the organization. Take, for example, Boeing's decision to commit their company to the introduction of the first commercial jet aircraft when everyone else believed that jets were only appropriate for military use. A BHAG challenges the norm and seeks to push the organizational boundaries, moving beyond the expected and taking the organization to new levels. Be aware that BHAGs are not for the faint of heart. Boeing bet and nearly lost the company in its efforts to develop the first commercial jet aircraft, but subsequently dominated the commercial aircraft industry for several decades.

The innovation phase will undoubtedly witness the emergence of new organizations as well as the morphing of established ones, but without a doubt the implications of Web services are not an "if" scenario but rather a "when" scenario. A firm does not need to be on the bleeding edge of the Web services tsunami, but do not wait to get washed away by the organizations who truly understand the implications of Web services for business innovation.

Plan of Action

Innovation using Web services will build upon capabilities developed during the integration and collaboration phases, but perhaps more importantly will require some organizations to make cultural changes to support and nurture an entrepreneurial and innovation-friendly environment. Important activities during this phase include:

1. Complete the back-office build out of Web service from both an integration and collaboration perspective. A Service Oriented Architecture (SOA), see Chapter 7, "Architecting for Competitive Advantage," will provide greater flexibility to innovate and adapt as new competitive threats and challenges emerge.
2. Create a small multidisciplinary innovation team tasked with thinking "Out of the Box." This team should bear three key questions in mind:

    * How can Web services be leveraged for innovation of current processes and capabilities?
    * What do we really excel at? Can these capabilities be exposed as Web services to create new revenue streams?
    * Are there any Big Hairy Audacious Goals (BHAG) that Web services can help us achieve?

3. Network with peers to see how they are using Web services for business innovation. Now is not the time to experiment in isolation.
4. As Collins and Porras suggest in *Built to Last*, "Try a Lot of Stuff and Keep What Works." Where possible, experiment with Web services,

learn from what does not work, and build upon what does. You might be surprised by what you learn and will be able to leverage successes to achieve competitive advantage.

5. Be sure to monitor emerging players in your markets as they may be positioning themselves to change the rules. As with the example of Dell Computer, new entrants may be better positioned, less encumbered, and more nimble in their ability to implement new business models. Learn what you can from these new entrants and be prepared to adapt quickly to changing market dynamics.

6. Do not let your investment in Web services get out of control. It will be critical to balance innovation with governance to ensure that newly developed Web services are deployed when and where appropriate, and are leveraged by authorized employees, partners, and suppliers to achieve maximum business benefit.

7. Continue to monitor Web services standards to determine which new standards can be leveraged to further extend the capabilities and options open to both you and your competitors. As discussed in Chapter 2, the W3C, OASIS, and the WS-I are three standards organizations that are extremely active in the Web services space and well worth keeping on eye on.

The innovation phase of Web services adoption will eliminate major roadblocks to the widespread use of Web services. Web services will enable new business process innovation and, ultimately, new levels of business execution and performance.

PHASE FOUR: DOMINATION

The final phase of Web services adoption is the culmination of the previous three phases—integration, collaboration, and innovation. The dominance phase will be based on superior performance in business as well as on the use of Web services to achieve innovation. Dominance will be established by the few key players in each industry that are able to realize the full potential of Web services. Those that dominate will have achieved internal cost and efficiency gains, as well as having significantly improved their ability to collaborate with partners, suppliers, and customers through the implementation of Web services.

The winners in the dominance phase will emerge as commerce hubs at the center of Web services-enabled ecosystems. Dominant organizations will use Web services to link their internal value chain and extend it beyond the organizational boundaries to include partners, suppliers, and customers as illustrated in Figure 3.6. Through the use of Web services, these organizations will achieve reduced operating costs, improved organizational flexibility, and dramatically faster time to market.

Web services will enable the seamless integration of a networked eco-system of partners and suppliers, extending the value chain beyond the traditional organizational boundaries

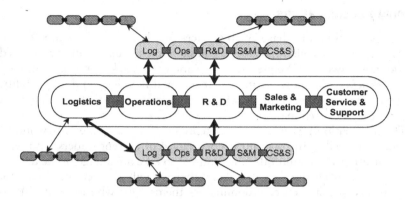

FIGURE 3.6   Extending the value chain with Web services.

Business Landscape

The dominance phase of Web services adoption will be characterized by the following traits:

- It is likely that leaders in the dominance phase will either be newly emerging organizations, or will have been early adopters of Web services during the integration and collaboration phases, and will have been the first to determine how to innovate using Web services.
- Extended business processes spanning multiple organizations will become commonplace. Organizations will operate as part of truly interconnected ecosystems of businesses.
- Dominance phase leaders will have demonstrated the ability to drive internal integration costs down, and will have learned the pitfalls of Web services.
- Leaders in the dominance phase will use Web services to enable new ways of delivering information-based value to the organization as well as to customers, partners, and suppliers.
- Dominance phase winners will have learned how to use Web services to achieve real innovation, perhaps fundamentally changing the dynamics of their chosen markets.

By the time dominance has been established by forward-thinking inno-vators, the technologies and standards required to build-out Web services will have matured considerably, to the point where they are a key component of most organizations' technology infrastructures.

Planning Considerations

During the domination phase, Web services will be used as core application building blocks in which applications will be implemented as an orchestrated workflow of networked Web services. The ability to quickly and easily modify these workflows will allow greater organizational flexibility and adaptability, which will be a key element in allowing organizations to maintain a dominant position in their chosen markets.

The domination phase will undoubtedly see the emergence of new industry leaders, as well as the continued domination of current leaders who have the organizational and cultural traits required to take advantage of the disruption created by Web services. It is likely that we will also see the decline of organizations, perhaps current dominators themselves, who are not able to effectively adopt Web services into their businesses. They will find that their internal systems are too inflexible to allow them to adapt to changing market dynamics, and that the ability to collaborate with partners, suppliers, and customers is undermined by competitors who have exposed selected processes using Web services to support extended business processes.

Remember, the key difference between the dominant organizations and the rest of the pack is the application of Web services to their businesses. Adoption of Web services technology will not be the biggest challenge for most organizations. Driving significant business value and competitive advantage through the use of Web services is the real opportunity and the real challenge.

Plan of Action

To attain market dominance using Web services, organizations will need to master the application of Web services for business value and market differentiation. The simple application of Web services to support current business practices will not be sufficient. Critical activities will include:

1. Look for innovation opportunities which will allow you to do the following:

    * Reduce costs and improve margins
    * Create new market opportunities
    * Increase the barriers to entry for competitors

2. The next disruptive influence is right around the corner, or perhaps is already arriving, so don't disband your innovation team. They should continue to think "Out of the Box" and should be tasked with looking beyond the horizon to determine how to leverage the next disruptive influence (for example, the semantic web and grid-computing).

The domination phase of the Web services adoption model will see the move to, and acceptance of, new business operating principles that leverage Web services at their core. New markets will be created that are enabled through the use of Web services. Current market leaders that do not leverage Web services will decline, and new leaders will emerge. Ultimately, Web services will fade into the background as they become part of the day-to-day fabric of how IT systems are implemented and how businesses operate as new disruptive technologies take center stage.

OBSTACLES TO ADOPTION

As discussed in Chapter 2, "Standards, Concepts, and Terminology," Web services standards are currently at varying degrees of maturity. On one end of the maturity spectrum the enabling standards are very solid, while on the other end of the spectrum the emerging standards are still very much in flux. As we look at the Web services adoption model, there are significant gaps in the emerging standards that need to be resolved to allow Web services to progress. These gaps represent potential obstacles to the Web services adoption model and, if left unresolved, will likely slow the adoption of Web services beyond basic integration and rudimentary collaboration capabilities. Figure 3.7 illustrates the four adoption phases and associated obstacles to adoption.

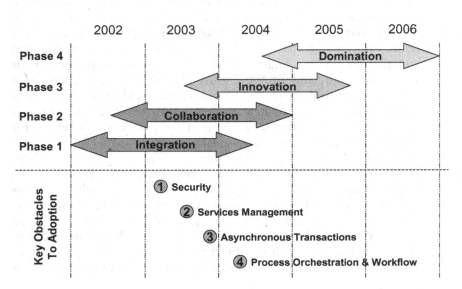

FIGURE 3.7 Obstacles to Web services adoption.

As Figure 3.7 illustrates, the obstacles to Web services adoption are primarily centered on the collaboration phase. As the collaboration phase gains momentum, the demands for greater collaboration will progressively require the following:

1. *Security*—Web services will undoubtedly introduce additional security risks for organizations that chose to expose services outside of the corporate firewall. Early collaboration initiatives can use Virtual Private Networks (VPNs) to create a closed network of trusted partners, but security standards for using Web services over the public Internet are only now being defined. Refer to Chapter 2, "Standards, Concepts, and Terminology," for more information on Web services security standards.

2. *Services Management*—As the number of Web services in use increases, it becomes increasingly important for organizations to understand what, when, where, and by whom services are being used. Much as with e-Commerce initiatives, it will become important to monitor the Quality of Service (QoS) that Web services are providing for partners, suppliers, and customers.

3. *Asynchronous Transactions*—As collaborative Web service transactions become more complex, they will gain longevity. Long-running transactions that persist indefinitely will eventually become common. In this environment, once a complex set of transactions has been started, it will be necessary to know the success or failure of a number of related transactions to determine an overall success or failure status. For example, if you are booking travel to Seattle, a booking system might include the transactions of booking the flight, the hotel, and the rental car. In this scenario you would only want to confirm the hotel and car rental if the flight is booked successfully. In recent months IBM, Microsoft, and BEA published the Web services Transaction (WS-Transaction) proposed standard to tackle this issue. WS-Transaction is still very much an emerging standard, and as such it is not yet clear if it will gain widespread acceptance and adoption for Web services transaction management.

4. *Process Orchestration and Workflow*—As the portfolio of available Web services, both within and across organizations, continues to grow, it will become increasingly important to orchestrate Web services as part of end-to-end business processes or workflows. For example, you might want to automate the booking process discussed above, using a process-driven booking and confirmation system. A booking agent or consumer might enter all the travel requirements via a Web site, and the orchestrated booking process manages the individual Web services

for each step of the overall transaction. Obviously, the ability to determine success or failure of each individual step of the process is an important prerequisite for the implementation of process orchestration.

Again, IBM, Microsoft, and BEA have published proposed standards to tackle the Web services process orchestration requirements. The Web Services Coordination (WS-Coordination) and Business Process Execution Language for Web Services (BPEL4WS) are leveraged together first to coordinate a group of Web services, and secondly to weave a coordinated group of services into a higher-level business process. As with WS-Transaction, WS-Coordination and BPEL4WS are emerging standards, and have yet to gain widespread acceptance and adoption.

These obstacles are only potential roadblocks, and in many instances major industry players like IBM and Microsoft are already actively engaged in proposing and developing potential solutions as with WS-Security, WS-Transaction, etc. The real test for these proposals is gaining the broad acceptance required to prevent the fragmentation of Web services standards, or if other organizations undermine them by pushing their own proposed standards.

Domination

•First movers begin to assert their dominance over respective markets and industries

•Industry dominance achieved by innovating new business models as well as out-executing competitors

•Web services leaders win through rapid innovation and cycles of learning

•Web services mastery creates new company and industry structures as boundaries are redefined

Innovation

•Lessons from integration and collaboration applied to new processes and business models

•New distributed WS processes and applications drive business change

•Dramatic business results are achieved as WS are applied in new ways, driving new value propositions

Collaboration

•Experimentation with WS outside firewalls

•Increasing interaction with trading partners & customers

•Close trading partners implement Web services to drive shared value

•"External" trading partners begin sharing information to drive industry value chain benefits

Integration

•Experimentation with Web services with small, internal integration projects

•SOAP-enablement of legacy applications and ERP, CRM systems

•Fast cycles of learning reach the limits of early Web Services, immature standards, and unprepared IT architectures

•Increase in shared information across the business

FIGURE 3.8 Benefits of Web services by adoption phase.

SUMMARY

The benefits of Web services will accrue as they are embraced along the trajectory of the adoption model depicted in Figure 3.8. In phase one of the Web services adoption model, the benefits of Web services will be realized primarily in internal integration. The use of Web services to accomplish simple integration tasks between legacy applications, enterprise computing systems and other business applications will be the primary theme for early Web services initiatives. Benefits of the integration phase include increased information availability and an eventual shift of IT resources and effort away from the integration of legacy and stovepipe systems toward driving front-end customer benefits and revenue-generating processes.

In the collaboration phase of Web services adoption, the benefits will build upon those realized in the Integration stage. Once the invisible yet seemingly insurmountable barriers of internal integration have been overcome, followed by B2B integration across organizational boundaries and firewalls, then the business benefits of collaboration can be realized. Benefits here include reduced transaction costs, an increase in shared information and extended business processes with trading partners, and closer relationships with customers, suppliers, and partners.

The innovation phase of Web services adoption will give rise to new ways of doing business across corporate boundaries, as well as new business models built on distributed business processes. New sources of value will be derived from rapid innovation of Web services solutions, and the first movers will reap tremendous benefits from their initial investments in Web service-enabled extended business processes, while late adopters will gradually cede leadership in their industries. The producer, consumer, and broker roles of Web services blur as Web services become the de facto method of conducting business. Once again, the benefits of Web services continue to build on previous phases, conferring significant advantage to the organizations that have progressed through the earlier phases of integration and collaboration.

By the time organizations reach the domination phase of the Web services adoption model, they will have separated themselves from their competitors. These organizations will leverage the innovations and ideas of the previous phases, turning them into new ways of providing value to new and existing customers. These organizations will become the dominant players in their respective industries, and will wield significant influence over contiguous industries as market boundaries blur.

The specific benefits of Web services in the adoption model will emerge as the standards and technologies of Web services are developed and stabilized. Many organizations are already well into the collaboration phase based on their early adoption of XML and SOAP. Not surprisingly, these are organizations that were first movers in using the Internet as a means of conducting business. The lesson from the Web services adoption model is clear: Begin using Web services now, and gain cycles of learning quickly. Apply Web services to real business problems, and deliver true business value from early projects. Wait too long and your future may be imperilled.

ENDNOTES

[1] www.cio.com, *CIO Magazine*, August 15, 2002, "Return on Investment," by Sari Kalin.

[2] Forrester Research, December 2001, "Reducing Integration's Cost," by Laura Koetzle.

[3] *EAI Journal*, January 2002, "Building A Business Case For EAI," by Christy Bass and J. Michael Lee.

[4] Forrester Research, December 2001, "The Web Services Payoff," by Simon Yates, 6.

[5] www.cio.com, *CIO Magazine*, September 1, 2002, "Web Services—Still Not Ready for Prime Time," by Ben Worthen.

[6] PC Magazine, June 30 2002, "Web Services Warm Up," by Sarah L. Roberts-Witt.

[7] www.intel.com, Processor Hall of Fame.

[8] Harper Business, New York, 1994, "Built to Last," by James C. Collins and Jerry I. Porras, pp. 90, 93–94, ISBN 0-88730-671-3.

CHAPTER 4

Strategic Implications of Web Services

"Nothing will ever be attempted, if all possible objections must first be overcome."

Samuel Johnson

"You are today where your thoughts have brought you. You will be tomorrow where your thoughts take you."

James Lane Allen

In order to truly understand and appreciate the current and future business implications of Web services, it is critical to first start with a strategic perspective. Only once the strategic implications are fully understood is it possible to appreciate how Web services might fundamentally change the business model and day-to-day operational imperatives for corporations. This chapter explores Web services from strategic, business model, and value chain perspectives, demonstrating that the decision to invest in this emerging technology will have an impact well beyond the confines of the information technology organization. These implications will require firms to revisit organizational structures and operating processes, and in some instances, will redefine the fundamental premises upon which an organization is built.

A BUSINESS PERSPECTIVE

The groundbreaking *Harvard Business Review* article, "Your Next IT Strategy,"[1] discussed a number of potential impacts that Web services might have. The authors speculate that the IT function might shift from a cost center to a profit center. This might be achieved, for example, where

Intellectual Property (IP), locked inside internal applications systems, is re-purposed and packaged as Web services, then offered on a fee basis over the Web. The barriers to entry for some markets will fall, as basic IT capabilities are delivered as "computing on demand."[2] This new model for delivery of IT capabilities will allow small and mid-sized organizations to scale their business capabilities more cost effectively, helping them to avoid much of the initial capital investment typically required to implement a firm's IT infrastructure. The funds released by this approach might be used as working capital to accelerate growth, or to minimize the need for expensive external borrowing.

These scenarios are a glimpse into the not-too-distant future of business capabilities enabled through the use of Web services. Today it is very difficult to determine when, or even if, these scenarios will become a reality. From a pragmatic perspective, it is certainly realistic to surmise that Web services will be used as the basis for developing new models for information delivery, IT systems procurement, and application deployment. These models will have a significant impact on how businesses operate, allowing them to consider new possibilities for which markets to enter, which markets to remain in, and which markets to exit. Those companies that are late to adopt Web services may well be forced to fundamentally reconsider their business strategies as market dynamics shift under the pressures generated by early adopters.

Organizations using Web services will identify new ways in which to implement their business strategies, removing or circumventing inhibitors in their business models and value chains. As firms leverage Web services, it will be critical that their implications be considered as part of the strategic planning process, ideally starting with the organization's business strategy and filtering down through the business model and value chain. As illustrated in Figure 4.1, Web services will have implications at each level of the strategic planning process.

The following sections look at elements of the strategic planning process, examining considerations for use of Web services as well as their implications.

Business Strategy and the Business Model

The process of developing a business strategy and implementing it as an operational business model is complex. This section does not delve into the specifics of developing a business strategy, but rather seeks to illustrate how Web services can impact or enhance an existing business strategy, opening up new target markets or changing the ways in which a firm interfaces with its partners, suppliers and customers. Web services will impact corporate strategy from a number of perspectives, such as the following:

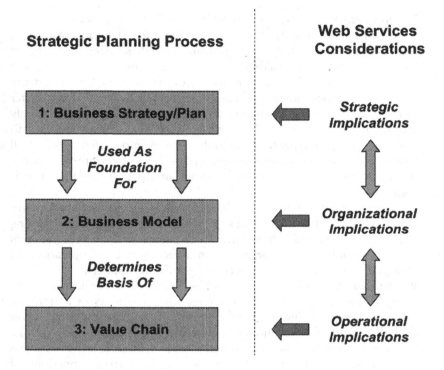

Strategic Planning Process

Web Services Considerations

1: Business Strategy/Plan ⟵ *Strategic Implications*

Used As Foundation For

2: Business Model ⟵ *Organizational Implications*

Determines Basis Of

3: Value Chain ⟵ *Operational Implications*

FIGURE 4.1 Web services as part of the strategic planning process.

- *Identification of Target Markets*—Decisions regarding the scope of products and services and the determination of target customers and geographies may all require scrutiny. Where appropriate, Web services will be used to augment products, providing remote monitoring, maintenance notifications, and other value-added information services. They will serve as a basis for competitive differentiation by changing the ways in which a firm operates internally as well as with its trading partners.
- *Corporate Performance Management (CPM)*—Historically, the ability to monitor business performance relative to business activity has suffered a significant time lag. Information derived from diverse and often disconnected sources needed to be collected and aggregated from disparate systems in order for it to be presented in a usable format, reflecting the organization's structure. With the use of Web services, executives can expect to receive information that is accurate, current, and relevant to the organization structure. Armed with this information executives can more rapidly and effectively identify those operations that are under performing or exceeding expectations.

- *Customers, Partners, and Suppliers*—Web services will play a significant role in how organizations interact in everyday trading relationships, particularly with customers. Web services will support supply chain visibility, enabling more effective inventory management across the supply chain and reducing on-hand stock levels and the frequency of stock outages. Channel partners will benefit from better visibility of inventory levels and customer demand across the supply chain. Customer service will be enhanced as Web services are used to integrate customer data from multiple systems into a single view. Call centers and customer service professionals will be able to provide better service by having more accurate customer information available at their fingertips.

- *Automation of Business Processes*—As Web services adoption progresses, new business processes will be implemented, automating manual processes and collaboration with partners. These processes will become the fabric of the organization, affecting internal operations as well as interaction with customers, partners, and suppliers.

- *Organizational Agility*—Agility will be enhanced as applications built using Web services are used to remove the constraints of a static IT infrastructure, creating greater flexibility for strategic planning. Over time the world of large, monolithic software installations may well be replaced by Just-In-Time (JIT) systems implementation, where business applications are implemented using Web services, from a portfolio of internally and externally published services. JIT system implementations will support new business models in which rapid IT response to changing business requirements is an accepted norm.

- *Organizational Structures*—Structures will change as the transaction costs associated with customer interaction, supplier interaction, and IT provisioning are dramatically reduced through the use of Web services.

- *IT Strategy and Management*—IT strategies will change, affecting the internal operations of organizations as well as the processes by which IT applications are researched, evaluated, tested, deployed, and eventually retired.

To take full advantage of Web services it will be necessary to develop a new approach to the use of IT. In order to maximize the business potential of available data assets, organizations must explicitly embed information-driven competitive differentiators within their business strategy and business model. Only once this has been achieved can the full potential for superior performance be driven from the business model.

Creating Intimacy with Customers, Partners, and Suppliers   The idea of getting closer to customers, partners, and suppliers has special relevance with the emergence of Web services. Given the high costs associated with integration and collaboration activities, Web services can be used to reduce the cost of sharing information, or linking with customers, partners, and suppliers. Web services provide open standards-based interfaces for access to information that will facilitate the partnering relationship.

On the customer-facing side (specifically commercial customers, not individual consumers) of the organization, shared information and linking can help align the core strategy of the organization with its value delivery processes. This assures that the products and services being delivered are truly valued by customers—of course, in this scenario value must be judged by customer-driven definitions. This linking element determines the value of products and services provided to customers and the feedback required to confirm that the products and services are what the market needs and wants. There may be opportunities to provide more value or different value that will differentiate one organization from another, resulting in market share gains and additional profits. Web services provide a critical vehicle for delivering additional value with products and services by forging a seamless information link to customers. They can provide lower cost interaction with customers at a more effective level, due to the ability to interface to systems for targeted business information exchange.

A critical consideration for creating intimacy with customers, partners, and suppliers is the need to define the organization's boundaries, which are based on what the organization performs in house versus sourcing from suppliers, or outsourced to partners. This situation introduces the notion of business transactions based on Ronald Coase's research.[3] This research suggests that if a particular business activity can be performed at lower cost outside the organization than inside, and it is not vital to the core corporate strategy to own the resources or the processes, then it may be outsourced. The way an organization determines what remains core and what is noncore can have serious implications for strategy achievement as well as the cost structure of the value chain. This becomes a vital linking element, especially given the information processes that must be implemented to achieve it. Web services promise to impact these decisions as the cost and effort of partnering, especially in forging tighter information links with new suppliers and partners, is reduced using open standard interfaces implemented using Web services. Ultimately, this means that more partners can be used to drive value on the input side of a business, which will result in structural changes to organization boundaries, based on outsourcing and co-sourcing strategies with suppliers.

The Friction Free Enterprise Web services will eliminate much of the friction in conducting internal and external business operations. They hold the potential to reduce an organization's internal transaction costs, but more importantly, they will dramatically reshape interactions between business partners. Transaction costs in existing value chains will be eliminated, and in some cases shifted to other areas of the value chain. Current industry structures will be challenged as the value propositions and viability of business processes, and in some cases entire businesses, are fundamentally impacted. This re-shaping of industry and business structures will be wrenching for organizations that do not anticipate them.

As discussed, Ronald Coase[4] suggests that transaction costs define the size of an organization as well as the business operations that it should perform. Firms that can perform business tasks more efficiently using internal capabilities and resources will keep those functions within the organization. As soon as it becomes less efficient to perform those business functions internally they should be outsourced, with the size of the organization shifting to accommodate the smaller set of internal functions. It is the distribution of transaction costs across a value chain that defines the economics of an industry and its structure.

Figure 4.2 illustrates how Web services will be embedded in every aspect of a business model, and therefore all corporate processes and functions, in order for organizations to reach higher levels of business perfor-

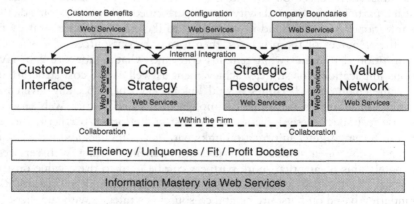

FIGURE 4.2 Web services and business models.

mance. This figure demonstrates how Web services will be pervasive, being adopted both within corporations as well as across industry value chains.

Change Is the Only Constant There will be far-reaching changes as Web services are infused into an organization's business model. Firms will need to adopt new modes of internal operation, from core strategy and strategic resource decisions to the ways in which it interacts with its customers and suppliers. These changes will extend to affect even the most basic preconceptions of how the company is configured to interoperate and drive business value.

The application of Web services can hold particular relevance for alignment of business and IT architectures, based on their inherent modularity and ease of integration into current business and IT architectures. Organizations that adopt Web services will have far more business and technical agility using smaller, focused application functionality versus large, monolithic enterprise applications. This means that changing the business architecture—the structure, processes, and capabilities of an organization—can be achieved more easily in support of information-based competitive initiatives. In parallel, introducing new business processes supported by information systems will be easier due to the anticipated ease of adding Web services-based applications to the IT portfolio. The actual footprint of Web services-based software applications, as they are eventually developed and marketed by software companies, remains to be seen, but the hope is that future applications will migrate away from the monolithic and complex enterprise applications of today, and will require far less custom integration to be incorporated into an existing IT portfolio.

Enabling Operational Flexibility and Agility Operating flexibility and agility provide an organization with the ability to refocus its strategy and resources quickly in response to new opportunities and threats. This ability may allow an organization to balance margin erosion in its core markets or product lines by quickly adjusting to provide new products, adding new value to existing products, or driving costs out of the current production processes.

Firms invest in flexibility and agility in a number of ways. For example, manufacturing companies have spent hundreds of millions of dollars investing in robotics, programmable logic controllers, and flexible tooling. All of these assets are reusable for new products and manufacturing lines due to their ability to be reprogrammed to suit the design data of new products. Web services hold a similar promise, through the use of lean, JIT, system development to rapidly respond to changing market and competitive conditions. Being able to tune and adapt a business model using Web services internally and externally will allow executives greater flexibility to respond to business challenges with unprecedented speed and agility. No longer will there be the typical 12-month plus lag between a business decision and the availability of systems to support the business direction. Coordination and alignment of the business and IT architecture to support corporate strategy and the business model will be a natural process, and it will provide competitive advantage to corporations as Web services become the basic building blocks for implementation of the enterprise systems architecture.

The preceding sections have illustrated the potential of Web services in several areas of an organization's business model, but actual implementations will vary by company and the markets in which a company competes. Viewing Web services from a business strategy perspective will help forge a dialogue between business and technology executives, resulting in shared purpose in driving new business value. Web services can provide the potential for firms to find new ways to grow revenue, realign costs, and improve productivity across the entire value chain. It will be this potential that will ensure that business impact and true business value drive the implementation of this emerging technology.

VALUE CHAIN ANALYSIS

It will not be the technical elegance of Web services that ensures their adoption, but rather the business value that they enable. If no incremental business value is created, if there is no competitive advantage in building and deploying Web services, then they will not gain the traction that many industry watchers anticipate. The sources of business value for an organization are derived from the composition and implementation of its business model. The business model is a vehicle through which business strategy is implemented, resulting in the basic structure of the firm, its core business process, and the strategic assets and intellectual property required to deliver value to customers and markets. An output of the business modeling process is a value chain, through which day-to-day operational imperatives are executed.

The value chain is comprised of the totality of activities required to perform processes and transactions for markets and customers. The result is the products and value-added services for which customers will pay a premium. In order to be a viable business entity, an organization must be able to perform these activities at a cost that is less than that which the market is prepared to pay for the products and services. Fundamentally, this is the basis upon which any firm makes money, and is how markets are defined—by the revenue potential markets hold, and the profits that might be earned by corporations servicing that market's customers.

Subsequent sections take a closer look at an organization's value chain, considering three distinct value chain perspectives:

* The business value chain
* The IT value chain
* The Web services value chain

Business Value Chain

Web services can drive the business value in several areas. Where and how they are applied can have a positive effect in the following areas:

* *Reduced Cost*—of internal systems integration, which allows shifting IT spending and staff efforts to other strategic initiatives.
* *Improve IT Agility*—by deploying smaller, standards-based business applications only as they are needed, and avoiding large, monolithic software applications that often are not fully utilized.
* *Improve Business Agility*—by easing the transition to new business models, new markets, and new business applications.
* *Improve Partner Interactions*—by easing trading partner integration and driving the cost of partnering down. This situation provides a path toward trading partner fluidity and reduces the transaction costs of doing day-to-day business with a particular organization.
* *Enhance Customer Service*—via portals, Customer Relationship Management (CRM) and call centers by providing cohesive, contextual data from multiple back office and front office systems.

The following sections consider the business value chain from a manufacturing and services perspective. Chapter 5, "Vertical Market Implications of Web Services," takes a more detailed look at the manufacturing and service industries, analyzing the potential impact of Web services on a number of specific industries.

Manufacturing Value Chain   Figure 4.3 illustrates three versions of a generic manufacturing value chain. Each version highlights possible areas of Web services impact on business operations.

These value chains illustrate the potential impact of Web services on supply chain management, product development, and sales and marketing.

* Supply Chain Management (SCM)—SCM initiatives will benefit from Web services by linking supply and demand information of a firm with its portfolio of partners and suppliers. This will result in lower

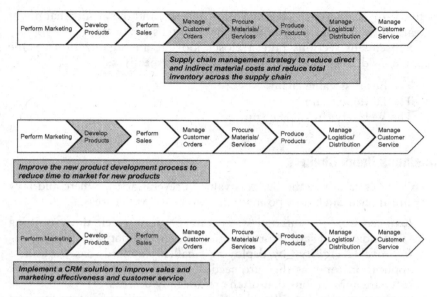

FIGURE 4.3   Web services and the manufacturing value chain.

inventory levels and reduced costs of inventory, as well as improved cash flow.

■ *Product Development*—Web services can improve the speed of new product development by facilitating collaboration with partners during the product design process in the form of sharing critical product specifications and design documents.

■ *Sales and Marketing*—In the third value chain, sales and marketing processes will be improved by forging closer relationships with current customers. This will improve the feedback loop to marketing and product development, as well as increasing customer service via CRM initiatives and other customer-facing business processes. Channel information flow to customers will be streamlined as Web services improve the distribution of product and pricing information to channel partners and direct customers. As a result, real-time customer and market intelligence will increasingly become available.

Service Value Chain   Web services can have an equally dramatic impact on a service organization's value chain, again in streamlining internal operations and eliminating the internal friction of business processes and information flow between information silos. As illustrated in the insurance industry example in Figure 4.4, customers and suppliers will bene-

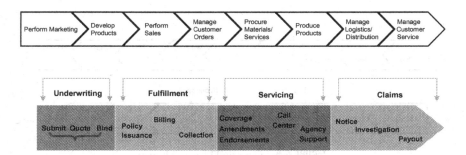

FIGURE 4.4   Web services and the insurance value chain.

fit from the ease of interaction with various insurance carriers, as the electronic interfaces between them are increasingly based on Web services standards.

Agents and brokers will be able to use Web services to create insurance applications and receive quotes from multiple carriers. Once a customer buys an insurance policy, the agent will be able to transmit the policy back to the carrier using Web services standards, and using that industry's data definition standards for particular documents.

The big challenge will be how IT organizations and processes of today's services organizations can deliver business value through the implementation of Web services. The business value chain and the IT value chain are increasingly interdependent, and with the use of Web services they will be even more closely aligned. The deep and broad effect that Web services will have on all organizations will enable the seamless merging of business and information processes.

Business will run more efficiently because of the ease with which information will be embedded into the basic operating fabric of the firm, enabling business processes to run more efficiently and smoothly, both internally and externally with trading partners. Information will flow across the gulfs of disparate systems and incompatible hardware, software, and application architectures, allowing the merging of content to support ever-changing business processes.

IT Value Chain

The IT value chain consists of all the activities required to deliver IT products and services to the business community of an organization. Very few executives have ever viewed their IT operation from a process or value chain perspective. Figure 4.5 shows a generic IT value chain, and includes

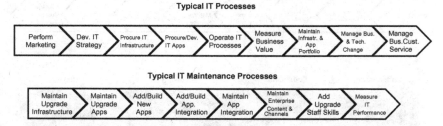

FIGURE 4.5 Generic IT value chain.

the typical processes that are required to establish and operate an information technology organization.

As illustrated, the generic IT value chain consists of processes related to designing, building, and operating an IT operation. Specifically, these processes are:

- *Perform Marketing*—Assess the needs of the operation, gather the requirements of the business community, build IT processes into all business processes, and develop the strategy for IT operations to drive and support all business process and departmental functions.
- *Develop IT Strategy*—In concert with the business strategy, develop an IT strategy that maximizes business value, drives top line revenue growth processes, facilitates cost containment and internal operating efficiencies, and positions the organization for agile responses to market and business changes.
- *Procure, Implement, and Maintain IT Infrastructure*—IT infrastructure represents the majority of an IT budget, averaging over 50% of the typical amount organizations spend on IT. The IT infrastructure consists of computing facilities such as buildings; raised floors; air conditioning and power backup and protection; the local and wide area networking; telecommunications infrastructure; large scale computing resources such as mainframes, servers, and enterprise storage; and related software and staff support. The infrastructure is the foundation upon which all other IT processes and applications rely to drive business value for the organization. A sound infrastructure provides an organization the agility and adaptability required to manage the IT application portfolio and effectively respond to and preempt business change.
- *Procure or Develop the IT Application Portfolio*—The IT application portfolio consists of the suite of business applications that run on the IT infrastructure and support business processes. The functions of the

application portfolio include secure and reliable execution of high volume business transactions (Enerprise Resources Planning [ERP]), financials, order management, financial management, procurement), providing online (or real-time) reports supporting business processes, generating printed reports as needed, and managing customer service and customer-facing interaction with the organization such as call centers and CRM systems. The application portfolio also includes portals, Web-based applications, online transaction systems, and all business systems that help the organization execute core business processes.

* *Operate IT Processes and Manage IT Assets*—Once the IT building blocks are in place and running, these assets must be operated and maintained to support the business. This consists of all the activities, processes, and personnel needed to effectively operate the infrastructure, run the IT applications, and provide the information delivery functions required to execute the organization's business model.

* *Measure IT Value to the Business*—A critical function of the IT operation is to continually measure its contribution to business operations. IT delivers business value to an organization in many ways that are often overlooked by corporate executives. It is imperative that the metrics of information value are captured and assiduously reported to the entire business community to make visible the IT value contribution to the success of the organization.

* *Maintain the Infrastructure and Application Portfolio*—One of the most critical challenges for an IT executive today is maintaining the infrastructure and application portfolio of the organization in response to and, preferably, in anticipation of business changes. For example, managing the capacity of mainframes and large servers as new computing requirements are addressed can be a challenge as more powerful machines are introduced to the market. Managing network capacity and traffic in lockstep with business growth must also be considered. Storage capacity across the organization is also an issue. A more pressing challenge is managing the application portfolio and maintaining legacy applications while continually adding new business processes and business applications on top of the existing portfolio. In addition, the integration needs of the organization must be managed as, increasingly, data from multiple enterprise applications is aggregated, transformed, and distributed to modern, cross-platform applications such as portals and other Web-based applications. These modern, Web-based, front-end applications can extend the silos of functionality built into enterprise and point solutions into more appropriate functionality customized to the business process,

department, or even user of the system based on profile and personalization information. This requires sophisticated integration capabilities that connect the systems, as well as aggregate and transform the content of these systems, to meet the needs of the ever-changing business context of the organization.

■ *Manage Business and Technology Change*—Similar to managing the infrastructure and application portfolio, managing business and technology change is perhaps more challenging. This is due to the nature and pace of change that is imposed upon the IT organization by two forces: changes in the external and internal business environment and changes in technology imparted by the technology vendors, standards bodies, and regulator agencies. The IT organization has to balance these forces against its internal processes for maintaining a stable and reliable computing environment on behalf of the organization. IT architectures must ensure that change can be accommodated from all of these potential forces by constantly evaluating and preparing itself for change.

■ *Manage Business Customer Service*—The IT operation of an organization must have processes and procedures for providing and managing customer service levels for its constituents, namely the business customers that utilize the IT products and services. This ensures a feedback mechanism for the value that IT delivers to the business community as well as a proactive tool for obtaining new requirements of the business and planning for them in advance.

This brief overview of the generic IT value chain addresses many of the typical processes associated with designing and implementing an IT architecture from a clean sheet perspective, or managing an existing IT architecture that has been inherited by an incoming Chief Information Officer (CIO). However, once these steps have been completed, there are many ongoing processes and activities, at a deeper level, that bear mentioning. These are also illustrated in Figure 4.5, and are described below:

■ *Maintain/Upgrade the IT Infrastructure*—Once installed and running, maintaining the IT infrastructure and managing new hardware and software releases is a major ongoing challenge.

■ *Maintain/Upgrade Applications*—Once applications are developed or purchased, configured, and deployed, they have to be rigorously maintained and tuned based on usage and performance. Application maintenance for existing applications, whether they are older legacy applications, more modern client-server applications, or Web-based applications, can consume a substantial proportion of the IT staffing and budgets depending on the nature of the application, its architecture, and performance and business criticality.

▪ _Add/Build New Applications_—Adding new packaged applications or developing new custom applications requires fitting them into the existing IT architecture and the application portfolio that, in all likelihood, they will interoperate with. They will potentially integrate with other business applications, and will surely share the networks, the printing resources, and other common IT resources leveraged by the entire spectrum of business applications. If new applications will integrate with existing applications, consideration must be given to what level of integration is required and for what purposes. Depending on the level of integration, tools such as Extract, Transformation and Load (ETL), Enterprise Application Integration (EAI), and others may be required.

▪ _Add/Build Application Integration_—If multiple business systems must be integrated in order to support a new business process requirement or reporting need, often organizations will utilize EAI or ETL tools. These specialized products are designed to tightly integrate business applications in support of new business processes and information requirements. Portals, for example, often aggregate data from multiple systems and present information to users based on highly personalized needs. This level of complex integration between multiple applications usually requires additional tools to construct and maintain connectivity. Often, commercial integration tools impose their own proprietary architectures upon the organization in solving the integration needs of the organization. In turn, this adds to the maintenance burden of the IT organization as it strives to maintain the environment as well as effectively manage change in the form of new software versions, operating system changes, database upgrades, et cetera.

▪ _Maintain Application Integration_—Maintaining application integration can be a challenge for IT organizations as applications change, versions are upgraded, hardware platforms are changed, and all other moving parts of the modern IT architecture and application portfolio are managed. As mentioned above, the EAI tools of today can effectively provide tight application integration to support business needs. In solving the application integration problem for organizations, EAI tools provide adapters for the major ERP, CRM, and SCM applications offered by most vendors, and also provide the tools to develop custom integrations as needed on top of the "canned" adapters. The EAI tools in many cases provide for robust point-to-point integration between multiple applications, which can support high transaction volumes and provide robust and reliable system integration connectivity. Architecturally, these tend to be point-to-point solutions, or hub and spoke implementations that require custom code to be implemented at both ends of the intended integration environment. These application integration strategies can often become their own integration nightmare, causing the same integration problems that they were purchased and implemented to solve. The real rub is that they are hardwired into the enterprise applications and any new applications that originally drove the need to implement EAI solutions. In short, EAI can result in a complex IT infrastructure that fails to provide the flexibility and agility that it promised. Thus, while integration should be a major focus of an IT strategy as the application portfolio is tuned and adapted to meet ever-changing business needs, current integration solutions often result in another monolithic application that requires dedicated IT staff to maintain, based on changes to the applications it was supposed to integrate. EAI solutions, in summary, are intrusive, proprietary, and architecturally rigid point-to-point interfaces that can add to integration headaches over time.

- *Add/Build/Maintain Business Integration, Enterprise Content, and Communication Channels*—While internal application integration is a real issue for IT organizations, the real opportunity lies with business and content integration across organizational boundaries. An emerging enterprise software category is addressing the diverse content distribution requirements of complex business models by abstracting the extraction, aggregation, transformation, and distribution of business content from the multitude of enterprise systems and from the universe of business content recipients. This category, called enterprise business communication, focuses on abstracting the back-end system connections, as well as the recipient channels, through a robust, many-to-many architecture that provides a content-centric business integration scheme, as opposed to a point-to-point system integration approach. The compelling difference between these emerging classes of solutions is that they are content- and business context-based solutions. They manage enterprise business content across business systems, processes, and users by virtue of their content-centric architecture. These are not EAI solutions solely focused on integrating disparate systems. They are content-based business solutions connecting users with the business content they need, the way they want to receive it, and in the format they want to receive it.
- *Add/upgrade IT Staff Skills*—Finally, an IT organization must upgrade its skills continuously as technology changes, and as the IT architecture and application portfolio are maintained in support of changing business priorities. Skills maintenance can be especially

challenging given the economic downturn, where training budgets are among the first to be trimmed, and where IT staffs are already stretched beyond their limits with maintenance and ongoing integration projects.

Given this discussion of the generic IT value chain, the compelling question is simple: "How will Web services change my business?" Again, the answer lies in establishing how Web services will alter the business and IT value chain for these same organizations. To do this we need to examine the Web services value chain.

Web Services Value Chain

The Web services value chain consists of the process of developing, publishing, finding, and generally ensuring the effective management and utilization of Web services. A complete view of the Web services value chain is illustrated in Figure 4.6.

The seven key elements of the Web services value chain are:

1. *Develop* (Also, *Author, Compose, Create, Encapsulate, Expose*)—This is the development process through which Web services are implemented using an Integrated Development Environment (IDE), application development tools, or encapsulating legacy functionality to be exposed as a Web service.
2. *Describe*—Once a Web service has been developed, a description of the service can be created and published in a UDDI registry. The description of the Web service will help potential users locate relevant services and determine their fit for current application development or application architecture needs.

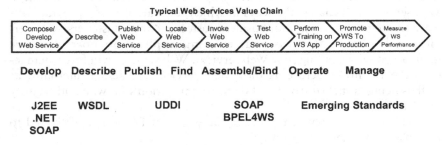

FIGURE 4.6 Web services value chain.

3. *Publish*—Publishing a Web service to a private or public UDDI registry provides a central location from which services can be found for current use or future reuse. In the future, a service can be updated or revised and any applications using the service will automatically use the revised version if so desired. Applications may be assembled from a number of Web services, each located via the UDDI registry. Once a service is located, based on search criteria, a description of the Web service is returned along with a pointer to the location of the Web service.

4. *Find*—This is the process by which published services are located in a UDDI registry. An individual or application may search a UDDI registry to locate services that meet a number of specified criteria.

5. *Assemble/Bind*—Once there is agreement between the service provider and the service requestor regarding a specific Web service, they are bound together into a new Web service application.

6. *Operate*—This is the process by which a network of Web services is executed. As the number of Web service-based applications increases, organizations will need to establish environments where services can be effectively tested and deployed.

7. *Manage*—The management of Web services applications and environments will be critical to ensure that individual services do not become a bottleneck and that effective load balancing of service is maintained across the physical hardware that they operate on.

Given this generic and very simple Web services value chain, how does this differ from the typical IT value chain, and what areas of the IT value chain will be impacted? Furthermore, how will the corporate value chain be impacted such that top-line revenue growth can be increased, or bottom-line profits can be increased through cost reductions or operating efficiency gains? Can Web services deliver that kind of value to an organization? When and how?

As we have stated previously, Web services will change the way in which IT applications are built and deployed in support of the business. Web services will change the ways in which software vendors provide software to their customers, both business customers and consumers. Web services will change the way that existing application portfolios are maintained while adding new Web services. Web services will force changes onto the IT infrastructure as these new services are added internally, as well as being launched from outside the organization's firewall and security boundaries.

Web services promise to change the way that IT value is delivered to the business in a number of ways:

- *Modular Building Blocks*—Business applications will be more modular, meaning fewer large-scale enterprise application implementations that can literally consume an organization for months or years. Ultimately, this translates into easier evaluation, acquisition, implementation, and faster time to business value, or ROI.

- *Services Oriented*—Some business applications may be delivered as services on a rental or transaction basis—remember the D&B example from Chapter 2—facilitating a pay-for-use model. For some software categories and capabilities, this may well spell the end of Volume Licensing Agreements (VLAs), where excess licenses are paid for, but left unused.

- *Open Standards*—Packaged applications will incorporate standards, including Web services-based; open interfaces; leveraging XML, SOAP, and WSDL. As the number of applications using Web services interfaces increases, the need for large-scale integration projects will steadily diminish.

- *System Development*—As Web services mature and are truly available on public networks, either manually or machine-searchable, they will be sought and evaluated by business users in conjunction with IT professionals. The business of acquiring information technology solutions will be initiated by the business in support of very specific needs. Small, modular Web services applications will be implemented in many cases without heavy IT involvement, management, or oversight.

These changes will bring the business and IT organizations together in seeking new sources of business value driven by information technology in general, and specifically using Web services.

Figure 4.7 shows how various elements of the Web services value chain might potentially impact the IT maintenance and the overall IT value chain. We will begin with the typical IT processes and work our way down to how Web services will radically alter the IT professional's world.

- *Application Procurement*—A major task of IT is to procure or develop new business applications in response to business needs. This also has a related task under maintenance of the IT architecture and application portfolio, as well as managing business and technology change. These are challenging tasks for a typical IT organization given the rapid rate of technology change, complicated by dizzying rates of business change and economic fluctuations worldwide. The move to a Web services-

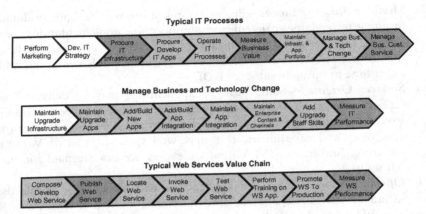

FIGURE 4.7   Web services value chain impact.

based "services on demand" model promises to dramatically reduce the complexity of IT procurement.

- *Application Development*—Many development tool vendors are already offering sophisticated products that will help retool legacy solutions into Web services. Microsoft, IBM, Sun Microsystems, Oracle, SilverStream (now owned by Novell), Cape Clear, and Blue Titan are all examples of tool vendors that are offering powerful visual integrated development environments for Web services, whether migrating legacy applications or creating new Web services from scratch.

- *Migration of Legacy Systems*—Legacy and existing business applications will be retooled as Web services. This will be accomplished by selectively encapsulating legacy system functionality into modular services and exposing legacy system processes as Web services. The selective use of Web services to "open up" legacy applications to allow other systems to interact with them is one way that IT organizations can begin to migrate their existing IT architecture and application portfolio toward a service-oriented architecture.

- *Integration of New Systems*—Currently, when a new business application is added to the portfolio, there are multiple system interfaces required to make the incoming application co-exist and interoperate with the other business applications. Integration with applications such as portals, messaging backbones, enterprise application integration servers, and data warehouses are common points of interface for a new system. Using the common approach of

EAI can be very expensive, as well as proprietary and architecturally rigid. Web services-based applications will be seamlessly added to an existing IT architecture with minimal integration effort required. Future applications will have Simple Object Access Protocol (SOAP) interfaces, and will use WSDL service descriptions to describe in advance just what services within the application do, how they do it, and what data they require to run. This will dramatically alter the value chain of IT, especially in the integration tasks required to add new applications or to maintain version currency of existing applications.

▪ *Application Maintenance*—Related to the process of managing business and IT change, and involves a number of maintenance processes related to the IT architecture and organization— infrastructure, application portfolio, integration connections, content and business integration, and even IT processes and skills of IT staff. Web services will have a tremendous impact on the processes related to procurement and maintenance of IT applications, as well as the processes of managing business and technology change.

▪ *Change Management*—Some of the most compelling value chain dislocations will be in the area of managing business and technology change. The middle value chain of Figure 4.7 shows the tasks a typical IT organization faces to manage change along the spectrum of infrastructure, applications, integration connections, business and content integration, staff skills and capabilities, and IT business performance. The immediate reduction in integration budgets for IT operations is clear and unambiguous based on the use of standard interface mechanisms and protocols for all Web services applications. Adding a new application that is built on Web services will significantly reduce the amount of integration effort required to make that particular application fit seamlessly into and function harmoniously with the existing application portfolio when compared to non-Web services applications.

These scenarios illustrate a number of areas where Web services will fundamentally alter the dynamics and economics of the IT value chain, thus impacting the entire IT industry. This section does not cover the entire spectrum of possibilities, but suffice to say that the changes will affect all aspects of IT value delivery. How technology vendors respond to changes in the value equation for information technology products and services will unfold over the next few years as Web services standards evolve, products and tools mature, and as adoption by organizations progresses.

SUMMARY

This chapter sought to demonstrate that the greatest impact of Web services, and the most effective way to implement Web services, is from a business perspective. We strongly suggest that initial Web services discussions begin at a strategic level, with a joint dialogue between business and IT executives. The framework introduced in this chapter illustrated several areas where Web services can, and eventually will, prove beneficial for organizations. An assessment of the implications of Web services should consider multiple perspectives, from corporate strategy to detailed value chain and operational considerations as illustrated in Figure 4.8.

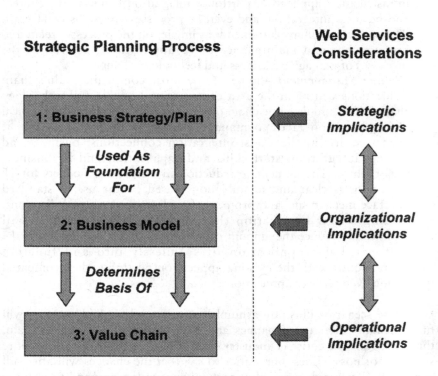

FIGURE 4.8   Web services impact across multiple levels.

Organizations should consider the implications of Web services across multiple levels of the aspects of the business:

- *Corporate Strategy*—Impact on vision and corporate goals
- *Business Model*—Impact on actual strategy, structure, organization, and processes
- *Business Value Chain*—Impact on specific value-creating processes
- *IT Value Chain*—Impact on IT processes creating and supporting business value
- *Web Services Value Chain*—How Web services will drive business benefit across the entire business

Careful analysis of the impact of Web services on the business model, on the corporate value chain, and, ultimately, on the IT value chain will help to identify business benefit for moving ahead with Web services and to determine the starting point for Web services initiatives, which is revisited in Chapter 6, "Where to Begin." It is critical to remember that the business value achievable through the use of Web services will be the greatest force for their adoption.

ENDNOTES

[1] *Harvard Business Review*, October 2001, "Your Next IT Strategy" by John Hagel III and John Seely Brown.
[2] CNET News.com, October 30 2002, "IBM talks up computing on demand" by John G. Spooner and Sandeep Junnaker.
[3] See Ronald H. Coase, "The Nature of the Firm," The Firm, the Market, and the Law. Chicago: University of Chicago Press, 1988, 33–56. See also Ronald H. Coase, Essays on Economics and Economists. Chicago: University of Chicago Press, 1994.
[4] Ibid.

CHAPTER 5

Vertical Market Implications of Web Services

"There will always be another reality to make fiction of the truth we think we've arrived at."

Christopher Fry

"Whatever you can do, or dream you can . . . begin it; boldness has genius, power and magic in it."

Johann Wolfgang von Goethe

The economics of Web services will dictate where they are used, how quickly organizations adopt them, and how much they will ultimately change the business and IT landscape. The use of value chain analysis in Chapter 4, "Strategic Implications of Web Services," shows how changes in business processes and cost structures might drive the adoption of Web services. However, the application of Web services to business processes, and their impact on cost structures, will vary from business to business and from industry to industry. This chapter expands on the use of Web services in specific industries and explores areas of greatest potential for their adoption.

VERTICAL MARKET ADOPTION AND DEPLOYMENT

The nuances of business strategy, business models, and organizational value chains can fundamentally differ by industry. Regardless of these differences, Web services can help organizations to increase revenue, reduce costs, and improve their cost structures. In so doing, it is possible to improve customer satisfaction and streamline interactions with partners. However, Web services are not a silver bullet or a panacea for all IT ills. There are many IT issues that remain unresolved by today's corporations due to an inability to view IT as a strategic asset. With the implementation of Web services, it is critical that organizations look to align business and IT strategy at all levels.

Previous chapters have advocated the use of Web services in solving business problems. Chapter 3, "Web Services Adoption," sets the stage for the adoption of Web services through the four phases of the adoption model: integration, collaboration, innovation, and domination. Chapter 4, "Strategic Implications of Web Services," proposed that the adoption of Web services can only fully be achieved through a strategic perspective of how Web service can be leveraged. Ultimately, changes to an organization's business strategy will have a ripple effect through the business model and value chain, requiring changes to organizational structures and business processes respectively. This concept is illustrated in Figure 5.1 below.

At the operational level, when leveraged within a firm to enhance the internal value chain, Web services can result in the following benefits:

- *Value Chain Compression*—to driving internal operational efficiency between business processes resulting in:
  - Reduced cycle times
  - Better order to cash management
  - Stronger customer relationships

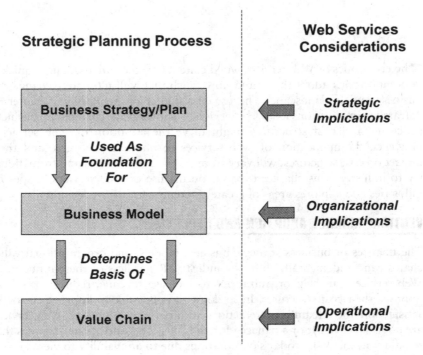

FIGURE 5.1 Business impact of Web services.

- *Improved Information Visibility*—to support executive decision making, enabling time to be spent on making better business decisions rather than collecting the information required to make decisions
- *Enhanced IT Capability*—to support business operations across the value chain
- *Greater IT Efficiency*—achieved through improved data integration capabilities and superior information distribution
- *Reduced Cost of System Integration*—freeing funds to better support mission-critical business needs

Beyond these internal operational benefits, Web services can be leveraged to achieve even greater benefits from inter-enterprise collaboration. In this scenario, organizations may perhaps participate in trading ecosystems, gaining an equal footing with larger competitors by virtue of the low cost and simplicity of participation enabled through the use of Web services.

Adoption Patterns

The adoption of Web services must be balanced against an organization's appetite for risk and the need for technology solutions to solve industry-specific problems. It is likely that some industries will be earlier adopters of Web services. On one hand, the early adopter will be those industries and companies that tend to be at the forefront of technology trends; quick to explore new approaches in an effort to achieve improved operational efficiency, revenue growth, and customer satisfaction; and overall, a basis for competitive advantage. On the other hand, the late adopter will be those firms that operate with more cautious, risk-averse stances toward technology adoption, waiting to see how others leverage a technology and follow suit.

In order to determine the focus areas and opportunities for adoption of Web services, regardless of industry, it is helpful to have a framework within which to evaluate Web services opportunities. This section reviews a number of alternative perspectives and subsequently develops a framework that provides a consistent, repeatable set of criteria for evaluating Web services opportunities.

As discussed in Chapter 3, "Web Services Adoption," in the near-term—over the next two to three years—the integration and collaboration phases will be the primary focus for most organizations, as illustrated in Figure 5.2. Those organizations that have excelled during the integration and collaboration phases will be among the first to enter the innovation phase and push toward the domination phase. Based on this adoption model, our framework will begin with the premise that integration and collaboration opportunities will be the initial targets for most organizations. However, there are additional perspectives to consider as companies contemplate their initial thrust into Web services.

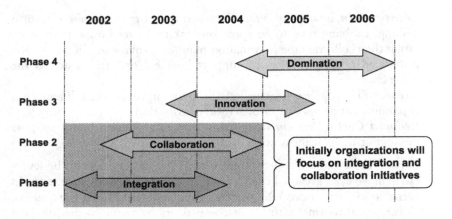

FIGURE 5.2   Initial focus on integration and collaboration initiatives.

Industry Perspectives

Forrester Research   Forrester Research,[1] a leading technology research organization, proposes three broad criteria for determining business process targets for the application of Web services:

1. *Recurring*—processes must occur with high frequency and be used by many users
2. *Dynamic*—processes are characterized by volatile information with high rates of change, and users benefit from receiving continually refreshed information
3. *Disconnected*—processes that are isolated by system silos, process and organizational boundaries, or organizational firewalls

According to Forrester, organizations should forego complex collaboration activities and instead target business processes that can benefit from visibility of information for the user community and other process constituents. As the technology barriers to more complex collaboration are overcome, and as the Web services standards evolve and stabilize, firms can begin to consider more complex Web services deployments. To that end, Forrester recommends focusing on process visibility related to the following business operations:

■ *Sales and Service Processes*—monitoring of customer order status, order fulfillment, Available To Promise (ATP) information, and pricing information for both customers and sales professionals

* *Procurement Processes*—real-time updates for purchasing forecasts and supplier commits, inventory levels and stock out alerts, and supplier delivery performance
* *Supply Chain Visibility and Management*—tapping into multiple enterprise systems to monitor inventory levels across the supply chain, supply ATP information, update customer order status, aggregate customer demand, and update production schedules based on real-time demand information

AMR Research   AMR Research,[2] continuing with this theme, suggests Web services are appropriate where:

* Stable and predictable business relationships exist
* Established business processes can be leveraged
* Low volumes of data are being processed
* Transactional integrity is not a mission-critical requirement

Stencil Group   Stencil Group[3] identifies five areas of business challenges being addressed with Web services. These areas are as follows:

1. *Reuse and Syndication*—This involves Web services-enabling existing applications and then provisioning them for use by partners and customers.
2. *Automation and Productivity*—This can be achieved with Web services by eliminating manual integration processes such as File Transfer Protocol (FTP), e-mail, and other data transmission and receipt processes that require human intervention for completion. Additionally, automating inter-enterprise collaboration can significantly reduce the manual effort required for activities such as gathering demand information from customers, distributors, and contract manufacturers, as in the electronics industry.
3. *Visibility into Operations*—This can be achieved using Web services to expose data from multiple systems, aggregating it, and publishing to portals or other business applications. Supply chain visibility can be improved by sharing inventory data from multiple locations to provide a single, global view of inventory levels and inventory costs. Gathering and consolidating information such as customer forecasts, customer demand, and customer orders can be used to provide global visibility for supply chain planning purposes.
4. *Exploring New Business Models*—From a long-term perspective, organizations may have the ability to explore new business opportunities. Early adopters of Web services are implementing basic

collaboration solutions with trusted trading partners. These firms are not yet deploying more sophisticated collaboration solutions based on business process management and complex workflows involving cross-firewall transactions. Early movement toward new business model development may come from Independent Software Vendors (ISVs) who will use Web services delivery models to deploy new software modules as subscription fee-based services rather than as perpetual licenses. Microsoft is already well down this path with its software licensing strategy, but the market place will likely determine how well accepted this business practice will become.

5. *Common Integration Structure*—As discussed, organizations will initially use relatively stable Web services standards (such as XML and SOAP) to integrate disparate back-end systems. This Enterprise Application Integration (EAI) use of Web services will drive increased sharing of information by building on existing EAI strategies and architectures. This system integration approach will spread from simple integration projects and EAI-augmenting initiatives to the implementation of a more robust Service-Oriented Architecture (SOA). These SOAs will support more complex integration within the larger enterprise, as well as extending the architecture to customers, partners, and suppliers. As the SOA extends to support more complex cross-firewall integration—as organizations truly move into the collaboration phase—we will see a rapid rise in business process and business model innovation.

Stencil Group suggests that over the next three years, there are three areas that will likely receive the most focus from Web services efforts:

1. *System Efficiency*—relates to both the integration of business systems as well as business operations, or "systems" in the larger, non-IT sense.
2. *Employee Productivity*—will be realized through better information availability and self-service initiatives for employees, partners, and even customers, which reduce employee workloads
3. *Revenue Generation*—can be accomplished via Web services deployed on the sell-side of an organization's value chain. For example, customer self-provisioning for purchasing transactions or sharing internal systems and intellectual property on a fee basis.

Further, Stencil Group suggests that initial Web services projects should consider the following pragmatic criteria to help ensure the best use of resources and the most appropriate test bed for learning how to successfully deploy Web services:

- *Repeatable Scenarios*—Will initial Web services projects be reusable and provide benefits for a large number of users across the organization?

▪ *Dynamic Data*—Does data frequently change, and does it impact other departments, business processes, or systems?
▪ *Self-Service*—Will a Web service provide self-service benefits to broad audiences of customers, suppliers, partners, and employees, or can a business function or process be syndicated to trading partners?

Beyond the initial pilot of Web services, ongoing projects should target solving the following types of business problems or provide some combination of the following benefits:

▪ *Unlock Information*—break down information silos and expose information from multiple systems for new users and new applications.
▪ *Free Up Resources*—redeploy employees otherwise focused on Electronic Data Interchange (EDI) mapping, internal integration projects and maintenance, EAI interface maintenance, dedicated hardware and software for proprietary interfaces, or communication processes that can be replaced by Web services.
▪ *Automate Processes*—eliminate manual processes and human intervention where errors can be introduced into a business process, such as data cleansing, data extraction, file transfers, and data scrubbing.
▪ *New Opportunities*—look for other options and ways in which Web services might solve cross-organization problems via shared information, shared processes, or shared system functions.

Conclusions This brief review of various perspectives on how Web services may initially be leveraged has some recurring themes. Figure 5.3 illustrates these themes using integration and collaboration as the high-level criteria, and further categorizing these themes into business challenges, business goals, and business benefits.

Organizations should look for challenges similar to those identified in Figure 5.3, which represents an aggregated list from the analysis above. Once the target processes or challenges have been identified, the goals of the Web services project should be considered. These goals represent the potential benefits promised by Web services as they are applied to the business challenges. Finally, the business benefits in the bottom row should be sought by initial forays into Web services. These business benefits are at a high level and should always be quantified for the actual revenue, cost savings, or operational efficiency benefits that can be achieved by a given Web services project.

Deployment Perspectives

The last piece of this analysis framework must now be developed before examining specific industries and identifying how Web services might be implemented. The following four criteria provide generic characteristics for any company, and can be used to identify likely Web services adoption scenarios:

	Integration	Collaboration
Challenges	•Recurring processes •Dynamic data •Disconnected organizations/ systems	•Distributed processes & relationships •Shared data benefits internal/external users
Goals	•Common integration scheme •Re-use of interfaces/content •Visibility of data or processes •Automation and productivity	•Syndication of processes & content •Frequent process coupling & decoupling
Benefits	•Self-service initiatives—integration of systems, data visibility •Sales and customer service—integration, data visibility •Supply chain visibility and management—integration and data visibility •Procurement and supplier management—data visibility and sharing •Enhance trading partner relationships—process integration •Develop or explore new business models	

FIGURE 5.3   Adoption framework for Web services.

1. *Industry Structure and Value Chain*—What are the predominant characteristics of the industry of interest? What is the overall industry structure? What is the clockspeed[4] of the particular industry? Consider the following aspects of industry structure:
   - Tightly bound or loosely coupled industry structures and relationships
   - High velocity versus slow velocity—industry clockspeeds, product clockspeeds, and process clockspeeds
   - Intensity of competition—dominated by a few large organizations or shared leadership by many organizations
   - Technology stance—characterized by early technology adopters versus technology laggards

2. *Organizational Structure*—What is the company's structure, both internal and external? How does the firm interface upstream and downstream with suppliers and customers? What is the organization's technology adoption pattern? What is the innovation rate of the company? Consider the following dimensions of organizational structure:

   - Internal structure—size of the organization, geographical coverage, industries participating in, markets served, and organizational structure to accomplish all the above

- Sell-side structure—complexity of distribution channel, number of customer tiers
- Buy-side structure—complexity of procurement processes, number of supplier tiers (driven by product complexity)
- Technology adoption tendencies—early adopters or technology laggards relative to competitors

3. *Product and Service Complexity*—The complexity of products and services, as well as the production assets and systems that generate the products and services, have a strong bearing on the structure of the organization as well as the structure of the overall industry. How complex are the products? Are the products assembled and modular, or are they processed products such as food, beverages, and consumer goods? If the products are services, what are the assets needed to compete (for example, physical equipment or intellectual property assets)?
   - Complex products consisting of discrete components and/or modules, such as electronics, consumer electronics, and automobiles
   - Complex products resulting from continuous or semi-continuous process manufacturing, such as pharmaceuticals, Consumer Packaged Goods (CPG), and food & beverage manufacturing
   - Complex products engineered to specifications, such as aerospace and defense, mining and harvesting equipment, and heavy machinery
   - Complex services requiring deep domain knowledge or expertise, such as consulting services, audit and assurance services, and business strategy services
   - Complex services with high fixed-asset requirements, such as transportation, logistics, and package delivery—Federal Express, UPS, US Postal Service, DHL, and so on
   - Complex services with high IT asset requirements, such as financial services, banking, insurance, healthcare, and so on
   - Simple services with high IT and related asset requirements, such as large scale retail and CPG, and database marketing
   - Simple services with low barriers to entry, such as temporary staffing agencies

4. *Process Complexity*—The complexity of business processes has significant bearing on the structure of a business and how a firm organizes itself to be managed and deliver value to its chosen markets and customers. How complex are business and production processes? How many tiers are there in the upstream (supply chain) and downstream (demand chain) and the overall value chain? Are processes tightly linked? How asset-specific and proprietary are production processes? How difficult to copy are they? Does process complexity create barriers to entry for competition?

- How complex are business and production processes? How difficult are the firm's business processes to copy and imitate? Does process complexity represent a significant barrier to entry for potential competition?
- How many tiers are there in the upstream supply chain? How complex are the procurement processes that support the inbound supply chain?
- How many tiers are there in the downstream demand chain? How complex are the sales and distribution processes that support the outbound demand chain? How difficult is the fulfillment process once a customer order has been received?
- Consider the core production processes of a business, regardless of whether these consist of the conversion processes of manufacturing or the information processes of a services business. What single set of core processes represent the central value proposition the firm provides to its targeted customers and markets? How complex are these? How are these managed? How well understood are they? Can they be replicated by a competitor?
- Think about Dell's business model and how many companies, such as IBM, H-P, and others, have unsuccessfully tried to imitate it. While business processes may seem simple in concept, the ability to execute processes demands experience and familiarity that derives from intimate knowledge of those very processes. What processes differentiate a firm from its most direct competitor? How unique are the company's processes in reality?
- Finally, consider process complexity from a higher level, spatial and time-based perspective. Are processes tightly bound in spatial terms, closely associated in a geography or within a facility, or are they loosely affiliated and modular? What are the logistics processes that support these processes? Are processes tightly interlinked in time? Wine making and beer bottling are related businesses but have significant time bases driving their production. Newspaper production is high-speed and real-time, similar to electronics production and other high-speed industries. The speed of the industry and the processes associated with them are important issues to understand.

These generic industry, organization, product and service, and process analysis questions can be summarized as follows with the potential Web services applications identified as well as potential benefits.

- *Complex Organizational Structure, High Business and Process Integration Needs*—Potential applications include employee productivity, operational efficiency, global operational visibility.

- *Complex Internal IT Environment, High System Integration Needs—* Potential applications include customer service, employee productivity, business performance.
- *Complex Distribution Channel, High Distribution Channel Integration needs—*Potential applications include customer service, inventory management, demand management.
- *High Product Complexity (Multi-tiered Bill of Materials), High Supply Chain Integration Needs—*Potential applications include supplier integration and management, Supply Chain Management (SCM), inventory management.
- *High Product Complexity (Production pProcesses and Asset Intensity), High Internal Integration Needs—*Potential applications include internal integration, operating efficiency, production management.
- *High Process Complexity (Production Processes and Asset Intensity), High Internal Integration Needs, Demand Management—*Potential applications include internal integration, operating efficiency, asset utilization.
- *Complex Procurement and Supply Processes, High Supplier Integration, and Supply Chain Management—*Potential applications include supplier integration, supplier management, and SCM.

As shown, there are many factors that influence the adoption of new technology into an organization and, more broadly, into an industry. The intent of this section is not to provide a detailed and formulaic approach to exactly how industries and the organizations within them will embrace and adopt Web services. Rather we hope to provide a framework outlining how an organization might approach the investigation and eventual deployment of Web services from a business perspective.

In the following section, we simplify the earlier analysis using the Web services adoption model detailed in Chapter 3, "Web Services Adoption." Again, it should be noted that integration and collaboration phases of the Web services adoption model should be the primary focus for executives over the next two to three years. Therefore, the analysis framework illustrated in Figure 5.4 is limited to these initial phases. Furthermore, based on the previous discussion, the integration and collaboration phases are each divided into subcategories for internal and external integration opportunities. This simple framework, when combined with the analytic framework discussed previously, provides filters to help focus Web services efforts on areas that provide rapid payback and real business value.

Every organization must perform its own analysis of the likely areas where, based on their unique competitive pressures, Web services might provide return on the investment. This activity will require long-term

Industry Structure			
Company Structure			
Integration		Collaboration	
Internal	External	Internal	External
•Data and system integration within a business unit •Data and system integration across organizations, departments and functions	•Buy-side supplier data and system integration, e.g. procurement •Buy-side partner data and system integration, e.g. R&D, new product development •Sell-side channel integration, e.g. distributors, contract manufacturers, sales reps, retailers	•Business process integration and management within a business unit •Business process integration and management across organizations, departments and functions	•Buy-side supplier process integration and management •Buy-side partner process integration and management, e.g. R&D, new product development •Sell-side channel process integration and management

(Left vertical labels: Product Complexity / Process Complexity)

FIGURE 5.4   Industry analysis framework for Web services adoption.

thinking and executive advocacy in order for business success to be achieved. Figure 5.4 combines the integration phase and collaboration phase of the Web services adoption model with the context provided from considerations of industry structure, competitive intensity, and organizational structure, as well as product complexity, product life cycle, and process complexity. These forces will have a definitive impact on the integration and collaboration challenges that an organization will face in contemplating where to begin with Web services. This framework provides a foundation for examining a number of industries for the potential impact and benefit of Web services, and will facilitate intelligent targeting of initial Web services implementations.

MANUFACTURING VERTICALS

Manufacturing verticals represent great diversity and opportunity for the adoption of Web services. For example, high-velocity industries such as electronics tend to have complex supply chains and high product obsolescence. This demands an intense focus on supply-chain execution and visibility across the entire industry. Conversely, while low-velocity industries such as aerospace and defense do not suffer from high-velocity or product obsolescence, they do need to manage extremely complex design and manufacturing requirements as well as a large number of suppliers.

The following section examines common activities that impact all manufacturing organizations, then examines selected manufacturing verticals for Web services potential.

Common Manufacturing Activities

For all manufacturing verticals there are a number of common activities that can be considered. These include:

1. Supply Chain Management
   - Supply chain visibility
   - Capacity planning
   - Production scheduling

2. Product Development
   - Product obsolescence
   - Product development cycles

3. Collaboration
   - Customer self-service portals
   - Supplier self-service portals
   - Designing portals to facilitate product development

To accomplish these initiatives, a combination of internal integration and collaboration is required. The following sections examine how manufacturers can achieve these goals using Web services.

Supply Chain Management SCM provides ample opportunities where Web services can be leveraged to drive significant changes in the ways organizations procure materials and services, transform them with value-added manufacturing processes, and ship them to customers and trading partners. There are several places in a manufacturing value chain where Web services not only make sense, but can dramatically change the value equation for a company.

Supply Chain Visibility First, supply chain visibility can be enhanced for all participants in an industry by sharing forecast and inventory data at both ends of the supply chain—buy side and sell side. In order to share data, manufacturing firms must tackle the internal integration problem first. This means vertically integrating in-plant manufacturing systems with in-plant Enterprise Resource Planning (ERP) systems and then tying multi-site ERP solutions to ERP and financial reporting systems. This scenario is not uncommon, as many large manufacturers have grown through Mergers and Acquisitions (M&A) and therefore have a variety of ERP and manufacturing systems running across multiple sites. In many cases, where the organization has several different product lines, different ERP systems are more appropriate for specific modes of manufacturing. Process manufacturing and discrete manufacturing, for example, are often handled by different ERP platforms.

In order to obtain accurate information from all manufacturing sites, it is necessary to tie all the plants into a single, real-time view of the total capacity of the organization as well as a single view of all inventory levels, customer orders, and inbound supplies. This information helps avoid stock outages of critical incoming raw materials, provides global visibility to all inventory and customer orders, and ensures steady throughput of customer orders through all manufacturing locations.

Capacity Planning Capacity planning is a very interesting potential application of Web services to vertically integrate manufacturing facilities into business planning systems. For example, Applied Micro Devices (AMD) uses Web services to aggregate data from multiple wafer fabrication tools in multiple plants to obtain a real-time view of its capacity (from fabrication tools, from Manufacturing Execution Systems (MES), from ERP systems, and so on). This type of vertical integration is increasingly used to aggregate manufacturing information to provide real-time production scheduling, global capacity management, and order status reporting. Similarly, Dell manages its manufacturing facilities in real time by publishing a refreshed manufacturing schedule to each of its production plants and partners every two hours. This improves the responsiveness of its supply chain in support of its direct order business model.

Customer Self Service It is increasingly common in manufacturing organizations to integrate Customer Relationship Management (CRM) with ERP platforms and order entry systems, which enables customer service professionals to access all customer orders and obtain real-time updates on order status, shipment location, purchase order status, and more. Increasingly, this level of integration is being used to support customer self-service applications along with customer service operations.

Web services provide a great advantage for these kinds of integration efforts because these connections do not have to be tightly integrated to one another. A Web service could be created for extracting inventory levels, customer order status, and shipment status without using heavy EAI integration schemes. This represents low-hanging fruit for achieving business value from implementation of Web services in manufacturing organizations.

Product Development Increasingly, companies are seeking competitive advantage by streamlining design processes and launching new products faster. In many high-velocity industries, the window of competitive advantage at the product level is narrow, and the obsolescence of components and finished goods is high. This rate of obsolescence puts extreme pressure on design groups to rapidly develop and release new products to production facilities without a glitch.

Web services can be leveraged to support processes such as Engineering Change Notifications (ECNs) and manufacturing effectivity dates for new components, sub-assemblies, or entirely new designs. These critical processes have a tremendous impact on the transition from design to production. These are simple examples of how leading organizations are adopting Web services for internal integration efforts in support of very real business problems.

Once the internal integration hurdles have been overcome with early implementations of Web services, many adopters will experiment with collaboration applications.

Collaboration Historically, collaboration efforts have been unsuccessful due to system integration issues. This was true where firms used a single vendor's suite of products, and was compounded when using SCM and ERP systems from different vendors. A best-of-breed approach for packaged software implementation often necessitated complex and expensive EAI projects to allow systems to interoperate. Web services will remove the integration barriers and enable seamless collaboration as organizations complete their internal integration efforts, and as ERP and SCM vendors provide open Web services interfaces for their systems.

Business models can benefit tremendously from value chain linking and synchronization using Web services. Firms have the potential to achieve these benefits by collaborating along a number of business process dimensions. Figure 5.5 shows how Web services might be applied across multiple value chains, from a supplier to an Original Equipment Manufacturer (OEM) to a retailer.

Figure 5.5 is an example of how value chains might be linked and synchronized across companies and vertical markets. Through the use of Web services, firms will be able to build inexpensive links between their SCM systems, from ERP systems and advanced planning and scheduling, to warehouse management and logistics systems.

Collaboration can produce results in a number of ways, such as optimizing supply chain throughput, improving time to market for new products, reducing inventory levels, streamlining procurement processes, and sharing information with trading partners. In the Web services adoption

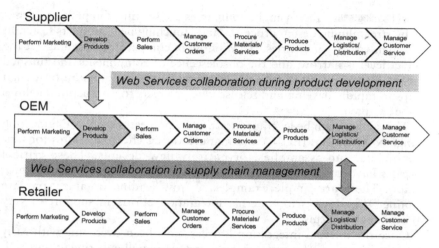

FIGURE 5.5 Web services in collaboration.

model, we have shown how collaboration follows internal integration. Once organizations have achieved a level of integration mastery with Web services, they will begin collaborating with close trading partners over secure private networks.

The standards and technologies for security, workflow, and related Web services functions are not yet mature enough to permit extensive collaboration across open networks. However, early adopters of Web services are already well down the collaboration path, as with the Dell Computer example discussed in Chapter 3, "Web Services Adoption." There are many cases where Web services collaboration can facilitate improved supply chain performance through shared information with partners.

Forecasting and planning are obvious areas for collaboration between organizations, and these were the early targets for B2B integration prior to Web services. On the buy side, customer collaboration for forecasting and orders helps provide more accurate demand information as an input to the Manufacturing Resources Planning (MRP) modules of ERP systems. In electronics, for example, Web services might be used to send requests to channel partners such as distributors, contract manufacturers, and customers for updated forecasts and replenishment orders. This information might then be used by advanced planning systems to calculate an accurate forecast. Even small improvements on the customer-facing side of the forecasting and planning process can produce dramatic results on the supplier side of the supply chain, improving procurement processes and reducing inventory levels.

Supplier collaboration may operate in a similar fashion, with Web service requests being sent to trading partners, or the reverse, partners may automatically send their updated forecasts and purchase orders to the OEMs. This scenario will again result in streamlined purchasing processes, reduced inventory levels, and fewer stock-outs of critical components required for manufacturing.

Selected Manufacturing Verticals

The following sections review sampling of manufacturing verticals to examine how Web services might impact them based on the industry adoption framework described earlier. The focus for these discussions will be the first two phases of the Web services adoption model, integration and collaboration.

Computers and Electronics Many companies in the computer and electronics industry will likely be early adopters of Web services for internal integration in support of SCM initiatives. This is critical because of the velocity of this industry and the associated rate of product obsolescence. Tight management of inventory through increased visibility of global capacity, inventory levels, customer orders, and inbound components can mean the difference between being profitable and losing money. Razor-thin margins on computers and electronics, as well as rapid price erosion of electronics in general, require superior visibility and control of all elements of SCM and execution.

This scenario, as exemplified by Dell Computer, can become a critical source of competitive advantage. Internal integration, combined with the increased use of collaboration with trading partners, will continue to drive industry performance and individual business results as Web services allow organizations to conduct more complex collaboration initiatives. The following is a brief summary of integration and collaboration opportunities in the computer and electronics industry:

- *Integration*—Solving the integration problems in electronics manufacturing using Web services greatly enhances SCM initiatives and visibility of orders, inventory, and potential shortages of key components and materials. Many electronics firms, especially in electronics assembly and contract manufacturing, have grown through M&A, and therefore have very different in-plant manufacturing systems that must be tied into business planning systems. In these situations, Web services can be used to integrate business systems to diverse distributed manufacturing systems by using standards-based XML/SOAP interfaces.

- *Collaboration*—Electronics manufacturers in general have already experimented with collaboration systems provided by their SCM software vendors. Web services will drive deeper adoption of collaboration across the entire electronics value chain as integration issues are resolved. Sell-side collaboration with contract manufacturers, distributors, and direct customers can demand multiple interfaces to forecasting and planning systems. Buy-side collaboration can dictate the same number and types of interfaces with distribution centers, suppliers and contract manufacturers for inventory information, forecasts, purchase orders, supplier evaluations, quality information, and more. Web services will reduce the costs of collaboration and will enable the electronics industry to dramatically expand the role of collaboration.

Automotive The automotive industry is ripe for Web services adoption in both the integration phase and the collaboration phase. GM, Ford, and Daimler-Chrysler (and most other global automobile organizations) have widely distributed manufacturing operations, and have retained much of their vertical integration with internal component and subassembly operations. In order to improve supply chain efficiency, Web services can be used to enhance internal integration within individual operations as well as to the corporate headquarters. The following is a brief summary of integration and collaboration opportunities in the automotive industry:

- *Integration*—Web services can be used in a variety of integration situations, both internally in assembly operations, as well as in managing global capacity, inventory levels, and sales information at the dealerships. Consider an assembly plant example, where components proceed through three broad manufacturing processes: body shop, paint shop, and general assembly. In the body shop, sheet metal parts are stamped, pressed, and bent, then ultimately welded together into the body of the vehicle (called the body-in-white). There are many tracking systems used to manage the scheduling process through the body shop as a vehicle proceeds to the paint shop. In the paint shop, there are different systems used to manage the routing of vehicles through paint booths based on the type of painting operation in the plant—in-line paint line or modular paint shop with robotics. In either case, there are complex scheduling algorithms used to determine the optimal sequence of vehicles as well as the color sequence used. Once a vehicle exits the paint shop, there are often re-sequencing systems that sort the vehicles to optimize the build schedule in the general assembly part of the plant. This is where the trim, electronics, engines, seats, and other components are added to produce a finished vehicle. The variety of systems required to support automotive assembly, as well as the delivery of components just in time to the manufacturing process, would benefit greatly from Web services. Broadcasts to suppliers for schedule changes, material pull signals, and other SCM systems could be managed using Web services as opposed to rigid, point-to-point integration using proprietary integration mechanisms.

* *Collaboration*—The automotive industry will also benefit from Web services in collaboration, especially given the complex network of suppliers to the automotive industry. The network of automotive suppliers, from large tier-one suppliers to medium tier-two suppliers and, ultimately, to the small tier-three suppliers, could use Web services as a common interfacing mechanism for inventory management, purchase orders, forecasting, and even logistics and shipment tracking purposes. Web services will be very powerful in this case because the smaller suppliers cannot afford the infrastructure of EDI. Web services can provide a way for smaller suppliers to exchange EDI-like transactions without having to invest in expensive EDI solutions. In addition, participating in exchanges such as Covisnt, the auto industry's procurement trade exchange, might be performed using standard Web services as opposed to implementing proprietary hub-and-spoke e-Commerce integration technologies to connect ERP systems to these exchanges.

Pharmaceutical The pharmaceutical industry is characterized by tremendous R&D expenditures and a high rate of M&A activity. Pharmaceutical organizations maintain an army of sales representatives to sell their products to hospitals and doctors around the world. There are several areas where Web services can deliver value to these organizations. They include the supply chain opportunities we have discussed already, but there are other unique requirements of the pharmaceutical industry that can also benefit from the adoption of Web services. The pharmaceutical industry has similar requirements to other manufacturing verticals in the integration and collaboration phases, but also has its own unique requirements:

* *Integration*—The pharmaceutical industry can benefit from Web services in integrating results from clinical trials into their reporting systems as mandated by the federal government, particularly the Food and Drug Administration (FDA). Web services can facilitate the integration of the multitude of systems across the entire new drug development and clinical trial process, as well as shortening the time for approvals. Another integration area for pharmaceutical organizations is in integrating acquired organizations into the parent organization. It is very likely that the acquired organization has different IT applications

than the acquiring organization, and therefore, using Web services as the integration mechanism makes sense.

■ *Collaboration*—Pharmaceutical organizations will adopt Web services for collaboration initiatives supporting drug research. The tremendous cost of R&D for these organizations, as well as the time required to develop new drugs, submit them for approval to the FDA, and move them through clinical trials to final approval is long and arduous. Web services can support collaboration research among organizations working together, which might help defray the cost of new drug development.

Retail/Consumer Packaged Goods (CPG)   The retail and CPG industry poses tremendous opportunity for Web services. The CPG industry uses the Collaborative Planning, Forecasting, and Replenishment (CPFR) standard to manage the flow of goods from UEMs to retailers. CPFR will require Web services integration activities within the organization, as well as the collaboration activities similar to those discussed for the electronics industry. Both of these verticals have complex supply chains as well as very complex information systems. Their IT architectures will make use of Web services as an integration technology to expose back-end forecasting systems, inventory management systems, and logistics systems.

The retail industry can benefit from Web services in a number of ways, most notably in supply chain visibility, logistics, and transportation management. Linking Point-Of-Sale (POS) systems with replenishment systems provides real-time information about demand in stores, which enables retailers like Wal-Mart to re-route shipments from regional distribution centers to those stores with the greatest need for replenishment. This is one example of how Web services can be used to integrate highly distributed and disparate systems together in real-time to drive improved business performance. Integration and collaboration in the CPG industries are briefly examined below:

■ *Integration*—Web services will support CPFR initiatives by helping retailers expose multiple back-end systems to logistics services providers, warehouses/distribution centers, and Third-Party Logistics Providers (3PLs). In addition, linking POS systems to forecasting and replenishment systems will improve supply chain response and help manage inventory across the logistics network. This integration problem is ripe for Web services.

■ *Collaboration*—Along with CPFR initiatives, which are the primary driver in retail and CPG, Web services can provide collaboration benefits by sharing data among suppliers and with other trading partners, which will accelerate supply chain responsiveness.

Aerospace and Defense   Aerospace and defense industries have SCM issues similar to all other manufacturing organizations. The complexity of the products, however, which are engineered to order, demands closer relationships with suppliers as well as with internal engineering organizations to support this mode of manufacturing. Aircraft manufacturing requires significant access to design data such as specifications, Computer Aided Design (CAD) and Computer Aided Manufacturing (CAM) data, and supporting product documentation. Managing the Bill Of Materials (BOM) for an aircraft is no small task, and coordinating suppliers across the supply chain can be extremely challenging. Although supply chain velocity is nowhere near that of the electronics industry, the complexity and sheer number of components is daunting, as are the systems required to manage the design and manufacturing processes. The following is a brief summary of integration and collaboration opportunities in the aerospace and defense industries:

- *Integration*—Web services in aerospace and defense will be used to tie internal design and manufacturing systems together, facilitating coordination between the army of suppliers. Again, although the supply chain does not have the same high-speed as some other industries, it is nonetheless complex, and therefore any efficiency gains will enable reduced costs and manufacturing cycle times. The internal integration challenge of aerospace and defense is similar to that of other manufacturing industries, where ERP, CRM, and SCM systems must be linked to provide a cohesive, real-time view of production status, inventory levels, and engineering changes.
- *Collaboration*—Web services will facilitate collaboration in aerospace and defense for internal purposes, as well as with suppliers and design partners. Many of these products are engineered products, which necessitates a close relationship between the suppliers, the design organizations, and the assembly operations. Collaboration via Web services will greatly enhance the ability of these organizations to cooperate in the design and manufacture of complex products such as military vehicles, missiles, jets, and other products. Collaboration via Web services will help speed up the workflow of the design cycle, as well as speed up manufacturing, all while reducing the inventory levels across this complex and costly supply chain.

Manufacturing Conclusions

Manufacturing organizations across the board will implement Web services to solve various business problems. While there are common themes across all manufacturing verticals, such as SCM and inventory visibility, the nuances of each particular vertical inevitably places demands on their systems, architectures, and application portfolios that Web services can ease. In particular, the complexity of internal system integration, combined with the increasing service levels demanded by customers, means that integration of disparate systems is critical for enhancing the customer experience and providing internal productivity and cost reductions.

While Web services cannot yet solve all of the problems of these verticals, they can facilitate the sharing of information internally as well as with trading partners, suppliers, and especially with customers. As Web services evolve and collaboration and workflow standards emerge, the attainable business benefits will become greater, and the pace of Web services adoption will accelerate.

FINANCIAL SERVICES VERTICALS

Financial services represent a diverse collection of businesses, including banking, brokerage and securities, and insurance companies. Each of these industries have their own particular nuances, such as their overall industry pressures and business drivers, tolerance for risk, and IT investment patterns. Banks, for example, have been relatively aggressive in introducing technology to facilitate customer service, improve internal productivity, and support the introduction of new products and services. Insurance organizations, however, have tended to be more conservative with their IT investments, maintaining a late adopter stance toward technology investments and seeking to extend the lifespan of legacy systems and technologies. These legacy systems can often create back-end integration problems when attempting to implement e-Business capabilities such as customer and broker portals, online applications, payment processing, and so on.

Selected Financial Services Verticals

The following section reviews the banking and insurance industries within the financial service vertical, examining how Web services might impact these organizations based on the industry adoption framework described earlier.

Banking   Banking, both wholesale and retail, is characterized by a diversity of systems required to support the various products and services offered to customers. Customers of wholesale banks include other banks, primarily retail banks, while the customers of retail banks are individual consumers and businesses. Mid-sized banks can have well over a hundred application systems running simultaneously to support their business needs, while large banks typically have many hundreds, if not thousands, of applications running at any given time. Lines of business for banking include loan origination, cash management, risk management, global trading services, payment processes, and online banking. Each line of business is supported by dedicated internal systems for reporting, billing statements, and online bill presentment. The array of financial products and services is supported by a host of applications and systems running on multiple hardware platforms and software systems provided by a plethora of vendors. Integration between these numerous systems has been built over many years and tends to be implemented as hard-wired, inflexible, point-to-point connections.

As banks add new customers, they must build additional hard-wired connections to these trading partners as they come online. Smaller banks, which do not receive the same levels of service, are not linked electronically to the extent that larger institutions are.

In general, the banking industry can be summarized as follows:

* Legacy systems dominate the application portfolio.
* A mixture of legacy, homegrown, and commercial applications require significant, on-going integration effort.
* Completing electronic transactions requires complex integration across multiple systems.
* Manual processing of transactions with complex, paper-intensive internal processes complicates the business workflow. Migration to electronic transactions over the next three to five years will make back-end system integration a high priority.
* Providing consolidated customer reporting across multiple channels requires the integration of systems, customer information, and identity management across all applications (retail banking only).
* There is an inability to obtain real-time views of banking transactions and investment and brokerage services and add new lines of business such as insurance.

Web services in banking can provide compelling benefits. A summary for the banking industry, based on adoption of Web services during the integration and collaboration phases, is detailed below:

* *Integration*—Banks, due to the complexity of their back-end systems and mixture of homegrown and commercial applications, will initially use Web services to integrate customer information from multiple back-end systems to CRM systems and portal applications. Retail banks differ from wholesale banks in their multi-channel interaction with their customers via ATMs, online banking, call centers, and in-person bank visits. The emergence of e-Business forced many retail banks to integrate their back-end systems in support of online banking, billing statements, and real-time balances. Web services will

provide similar benefits for retail banks except that integration will be based on open Web services standards, and over time the services created will be reusable to support the introduction of new products and services. These Web services will be reused across multiple channels. For example, completing a funds transfer via an ATM will likely use the same Web service as an Electronic Funds Transfer (EFT) from an internal banking system. The reuse of services will significantly reduce application development costs as well as improve time-to-market for new financial products through reduced systems development time.

■ *Collaboration*—Collaboration in the banking industry is less mature than in many other industries, such as high-tech manufacturing. However, as integration issues are tackled both internally and externally, collaboration via Web services will begin to gain traction. Before Web services collaboration can become a reality in the banking industry, security, reliability, and transactional consistency standards will need to stabilize and mature, creating the foundation upon which collaboration initiatives can be built.

Insurance   Insurance organizations have generally been late adopters of technology, and their mixture of homegrown and commercial systems reflects this pattern. Many insurance carriers are only now implementing CRM initiatives to provide a single view of the customer across product lines. This is a challenging task as the systems for each particular line of business (for example, homeowners insurance and automobile insurance) will often have separate systems for quoting, underwriting, claims management, and renewals. This means that in order to provide a single, coherent customer experience, insurance companies will likely need to use Web services to integrate their disparate back-end systems into CRM and portal applications. Internal integration projects will be a primary theme for some time to come in the insurance industry.

In general, insurance organizations face the following issues:

■ Multitude of front-end and back-end systems.
■ New products and services are difficult to create and market.
■ Combination coverage and bundles of coverage rely on connecting back-end systems.
■ Claims processing is transaction-intensive, and systems do not link to CRM and other customer systems.
■ Linking with online insurance marketplaces is difficult with legacy back-end systems.
■ Integrating agents and brokers into carrier systems is a critical need to drive new business and maintain sales channels.

From this list of issues it is clear that the insurance industry is fertile for the adoption of Web services. The combination of complex legacy systems, high transaction volumes for claims processing, renewals, and new policy issuance, combined with interaction across numerous customer acquisition channels (agents, brokers, exchanges, Web sites, and so on), provides opportunities for the implementation of Web services. A summary of the insurance industry, based on adoption of Web services during the integration and collaboration phases, is detailed below:

- *Integration*—Insurance organizations face similar issues to banks in their need to integrate multiple back-end systems. This is especially true for the integration of front-end quoting and underwriting systems with back-end claims processing systems, as well as integrating these systems to a CRM solution that provides a single view of, and point of reference for, its customers. It is common for insurance carriers to offer multiple products, for example, workers compensation, commercial automobile, liability, and property coverage, and yet they have separate systems for the front-end and back-end processing activities for each of these products. This results in a very complex IT environment. Web services can be leveraged as the basis for integration of these systems to portals, Web sites, CRM systems, and more. Further, Web services will be used to connect these diverse systems to insurance exchanges and other e-Markets to support new distribution channels for products and services. Because of the proliferation of legacy systems, Web services will likely be leveraged in solving diverse integration needs in support of new customer service demands.
- *Collaboration*—Web services can offer a range of benefits to insurance companies in the collaboration phase of adoption. Integrating agents and brokers into their distribution model will play a critical role in reaching customers with new products and services. While there are standards for the insurance industry, for example the Association for Cooperative Operations Research and Development (ACORD) standards, back-end systems are nonetheless very different from company to company. Web services will be used to expose these back-end systems to the agency management systems used by agents and brokers. After an insurance quote is shopped around to multiple insurance organizations and the customer is satisfied with a particular policy, the agent might submit the application information to the selected underwriter using a common interface mechanism enabled using Web services. This approach will streamline the quoting and policy issuance process as well as integrate the agents and brokers more tightly with insurance carriers.

Financial Services Conclusions

Financial services are fertile ground for the deployment of Web services. The structure of the industry, whether it is retail banking, insurance, or other financial services verticals, will allow Web services to provide significant improvements in processes that affect the relationships of companies to their customers and suppliers. There are real and immediate opportunities For Web services as an integration platform based on the complexity of back-end IT systems and the tendency of some financial services segments to under-invest in their infrastructure and IT application portfolio. Once these are explored and the opportunities are exhausted in the integration arena, attention will shift to collaborative opportunities, working more closely with business partners to provide new sources of value to customers and creating new sources of competitive advantage. Financial services will be a very interesting vertical to watch over the coming few years as the early adopters distance themselves from the late adopters.

ADDITIONAL BUSINESS SCENARIOS

There are a number of generic business processes that are represented in all organizations regardless of the industry or vertical. These range from simple portal integration initiatives to the use of Web services to support the business integration requirements of an M&A strategy. From the Web services adoption model developed in Chapter 3, we showed how initial forays into Web services will be focused on internal integration, solving integration issues between back-office, enterprise applications and front-office systems such as portals, Web-based front-ends for CRM, and other related customer-facing systems.

Mergers and Acquisitions

Of all the possible business issues faced by executives, one of the most common is the need to integrate an acquired firm into the acquiring organization. This task can be challenging on many levels, including business strategy, organizational structure, business process, and technology infrastructure. All of these forces of change must be considered and explicitly addressed in order to achieve the synergies of an acquisition that most executives point to as justification for the decision. Of course, recent accounting insights have shown that M&A activities have not generated the value that was promised, and more often than not have resulted in the destruction, rather than the creation, of shareholder value. One key issue with M&A strategies has been the speed with which an acquisition can be absorbed in order to achieve the intended synergies of the merger.

A typical first step in M&A absorption is financial integration, followed by the strategic integration of business operations to eliminate redundant operations, trim excess costs, and eliminate duplicate functions. Ultimately, back-end integration of all business systems may be required depending on how integrated the organizations must be to support the M&A objectives. Strategic mergers, where the entire operations of the acquired firm are integrated, require the rationalization of duplicate staff, of duplicate processes and IT systems, and duplicate capacity.

Web services can be leveraged to very quickly integrate the financial and operational systems of the acquired firm. The use of Web services significantly reduces the time and cost of integration and provides executives with an integrated view of the combined organization's operating metrics—typically a significant post-merger challenge. This allows executives to more effectively ensure that the merger can achieve its targeted objectives. However, from a medium- to long-term perspective, it is still critical for a post-merger organization to develop a consolidated enterprise architecture and retire duplicate and legacy systems. Consolidation of systems will enable the full benefits of an M&A strategy to be realized. As will be discussed in Chapter 7, "Architecting for Competitive Advantage," Web services should be a key consideration when creating a consolidated enterprise architecture.

Public Trade Exchanges

Participating in public trading exchanges is another area where Web services hold great promise for organizations in multiple verticals, regardless of whether their core focus is manufacturing products or providing services. Previously we have discussed participation in trade exchanges for procurement of components and raw materials, as well as using trade exchanges to sell finished goods. These exchanges require access to ERP data, the ability to process purchase orders on the procurement side, and also to expose production data and order status on the sell side.

Web services are compelling for exchanges because they offer a low-cost, standards-based approach for integration of the systems necessary to exchange commerce transactions electronically in an exchange or online market. Previously, integration with exchanges, whether private or public, demanded expensive interfaces via EDI, EAI, or other means. The cost of integration to exchanges was often beyond the budget of smaller vendors, who often still rely on fax and phone channels of communication for orders, forecast sharing, and other related information.

Web services will drive down the integration costs for suppliers, trading partners, and customers, such that partnering and participating in online trade exchanges will become not only easier, but more economically viable for small- and medium-sized firms. This development will change the structure and cost basis for many industries as efficiencies are gained in the exchange of information, products, and services.

SUMMARY

This chapter provides some insight into how Web services can be adopted by a variety of vertical markets based on the Web services adoption model and the Web services deployment framework. We have shown that there are generic business challenges that are natural starting points for the development and deployment of Web services, and as our framework suggests, there are certain Web services goals that should be targeted as outcomes or guiding principles of these initial projects.

There are a number of obvious business benefits that should result from the successful application of Web services to these business problems. In order to truly evaluate the success of these initiatives, cost-benefit analyses must be performed to identify the business value sought and an analysis must be conducted to measure the actual business value realized. The frameworks provided in this chapter facilitate the targeting, analysis, and goal orientation for initial Web services projects, and will help to ensure a successful foray into the world of business-driven Web services.

ENDNOTES

1 Forrester Research, The Web Services Payoff, p. 6, December 2001.
2 AMR Research, "Web Services: Changing the Dynamics of Integration and Application Vendors," August 2002.
3 Stencil Group, "The Laws of Evolution: A Pragmatic Analysis of the Emerging Web Services Market," p. 24, April 2002.
4 Charles Fine, Clockspeed, 1998.

CHAPTER 6

Where to Begin?

"Whenever you are asked if you can do a job, tell 'em, 'Certainly I can!' Then get busy and find out how to do it."

Theodore Roosevelt (1858–1919)

"Good plans shape good decisions. That's why good planning helps to make elusive dreams come true."

Lester R. Bittel, The Nine Master Keys of Management

We are all familiar with the story of the young shepherd who cried "wolf!" just one too many times. Perhaps the vendors in the software and services industries could learn a lesson or two from this old story. With the still-too-present memory of the dot-com boom and bust, the huge investments that many organizations have made implementing e-Commerce storefronts, combined with the tremendous media hype surrounding Web services, it is not surprising that many CIOs are trying to separate Web services hype from reality.

In Chapter 3, "Web Service Adoption," we took a pragmatic look at the potential that Web services undoubtedly bring—examining both the tactical and strategic implications of Web services and discussing the implications of Web services adoption over time. In this chapter, we differentiate between reality and hype, outlining a comprehensive framework to help determine where to begin implementing Web services in an organization. We will offer a step-by-step approach for building an initial Web services plan, to obtain the real benefits that Web services can deliver today.

REALITY VERSUS HYPE

The emergence of a new technology in the software industry has a tendency to generate media attention and hype. Web services has perhaps been the most heralded and hyped new technology to date. The Gartner Group refers to this phenomenon as the "Hype Cycle."[1] Figure 6.1 illustrates Gartner's Web services hype cycle from late 1999 through 2005. Gartner believes that Web services will reach the peak of its hype cycle by early 2003 and then descend into the "Trough of Disillusionment," where Web services are unable to live up to the mystical image created by the software industry.

Considering how over-hyped Web services are today, one could envision reality versus hype as two ends of a spectrum. On one end of the spectrum, there are the very real and tangible business benefits that can be attained today. On the other end, there is the speculation of what might be attained in the future. This concept is illustrated in Figure 6.2, the Web services reality versus hype spectrum. Although the hype of today is not what we will see and implement tomorrow, it is important to remember that over the coming years

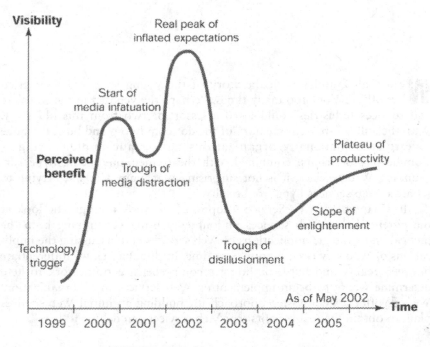

FIGURE 6.1   The Web services hype cycle.
Source: Gartner, 2002

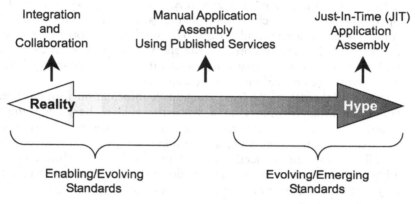

FIGURE 6.2 The spectrum of Web services reality versus hype.

it is possible—even likely—that Web services will bridge the gap, making today's hype tomorrow's reality.

The Reality

At the reality end of the spectrum, early adopters will gain significant benefits from Web services through internal integration and closer collaboration with partners, suppliers, and customers. The capabilities and standards required for the first steps of integration and collaboration pilots are already in place. Earlier pilots will primarily leverage XML messaging from the enabling standards tier and SOAP binding from the evolving standards tier. Early pilot projects will focus on cost reductions and efficiency gains through the following initiatives:

- *Reduced System Integration Costs*—Web services, using XML and SOAP, will become the de facto mechanism for systems integration. As an organization's application portfolio migrates to a service-oriented paradigm, all systems will use Web services as a primary interface mechanism, removing the need for custom integration projects. This standards-based approach to application integration will significantly reduce the time, effort, and cost of future integration projects.
- *Faster Time to Market*—By exposing current application functionality as services, the promise of software reuse can at last become a reality. Reuse of services, rather than the more traditional "let's reinvent the

wheel" approach, will enable greater flexibility and faster time-to-market for implementation of capabilities or services.

- *Real-time Operational Visibility*—Without exception, every organization seeks to improve the availability, accuracy, and visibility of key operational metrics such as sales forecasts, operating expenses, cash flow, inventory levels, and so on. The implementation of real-time executive dashboards tailored to the specific needs of each executive will provide real-time mission-critical information, enabling better management of internal business execution.

- *Closer Collaboration*—Sharing much more information with partners, suppliers, and customers on a system-to-system basis, making it possible to take slack out of the value chain for a firm and its partners. For example, much like Dell, a firm might be able to improve order visibility, enabling reduced levels of on-hand stock—thus creating additional space to add new production lines. This situation in turn could increase production capabilities and improve purchasing economies of scale.

- *Redeployment of Valuable Resources*—By enabling both greater reuse and improving collaboration, it will be possible to greatly improve operational efficiencies.

Dell Computer is a great model of how Web services capabilities can be applied to achieve the advantages above. In their article "Break on through to the Other Side: A Missing Link in Redefining the Enterprise,"[2] John Hagel III and John Seely Brown discuss how Dell has continued to change the rules in the PC market:

> *Direct material purchases represent as much as 70% of Dell's revenue, so even modest savings in the area can deliver significant bottom line impact. Equally important to Dell is the inventory asset exposure—in an environment where product prices recently have been declining at 0.6% per week, any excess inventory can become very costly. It is not surprising that Dell sees significant benefits to more effective supply chain management.*
>
> *Dell began by focusing on its network of third-party logistics providers who operate distribution centers ("vendor managed hubs") where raw material inventories are maintained for Dell's assembly operations. Dell's "ship to" target from the time of receipt of a customer's order is 5 days, yet the average fulfillment time of their suppliers is 45 days. To meet their "ship to" targets despite the 45-day delivery time from suppliers, Dell used three business approaches at the outset: maintain a 26–30 hour inventory buffer at the Dell assem-*

bly plant, ensure vendors maintain a 10-day inventory buffer at the vendor managed hubs and distribute on a weekly basis a 52-week demand forecast to suppliers. The vendor-managed inventory at the hub helps to deal with unanticipated supply disruptions and inaccuracies in the near-term forecast.

In the first stage of its initiative, Dell focused on reducing the 26–30 hours of inventory held at their assembly plants. Using i2 supply chain software, Dell now generates a new manufacturing schedule for each of its plants every two hours to reflect customer orders received over the previous two hours. Publishing those manufacturing schedules as a web service via Dell's extranet, Dell alerts the vendor-managed hubs regarding what specific materials are needed and directs them to deliver those materials to a specific building and dock door so that the materials can be fed into a specific assembly line. These alerts are sent in an XML format so that they can be integrated directly into the disparate inventory management systems maintained by its vendor-managed hubs. The distribution centers are implementing the capability to respond to the material requests automatically through the extranet and then have 90 minutes to pick, pack, and ship the required parts to the factory. With this automated, web services-based approach, Dell has been able to reduce its own holding of raw material inventories from 26–30 hours of production to 3–5 hours—a reduction of more than 80%. Eric Michlowitz, Director of Supply Chain E-Business Solutions for Dell explains, "what we've been able to do is remove the stock rooms from the assembly plant, because we are only pulling in materials that we need specifically tied to customer orders. This enabled us to add in additional production lines, increasing our factory utilization by one-third."

Of course, lean manufacturing approaches often push back inventory exposure from the manufacturer to the supplier. Dell's goal is to eliminate excess inventory, not simply push it back up the supply chain. This drove its next wave of initiatives designed to eliminate the need to hold buffer inventories in the vendor-managed hubs because of errors in the supply chain. To do this, they focused on checking the reliability of supplier delivery schedules early enough in the process to allow effective contingency planning to mitigate against unanticipated disruptions in supply (e.g., by temporarily withdrawing certain models on Dell's web site). Michlowitz's team is deploying a web services-based event management system to do this through its extranet. This approach avoids the need to directly access the *application systems of its suppliers and instead relies on an approach consisting of automatic exchanges of inquiries and confirmations with its suppliers (e.g., inquiring whether the supplier shipped as promised). Because the system is automated, the supply chain team is able to focus its energy on handling the exceptions. Dell expects to be able to reduce inventory exposure in the vendor-managed hubs by 10–40%, while at the same time significantly improving gross margin performance through more effective matching of demand and supply.*

In this example, Dell demonstrates superior performance using only basic Web services capabilities. As Web services standards evolve, Dell may be able to identify further opportunities to improve efficiencies, reduce costs, and increase profitability.

The Hype

At the hype end of the spectrum, a disproportionate amount of early Web services discussion has focused on the conceptual ability to automate application assembly on a Just-In-Time (JIT) basis. In this scenario, it is proposed that applications will be automatically and dynamically assembled as needed by using services published in public registries on the Internet, typically using the UDDI standard. This capability, although technically feasible, faces significant obstacles including the following:

- *Trust*—The fundamental ability to put trust in the source of a public service is an obstacle. Unless one knows that a public service is trustworthy, as with the Dunn and Bradstreet example in Chapter 2, "Standards, Concepts, and Terminology," would a firm really be willing to use it? How does one know whether the service does what it is supposed to do? What if the service is malicious? The ability to trust the provider of a service will initially limit the use of Web services to collaboration with partners, suppliers, and customers where a pre-existing trusted relationship exists. It is unlikely that significant markets will emerge for publicly available services unless those services are provided by organizations that are deemed trustworthy by a large target audience.

- *Security*—It is possible to secure a private network with trusted partners, suppliers, and customers by using Virtual Private Network (VPN) capabilities today. But as the desire to use services that exist outside of a private network increases, the emerging Web services security standards will need to mature significantly. In the medium-to-long term we do not anticipate that security will remain an inhibitor to Web services adoption. A number of new security standards have recently been proposed by the WS-I organization to close the security gap (for example, WS-Security and WS-Policy).

▪ *Management*—A range of support tools are emerging that will be applied to the broad category of Web services management. This category includes tools for performance management, quality of service, logging and auditing, and so on. All of these capabilities must be evaluated as the number of Web services being used by an organization grows. To date, management requirements have received less visibility than Web services security, and there has been less attention focused on creating management standards. As a result, proprietary solutions have already begun to appear, and these may be followed by the eventual emergence and adoption of Web services management standards.

THREE STEPS TO SUCCESSFUL WEB SERVICES

Taking the first step—the "leap of faith"—with any new technology can be daunting. This section identifies three steps that will help a company get started with Web services and avoid any hurdles. The three steps detailed in this section are as follows:

1. *Start Preparing*—What does a firm need to consider before beginning the implementation of Web services?
2. *Selection of a Pilot Project*—How should a firm select the first Web services pilot?
3. *Incremental Adoption*—What should the primary considerations be as Web services are deployed across the organization?

Step 1: Start Preparing

In Chapter 3, "Web Services Adoption," we discussed the four phases of the Web services adoption model: integration, collaboration, innovation, and domination. Here, we focus on the tasks required to get ready for the integration and collaboration phases, discussing the steps that should be considered when preparing for the first Web services project. Think of this section as a pre-project checklist of steps that ideally should be completed before starting the first Web services project. The key topics that are covered in this section include the following:

▪ *Questions to Ask*—What questions should be asked today? Also, what questions should the executive team be asking?
▪ *Awareness and Training*—Who needs to understand the concepts and capabilities of Web services? Also, who should receive training on how to implement Web services?
▪ *Getting Started*—Are there any key tasks that should be considered before starting the first Web services project? What can be done to get started today?

Chief Executive	Next Steps
How can I accelerate the implementation of our business strategy?	Review the business strategy with the executive team and identify opportunities where Web service can be used as an enabler.
How can I gain greater visibility of business operating metrics?	Investigate the implementation of a real-time executive dashboard, enabled using Web services.
How can I increase my firm's value proposition?	Work with the executive team to identify opportunities where Web services can support entry to new markets.

IT Executives	Next Steps
How can I increase the strategic value and role of the IT group?	Investigate how Web services can be used to create new market opportunities, perhaps exposing an existing IT capability as a public service.
How can I deliver increased business value using the resources available to me today? (more with less!)	Determine which existing applications should be used as a foundation for creating *virtual services*.
How can our architecture better support short-term and longer-term business objectives?	Dust off your enterprise architecture and revisit it with an eye to Service Oriented Architectures (SOA) and Web services. See Chapter 7, "Architecting for Competitive Advantage."

Operations Executives	Next Steps
How can I reduce operating costs?	Identify manual processes that can be evaluated for automation using Web services.
How can I achieve greater visibility of business operations?	Investigate the implementation of a real-time executive dashboard, enabled using Web services interoperability.

Business Managers	Next Steps
How can I create closer relationships with partners, suppliers, and partners?	Work with the management team to identify key partners, suppliers, and customers that can be early candidates for Web services collaboration.
How can I remove labor-intensive duplication of data entry?	Work with IT to implement Web services integration projects that will remove the need for duplicate data entry.

IT Managers	Next Steps
How should I best leverage my current team?	Talk with your team to determine who has already been working with Web services. Leverage a core team for early pilots.
What skills does my team need to gain for implementation of Web services?	Determine if you are going to focus on implementation of Web services using J2EE or .Net and develop a skills development plan. Make sure that the IT team is up to speed with core Web services standards (specifically XML, SOAP, & WSDL).

FIGURE 6.3 Questions to ask today.

Questions to Ask Today   As a firm is considering Web services, Figure 6.3 out-
lines some of the initial questions that should be considered by any organization beginning its Web services journey.

Awareness, Skills, and Training   A Web services project is no different than any
traditional technology project in that it should be a collaborative effort
between the business unit(s) and IT. But as with any new technology, the
application of Web services can only be conceived and implemented as well
as the skills and experience within the organization allow. Awareness of
Web services in both the business and IT communities will be critical to
fully leverage Web services and enable new business capabilities.

Business Awareness   Web services will ultimately impact all aspects of an
organization. Therefore, a priority for any company planning to launch
Web services should be basic awareness and training across all functions
and at all levels of the organization. Make sure that managers and executives across the organization understand the basic principles of Web services and that they receive regular updates on how Web services are being
used and can be used in your organization.

Primary considerations for creating business awareness of Web services
include:

- *Executive Awareness*—It is critical that senior executives and company
  leaders are aware of the strategic value that Web services can provide.
  Communicate the capabilities and implications of Web services to the
  executive team, and make this goal the highest priority.
- *Executive Buy-in*—Without executive awareness, buy-in, and support,
  a firm might have the in-house Web services implementation skills but
  will lack the necessary mind-share to move early projects forward.
- *Strategic Planning*—Beyond the mind-share required to get the first
  project underway, the executive team requires a broad understanding
  of the medium- and long-term strategic implications of Web services.
  Ensure that Web services are considered in the context of the strategic
  vision and strategic planning. They may be a key enabler, or perhaps
  will require fundamentally rethinking the business focus. Look for
  strategic value in Web services. There might be opportunities to
  migrate from a low-margin manufacturing service to a high-margin
  services business.

If a firm does not gain executive mind-share and formulate a Web services
strategy during the integration and collaboration phases, it will likely not be
among the winners in the innovation and domination phases. In order to
really make Web services deliver true business value, the corporate strategy

and business model must be explicitly interlocked with the Web services strategy, implementation plans, and the initial projects under consideration.

Java versus .Net   Web services today are implemented in two primary ways: Java 2 Enterprise Edition (J2EE) or Microsoft .Net. The relative advantages and disadvantages of these two implementation models are discussed in Chapter 7, "Architecting for Competitive Advantage," but fundamentally either or both can be used to develop interoperable Web services.

From a technical training perspective, primary considerations should include "What are the current in-house skills?" and "What are the majority of existing applications and infrastructure implemented with?" The answers to these two questions will likely determine whether a firm uses Microsoft .Net or J2EE for the implementation of its first Web services projects.

Technical Training   Beyond the question of Java versus .Net, primary considerations when looking at capabilities and training should be the following issues :

- ■ *Development Tools*—A new breed of development tools, referred to as authoring environments or Integrated Development Environments (IDEs), are emerging to aid developers with Web services implementation. These tools promise to significantly reduce the time and effort required to implement Web services by automating the creation of access protocols (specifically SOAP) and service description documents (specifically WSDL). Further information regarding Web services software vendors and development tools can be found in Chapter 8, "Web Services Vendor Landscape."
- ■ *Technical Team Perspective*—Obtain architects', designers', and developers' perspectives and feedback on Web services and the associated Java or .Net development tools. It is likely that they have already been reading up on Web services and testing their capabilities on "skunk-works" projects, using any one of the multitude of downloadable trial development environments available from Microsoft, IBM, BEA Systems, Sun, and others.
- ■ *Prioritize Training Needs*—Formalize needed Web services capabilities and skill sets. It is probably not practical to train the entire team at one time, so identify a SWAT team of architects, project managers, and senior developers who will form a bridgehead for formal Web services training and skills development. This group should also contain the individuals that will lead the initial pilot projects.

If in-house planning and development resources are limited, consider working with a Systems Integration (SI) partner to kickstart Web services efforts. Be sure to ask for Web services references and check them diligently, vetting the proposed team members to determine their real hands-on skills with Web services. Make sure that it is possible for key resources from the core team to participate as project team members, or shadow resources, alongside the SI team. Early projects with SI partners will create an ideal opportunity to obtain on-the-job Web services training and knowledge transfer for your staff.

Getting Started Today Having determined the training needs, a firm must start preparing its applications and architecture for the first Web services project. Two key areas to start work on are the standardization of data definitions and XML-enabling legacy systems.

Standardize Data Definitions It is critically important to define and then garner agreement for the data definition standards that will be used across the organization. Web services provide the protocols and standards to significantly reduce the complexity associated with system integration, but they do not guarantee shared terminology and agreement on the meaning of data shared between organizations. In Chapter 2, "Standards, Concepts, and Terminology," we discussed the flexibility that XML provides but also introduced the challenges of aligning data definitions, jargon, and vocabularies within and across organizations. For example, is what you mean by a "widget" the same as my understanding? Or, for example, in an XML document containing a product catalogue, is the "Price" field the gross price or the net price?

These examples represent just the tip of the semantic iceberg. Recognizing these challenges, a number of standards organizations are actively engaged in defining data schemes for shared agreement and understanding (for example, OASIS, RosettaNet, and so on). Unfortunately, getting agreement on these standards is proving to be a slow and arduous process as Dell Computer experienced firsthand working with RosettaNet:

> *After three years, members of the computer-industry standards group RosettaNet haven't agreed on specifications, so Dell Computer Corporation just dropped out. Instead, it is moving ahead with its own system for linking suppliers. "I think it'll take years to get an adoption of RosettaNet standards. We're all for it, but I'm not waiting," says Richard L. Hunter Jr., Dell's vice-president for Americas manufacturing operations.[3]*

Some industries have achieved broader agreement on data definition standards than others (for example, ACORD in the insurance industry and FITS in brokerage), so it is not always necessary to go it alone as Dell decided to do.

Regardless of whether existing industry standards are used or a firm defines its own, it is critical to enforce data definition standards within an organization. This task is perhaps the single most important activity that can be completed in preparation for implementing Web services. As the need for data definition standards in an organization is examined, consider the following activities:

- Check with industry bodies to determine if industry-specific data standards have been developed that can be leveraged. Perhaps the standards for your industry are a "work in-progress," where a firm can participate in and influence their direction.
- Investigate if any previous projects have started the process of data definition for your organization. Perhaps a glossary of terms, a data dictionary, or data modeling project can be leveraged as a starting point for your data definition standards.
- Making sure that a definitive source of defined standards is published and maintained (once you have defined your data definition standards).
- Making sure that data standards are applied consistently for all projects going forward.

Cutting corners on data standardization now will create a snowball effect later, so invest the time and energy to develop data definition standards as soon as possible.

XML Enabling   XML-based messaging is a central enabler for Web services, providing a more simple, flexible approach to connecting systems than traditional custom interfaces and current Enterprise Application Integration (EAI) offerings. XML is literally the keystone of Web services, enabling the creation of standards-based integration across an organization.

XML and Web services go hand in hand. Therefore, XML-enabling core systems pay dividends when implementing Web services. As a firm leverages XML across its organizations, consider the following actions:

- *Investigate Emerging Tools*—Early adopters of XML, such as Fidelity Investments, hand-coded the software to generate XML documents. Now, a range of XML and Web services enablement tools are on the market, which significantly reduces the time and effort required to generate XML extracts from newly developed or legacy systems. Examples of such tools include XMLSpy and exteNd Composer.
- *Consult Key Application Vendors*—Many software vendors are already XML- and Web services-enabling their applications. Talk with

key application software vendors to determine when they intend to release XML or Web services-enabled versions of their software. Determine whether software releases supporting XML and Web services will be minor updates or major new releases.

- *Determining Application Upgrades*—Determine the effort required to update or upgrade packaged applications to provide XML and Web services support. Decide which packages will be updated or upgraded, and for which a firm will develop its own Web services support.

Step 2: Select a Pilot

Having begun the preparation tasks, a firm will be well on the way toward laying a solid foundation for its first Web services project. Now, it is time to identify and prioritize candidate pilot projects. Three activities required for this are listed below:

- *Guiding Principles*—Are there any guiding principles that should be known and followed before the project begins?
- *Application Inventory*—What applications systems exist today? How can the existing application portfolio be leveraged using Web services?
- *Pilot Project*—How should the pilot project be identified?

Guiding Principles As a firm targets candidate projects, use these three key principles to facilitate selection process:

- *Remember the "Usual Suspects"*—The biggest challenges of implementing Web services projects will inevitably be similar to the challenges experienced during a typical IT project or program. These include the following:

  1. Lack of executive sponsorship
  2. Lack of stakeholder input
  3. Unrealistic or poorly managed expectations
  4. Not dedicating business and technical resources
  5. Lack of change management
  6. Scope creep

  Far too often, these challenges are overlooked as it is easier to focus on the technical obstacles or limitations. The reality is that if these six challenges are not a primary focus, then overcoming technical limitations will be the least of a firm's worries.

- *Keep It Simple*—The adoption of any new technology inevitably has its fair share of unexpected pitfalls. Unfortunately, these pitfalls only become obvious after the fact. Do not choose a highly visible or mission-critical project as an early pilot. Remember that one high-visibility failure has the potential to cost far more in lost credibility than it could ever return as a run-away success.

▪ *Web Services Are not Hammers for Every Nail*—Web services are a valuable tool to be added to the IT arsenal, but they are not right for every project. For example, Web services are a good fit for interoperability and loose coupling, but where high volume and high throughput is essential, Web services add a performance overhead that make them a poor choice.

Application Inventory   Before deciding where to start implementing Web services, a firm must know what application systems already exist. Many organizations maintain an application inventory of production systems, but if it does not exist or if it is not up to date, then take the time to review and document the application portfolio. As the application inventory is updated or created, capture information that will help identify initial Web services opportunities. Use these four categories as a basis for identifying Web services "hot spots:"

1. *Data Silos*—Where information is held within enterprise application silos, limiting operating visibility. This is a primary candidate for Web services-enabled "executive dashboards." Using XML and Web services, data can be extracted from multiple systems and aggregated, in near real-time, to provide unprecedented visibility of operational metrics. Dashboards can be tailored to the specific needs of business and executive management roles.
2. *Manual Duplication of Data*—Reducing or eliminating manual data entry is a glaring opportunity for Web services application integration. Look for process and automation breaches where there are gaps that require manual data entry or repetitive fax and print operations augmented with manual effort.
3. *Proprietary Interfaces*—Applications that have proven difficult to integrate, perhaps using proprietary interfaces requiring specialists' skills, can be encapsulated using SOAP to provide a standard Web services interface. Once a SOAP interface has been implemented, the new service can be reused by other applications without the need for additional development effort.
4. *Manual Touch Points*—Use Web services to enable more effective collaboration with trusted partners where manual processes exist. Look at large partners, suppliers, and customers. Where orders are processed manually, consider implementing collaboration Web services to reduce transaction costs, remove transcribing errors, and develop "stickier" relationships. Talk with trusted partners, suppliers, and

customers to see who is using Web services or considering their use. If any trusted partners, suppliers, or customers are using Web services, then there may be an ideal opportunity to jumpstart Web services collaboration efforts. Closer collaboration with key partners can deliver dramatic results, as with the Dell case study illustrated earlier in this chapter.

Upon completion of the application inventory, identified primary Web services hotspots will fall into these four categories. This analysis will help identify the first Web services pilot project.

Pilot Projects As long as a company has applied the guiding principles and updated its application inventory, using the categories identified previously, there should now be a good short list of candidate pilot projects. As the risks of failure are significant on a pilot project, especially when using new technologies and capabilities, further filter the short list to minimize risk and maximize return. Figure 6.4 illustrates a four-quadrant view for mapping short-listed pilot projects. Clearly, look for projects that fall within the top-right Sweet Spot quadrant.

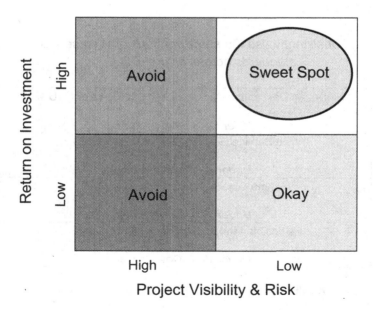

FIGURE 6.4 Maximize return and minimize risk.

Now that a pilot project has been selected, make sure there is agreement on the set of Web services standards that will be used. One of the fundamental goals of Web services is to enable systems interoperability, but the accelerated rate at which standards are evolving can undermine this goal.

As discussed in Chapter 2, "Standards, Concepts, and Terminology," to ensure interoperability first agree on the core standards and versions that will be used to deploy Web services. The Web Services Interoperability (WS-I) organization has defined the WS-Basic Profile, as illustrated in Figure 6.5. The WS-Basic Profile provides standards that are a good starting point for early Web services projects.

Step 3: Incremental Adoption

In moving beyond the first pilot project, a firm will have learned a tremendous amount about the real-world deployment of Web services—gaining a better understanding of their capabilities and limitations. It is important to remember that the early Web services primarily focus on integration and rudimentary collaboration, but as standards gain greater acceptance, the Sweet Spot will grow to encompass extended collaboration and innovation opportunities.

For now, limit early projects to integration and collaboration and learn from early successes and failures to prepare for more complex Web services projects. Specifically:

Consistently use the same versions of Web services standards across all projects.

WS-Basic Profile	Universal Description Discovery and Interoperability (UDDI) Version 2.0 *Under OASIS Governance*
	Web Service Description Language (WSDL) Version 1.1 *Under W3C Governance*
	Simple Object Access Protocol (SOAP) Version 1.1 *Under W3C Governance*
	eXtensible Markup Language (XML) Schema Version 1.0 *Under W3C Governance*

FIGURE 6.5   The WS-Basic Web services standards.

- *Don't Bite off More than You Can Chew*—Keep early projects simple and well defined. It is appropriate to push the boundaries of internal skills as well as Web services technology, but do not push these capabilities too far or too fast. Consider focusing early projects on a single departmental application or single enterprise application at a time. By taking a step-wise approach, your Service-Oriented Architecture (SOA) will come together over time.
- *Leverage Key Vendors/Partners*—Identify which software vendors your firm spends the most with (such as Microsoft, Oracle, HP, IBM). All major vendors, and many others, are actively promoting their ability to deliver Web services. Leverage relationships with these organizations to receive Web services briefings and demonstrations. Their in-house experts can be valuable resources when determining how far to push the capabilities of Web services.
- *Leverage Your Peer Network*—Talk with peers in formal and informal settings to gain better visibility of what others are doing with Web services. There are a number of peer networking groups you can join that help executives share best practices, lessons learned, and success stories. Examples include Beacon Hill Group, a regionally based in-person network (beaconhillgroup.com), and Chief Officer (chiefofficer.com), an online community with more than 2,000 members. These networking groups provide exposure to cross-industry best practices that can be leveraged to identify realistic Web services benefits, rather than needing to rely on media hype.
- *Don't Forget the Basics*—Forgetting project fundamentals such as executive support, expectation management, and scope management lead to project failure far more frequently than technical issues or limitations. Make sure to remember these basics for any Web services projects.
- *Learn from Your Successes and Failures*—In the early adoption stages of any new technology, both successes and failures can be used as a basis to gather lessons learned. Capture what works and what does not and build this body of knowledge into training for business and IT personnel.
- *Get Integration and Collaboration Right, and Innovate From There*—Lay a Web services foundation from a skills and capabilities perspective as well as from an infrastructure and architecture perspective first. Once the right foundation exists, innovation opportunities will be far easier to realize.

WHERE-TO-BEGIN CHECKLIST

Figure 6.6 contains a checklist to use when starting out with Web services. Use this checklist to remain on track with Web services in the categories of training, identification of Web services opportunities, automation of business processes, and Web services architecture.

1) Skills, Experience, and Training	
Has the executive team received a Web services primer?	☐
Are the organization's business and IT leaders trained to understand and exploit the Web services opportunities afforded them?	☐
Have all IT staff been trained on Web services development, assembly, testing, and deployment?	☐
2) Identification Web Service Opportunities	
Do the organization's business and IT leaders understand where Web services can drive competitive advantage, cost savings, revenue opportunities, or customer satisfaction?	☐
Have opportunities been identified for internal integration projects that will use Web services?	☐
Have opportunities been identified for Web services collaboration internally, with partners, suppliers, and customers?	☐
3) Business Process	
Has the organization identified distributed business processes that can be streamlined and implemented using Web services?	☐
Have business processes been decomposed such that they can be implemented as a set of services encapsulated and executed as Web services?	☐
Are organizational structures established such that they can empower the business to operate maximally with Web services?	☐
4) Architecture	
Has the IT organization completed an inventory of the current application and system portfolio?	☐
Have key application vendors been contacted to evaluate their Web services strategy? Do you know when Web service-enabled releases of key applications will be available?	☐
How agile is the firm's architecture?	
Can the architecture support multiple business and IT options over time by virtue of its flexibility and agility?	☐
Has the IT organization developed a Service Oriented Architecture (SOA) using Web services to enable the implementation of an enterprise architecture?	☐

FIGURE 6.6 Where-to-begin checklist.

SUMMARY

In this chapter, we have sought to separate the realistic business capabilities that Web services can deliver today, from the media-hyped capabilities that may be possible in the future. Building upon a perspective of what is hype and what is reality, we detailed a pragmatic three-step approach that can be used as a basis for kick-starting early Web services initiatives. Specifically these three steps are as follows:

1. Preparation for Web services
2. Selection of a pilot project
3. Incremental adoption of Web services

Each step goes beyond a pure technology discussion and examines people, process, and organizational considerations that must be examined when looking at the implementation of Web services. We have concluded this chapter with a "Where-to-Begin Checklist" that can be used as a quick reference to determine Web services readiness for any organization.

Our hope is that this chapter has been able to answer many of the questions regarding how and where to get started with Web services, and made it possible to identify a set of immediate next steps to execute tomorrow.

ENDNOTES

[1] Gartner Group, September 2002, "Navigate the Web Services Hype Cycle" by Mark Driver.
[2] "Break on Through to the Other Side: A Missing Link in Redefining the Enterprise" by John Hagel III and John Seely Brown, pp. 12–13.
[3] March 18, 2002, "The Web at Your Service" by Jim Kerstetter.

CHAPTER 7

Architecting for Competitive Advantage

"The architect must be a prophet . . . a prophet in the true sense of the term . . . if he can't see at least ten years ahead don't call him an architect."

Frank Lloyd Wright (1868–1959)

"What business strategy is all about; what distinguishes it from all other kinds of business planning—is, in a word, competitive advantage. Without competitors there would be no need for strategy, for the sole purpose of strategic planning is to enable the company to gain, as effectively as possible, a sustainable edge over its competitors."

Keniche Ohnae

This chapter introduces the enterprise architecture and discusses how it can be used to create competitive advantage for an organization. We examine the business realities and challenges that have made it so difficult to maintain a coherent enterprise architecture in recent years and how a Service-Oriented Architecture (SOA), implemented using Web services, can be used to make the enterprise architecture a more achievable and manageable objective.

Finally, we consider the implementation considerations for an enterprise architecture and investigate the relative positions of Java 2 Enterprise Edition (J2EE) and Microsoft .Net as the foundation for implementation elements of an SOA.

EVOLUTION OF COMPUTER SYSTEMS

Since the development of the Electrical Numerical Integrator and Calculator (ENIAC), the first high-speed electronic digital computer developed in the mid 1940s, we have pursued an inexhaustible race to build faster and more powerful computer systems. In the realm of computer hardware we have seen significant developments over the last sixty years, including development of the first digital computer, the first transistor-based computers, and the first integrated microprocessor. Now, as we approach the physical limitations of the microprocessor, we are on the verge of new hardware paradigms that will perhaps use quantum theory to operate at the subatomic levels or even use DNA strands to process information.[1]

Along a similar path, computer programming languages have made considerable strides. Early computers such as ENIAC were custom programmed using machine code, the basic binary "1" and "0" language that all digital computers use at their core. Over the past two decades, we have seen a broad range of third- and fourth-generation programming languages (3GLs and 4GLs), including Java, Visual Basic, Smalltalk, and so on, emerge. In many respects, these 3GL and 4GL languages are closer to our natural language than the native language that computers understand. 3GLs and 4GLs have enabled the development of increasingly more complex software in ever more rapid timeframes.

Beyond the custom development of applications, the past decade has seen the emergence and near dominance of packaged software solutions such as Enterprise Resource Planning (ERP), Customer Relationship Management (CRM), and Supply-Chain Management (SCM) systems. The majority of mid- to large-sized organizations use enterprise applications from SAP, Oracle, Siebel, Peoplesoft, and others to support and manage significant aspects of their business. These enterprise systems are not all-encompassing, one-stop solutions, and thus they must co-exist with home-grown custom systems and niche package applications that perform a multitude of ancillary functions across the enterprise.

The point of reviewing the evolution of computer hardware and software is to emphasize the tremendous pace of change that businesses have seen in how and where computer systems and business applications are deployed. These changes, combined with the ever more rapidly moving dynamics of the business landscape, create a unique set of challenges for effective IT management. The management of an organization's IT infrastructure is a constant struggle to maintain and support aging legacy systems and implement new systems to meet emerging business needs, while also ensuring that the overall IT infrastructure is dynamic and flexible enough to enable rather than inhibit changes in business direction and strategy. In an effort to bring balance to these competing perspectives, many organizations define an enterprise architecture to map out their IT plans.

THE ENTERPRISE ARCHITECTURE

The enterprise architecture defines the building blocks that comprise an organization's overall system architecture and provides a framework into which new applications can be incorporated while maintaining the integrity of the whole. The enterprise architecture can be used to optimize current IT investments and ensure that future investments are aligned with the organization's business goals and objectives.

The creation of an enterprise architecture is achieved through balancing the organization's infrastructure and application architecture needs with business and information requirements, as illustrated in Figure 7.1. The enterprise architecture will typically identify a current state, an anticipated future state, and a plan of coordinated activities to guide an organization from the current state to the desired future state.

Each of these four perspectives, or inputs, must be considered to create a single, cohesive enterprise architecture view. Ultimately, the value of the enterprise architecture is only realized by balancing the interactions, relationships, and dependencies of these four perspectives. To find the

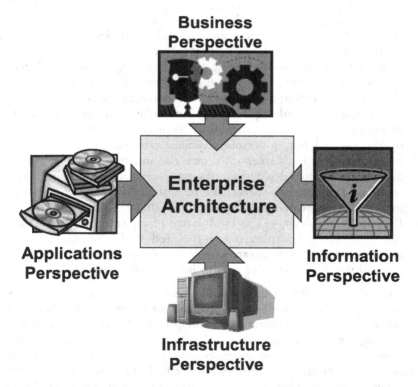

FIGURE 7.1 Influence on an enterprise architecture.

appropriate balance between these disparate perspectives, there inevitably must be give and take and the development of mutual understanding and respect between IT and business stakeholders.

Enterprise Architecture Benefits

Today's executives know that effectively leveraging valuable information assets using information technology is necessary for achieving business goals and objectives. The enterprise architecture addresses this need by providing a strategic context for the evolution of applications in response to constantly changing business needs and market dynamics. Creating and maintaining an effective enterprise architecture can be a key enabler to achieving competitive advantage and will become an increasingly important requirement for organizational survival.

When developed and maintained as a strategic tool, an enterprise architecture can be leveraged to achieve the following:

- *Lower Costs*—A well-defined architecture can provide system modularity. Modularity and reuse are important attributes of a streamlined architecture as they enable lower system development, support, and maintenance costs, while also improving system interoperability.
- *Increased Flexibility*—By defining and maintaining the key touch points between components of the overall architecture, it is possible to increase support for organizational growth and restructuring requirements (for example, mergers and acquisitions). A modular architecture can also be leveraged to increase organizational flexibility, and maintain a firm's options to build, buy, or outsource systems as needed.
- *Improved Time-To-Market*—An enterprise architecture can be leveraged to support the rapid deployment of mission-critical business applications, achieving faster time-to-market for new products and services. This, in turn, leads to increased growth and profitability.
- *Reduced Complexity*—The modularity of an enterprise architecture can reduce the complexities associated with the integration of information across disparate systems, maximizing the visibility and value of the organization's available information assets.

Once the enterprise architecture has been created, it cannot be left to gather dust or end up at the bottom of a stack of documents. Creation of the enterprise architecture requires an ongoing commitment to updating and maintaining it as business priorities and information needs change over time. Unfortunately, it is not easy to maintain an up-to-date enterprise architecture, especially in recent years as priorities have shifted to e-Commerce storefronts and other e-Business imperatives. In the flurry of activity during the Internet bubble, many organizations allowed their enterprise architecture plans to become outdated. It is therefore important for executives to take a moment to ask themselves whether their enterprise architecture truly reflects the systems and applications they have in place today, and if it is aligned with the strategic needs of the business. It is likely that the answer will be an emphatic. "No!"

Today, as IT budgets continue to be trimmed, IT executives are being asked to do more with less. In this environment, the enterprise architecture is once again coming to the forefront, but it is still challenging to maintain an enterprise architecture that balances business's tactical imperatives and strategic goals—especially with the ever-increasing rate of change and demands on today's economy.

Today's Reality

Today's reality is that most organizations have struggled to maintain an effective enterprise architecture. Over the medium to long term, no one has been able to accurately predict how technology might change and what the implications of those changes might be. As such, enterprise architectures have developed through a combination of best guesses and informed hunches—resulting in an accidental architecture, implemented with an array of heterogeneous hardware and software platforms adhering to their own proprietary standards and protocols. Add to this the tremendous business demands placed on the IT organization, in which "We need that new system yesterday!" is not an uncommon cry. The result has been an environment in which tactical business needs supercede the enterprise architecture plans, forcing organizations into an ad-hoc approach to system implementation with the well-intended goal of folding tactical initiatives into a more cohesive architecture when current pressures and demands stabilize. The reality is that the pressures do not abate, the demands do not stabilize, and the enterprise architecture is lost in the myriad of tactical initiatives. As George Paras and John Zachman, respectively, wrote:

> *"The wild e-everything ride is over. Budgets are tighter and reality has set in. Executives tell us they must provide a solid, cost-effective IT foundation and simultaneously increase flexibility to respond to the increasingly diverse demands of the business. The effective use of information, technology, human resources, and investment capital must be balanced to achieve these goals. The solution is a portfolio focus, a return to disciplined, pragmatic approaches for strategy development and enterprise design, combined with robust processes for managing the enterprise portfolio of programs."*[2]

> *"[Enterprise] Architecture requires actual work. We keep looking for the 'quick fix,' a technological solution, a tool, a package, a*

new processor, the perennial 'silver bullet.' We wish we could simply throw money at the problem and have the pain go away."[3]

Although frustrating and extremely expensive, there was little that organizations could have done to sidestep this issue and avoid the crumbling of their enterprise architectures, other than perhaps consult a crystal ball—and even those have been of limited value of late. Over recent years computer systems, and the applications that run on them, have made huge leaps and bounds, but it has been incredibly difficult to build and maintain a cohesive enterprise architecture.

The cost associated with support, maintenance and integration of heterogeneous architectures has been huge, demanding an ever-greater proportion of the annual IT budget. It is estimated that on average organizations spent $6.3 million on integration projects in 2001 and that this number will rise to $6.4 million in 2003.[4] So, what can executives do to reduce this level of expenditure while also creating a flexible enterprise architecture that supports the business needs today, as well as the long-term business strategy? The answer is a new architectural paradigm referred to as the Service-Oriented Architectures (SOAs).

THE SERVICE-ORIENTED ARCHITECTURE

Over the past 40 years, we can clearly identify four distinct architectural paradigms. The earliest paradigm being the monolithic architecture, implemented on early mainframe systems, followed by the client-server architecture, and then the distributed or component architecture. Now, as we move into the

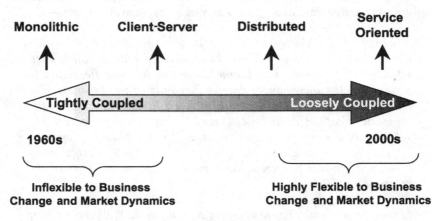

FIGURE 7.2 Evolution of systems architecture.

new millennium, the fourth architectural paradigm—the Service-Oriented Architecture—is beginning to emerge. Figure 7.2 illustrates the progression from the monolithic architecture to the SOA during the past 40 years.

As discussed, most organizations have heterogeneous business systems that utilize significant elements of monolithic, client-server, and distributed architectures, which are extremely difficult to support and maintain within the context of enterprise architecture. The emergence of SOAs, implemented using Web services, will make it significantly easier for organizations to implement and maintain an enterprise architecture while also ensuring that the enterprise architecture has the much-needed flexibility to adapt to rapidly changing business needs and market dynamics. Figure 7.3 illustrates the key constituents and relationships within an SOA.

This discussion brings up a logical question: "What is the relationship between an SOA and Web services?" The concept of SOA is not specific to the technology used for implementation. Conversely, *Web services are a specific set of standards and technologies that can be used to implement an SOA.* As discussed in earlier chapters, an SOA implemented using Web services does not require a "rip 'n replace" approach. Web services can be used to implement an SOA in which functionality from legacy systems can be exposed as "virtual services," and in which systems are integrated using Web services standards.

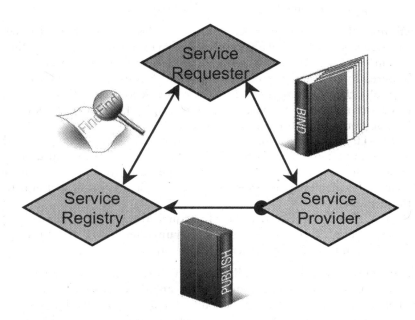

FIGURE 7.3 Constituents of a service-oriented architecture.

As illustrated in Figure 7.3, an SOA has three key constituents:

* *A Service Requester*—The service requester is a software component in search of a service to invoke. The service requester finds the service by discovering—through the service registry—the set of available services that meet pre-defined criteria. Once a suitable service has been discovered, the service requester binds to the service publisher to invoke the service.
* *A Service Registry*—The service registry is a centralized services repository that facilitates service discovery by service requesters. The service registry brokers the relationship between the requester and provider. If the requester and provider have a pre-existing relationship (For example, they are trusted partners), the requester can obtain the service description directly from the provider. In this case the service registry can be considered an optional component of the SOA as it is by-passed by the requester and provider.
* *A Service Provider*—The services provider, typically the owner of the service, submits a service description to be published in a service registry. The service registry brokers the relationship between the requester and provider, but it is important to note that services are typically hosted and executed by the service provider.

To facilitate interaction between the service requester, service registry, and service provider, three key operations are required:

* *Publish*—The service provider publishes a description of the service. The description details the necessary information for requesters to find and interact with the service. The description includes the information required by a requester to bind—meaning to connect—with a service. Typically the description includes the network location of the service, transport protocols to be used (for example, HTTP), and message formats for input and return parameters.
* *Find*—The find operation is initiated by the service requester and submitted to a service registry. The requester might be an end user or another service. In response to a find operation, the service registry locates the matching service(s) and returns the service description to the requester.
* *Bind*—Once the service requester has found the requested service, the service can be directly invoked at runtime, using the binding information provided in the service description.

It is important to be aware that the service requester, service registry, and service provider constituents of an SOA can all exist within the context of a single organization, or could equally as well be distributed across the Web. As discussed in Chapter 3, "Web Services Adoption," early implementations of SOAs using Web services will undoubtedly operate within the boundaries of a single organization, but once the SOA is in place the model can easily be extended to leverage services published by third parties over the Web.

Services versus Components

The following section takes a closer look at the attributes of an SOA, but before we dive into the details of SOAs, we will examine the key attributes of a service architecture versus a component architecture. It is not uncommon to hear the terms "service" and "component" used interchangeably. However, components and services should be considered distinct. Components and services can be thought of as being at different levels in a system implementation hierarchy, as illustrated in Figure 7.4.

As illustrated, components are typically fine-grained, meaning that they implement low-level technical functions (for example, user login functions for security and authentication), whereas services are coarse-grained and implement business level services (for example, a user administration service). As illustrated in Figure 7.4, the logistics management application uses a number of services, including the coarse-grained user administration service. The user administration *service* is itself composed of a number of fine-grained *components*, including the "User Login" component used to manage security and authentication.

Figure 7.5 illustrates the key differences between the implementation of services and components and the following sections discuss the characteristics of services and SOAs in more detail.

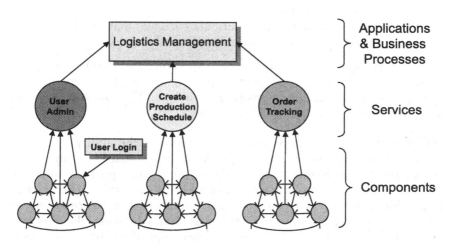

FIGURE 7.4 System implementation hierarchy.

Component	Services
Tightly Coupled	Loosely Coupled
Fine Grained	Coarse Grained
Static Reference	Dynamic Reference
Transport using TCP/IP	Transport using HTTP

FIGURE 7.5   Component versus service.

Service-Oriented Architecture Characteristics

Chapter 2, "Standards, Concepts, and Terminology," introduced many of the key concepts of an SOA within the specific context of the Web services enabling, evolving, and emerging standards. This section takes a step back from the Web services specifics and examines the characteristics of an SOA in general, but ties the characteristics back to Web services standards to clearly show how Web services can be used to implement an SOA.

There are four primary characteristics of an SOA that together differentiate it from previous architectural paradigms:

- *Interoperability*—Open interface standards, as opposed to systems or vendor specific standards
- *Coarse Grained*—Business level services, as opposed to fine-grained code or components
- *Loosely Coupled*—Flexible, loosely coupled services, as opposed to tightly coupled units of code
- *Dynamically Discoverable*—Distributed services that are dynamically located at run-time, as opposed to hard-wired references

From the context of Web services, some of these characteristics are basic capabilities, while others are either design principles or are attained through the use of additional evolving standards. The following sections discuss the four SOA characteristics in more detail.

Interoperable   A basic characteristic of an SOA is the ability to deliver greater system interoperability. As previously illustrated in Figure 7.3, a service provider publishes a service description, which provides information regarding where to locate and how to invoke a service. This invocation information informs the service requester of the information the service requires and the information it will return. In effect, this function makes the service a "black box," where knowledge of its inner workings is not needed.

As long as the service is trusted and you believe that the service will do what it describes, then the details of how the service has been implemented are unimportant. The physical location of the service, the programming language used to implement the service, and the hardware that the service runs on are all implementation details that can be hidden in an SOA.

Although the implementation details of a service are hidden, that is not to say that they are unimportant. In fact, as an organization's SOA evolves, it will be critical to closely monitor and manage the availability of system resources, including the following:

- *Network Bandwidth*—An SOA can significantly increase network bandwidth requirements. The use of XML can increase bandwidth requirements by three to four times; as such, it is important to monitor network usage as the SOA is implemented.
- *Load Balancing*—From a Quality of Service (QoS) perspective, it is important to monitor the peak loading of machines that are running services to ensure that performance bottlenecks do not appear. For example, as systems come online, one single service might experience very heavy usage. This service could become a system bottleneck due to either network or processor bandwidth limitations.
- *Identity and Security*—Even when implementing an SOA within the enterprise, it will be increasingly important to ensure that appropriate identification and security is implemented to ensure that access to services is secure and authenticated. Logging information regarding who is running which services and when will provide an important audit trail should a service be accessed without authorization.

Coarse-Grained As previously illustrated in Figure 7.4, at the lowest level object-oriented languages such as Java, COM, and CORBA expose their interfaces as fine-grained components. These components are then aggregated into larger, coarse-grained services that more closely resemble real business functions. A coarse-grained service might itself be further aggregated into other services, or incorporated into an application or coordinated business process.

The decision to create a coarse-grained service rather than a fine-grained service is primarily a design and implementation decision. As such, it is quite possible to create fine-grained services; however, component-based architectures are better suited to this task.

Loosely Coupled Traditionally, systems are integrated using hard-coded connections in which the call parameters, interface name, network location, and so on are all hard-wired when an application is implemented. This approach creates tightly coupled systems which are highly sensitive to even minor changes in system configuration. For example, changing something as simple as a server's network address could cause a number of systems to no longer operate correctly. This concept is illustrated in Figure 7.6.

From a Web services perspective, loose coupling is achieved through three progressive levels of abstraction. These are:

1. *Services Communication*—SOAP provides the first level of abstraction. At this level, the details of which development language the service was implemented in is hidden. For example, a service implemented in Java can work hand-in-hand with a service implemented in Microsoft .Net. However, the service parameters and network location of each service must still be specified manually.

2. *Services Description*—WSDL provides the next level of abstraction. At this level, the service description contains the details of the service parameters and network address. The service description must itself be manually located, but once located, it can be manipulated programmatically to determine the additional information required to locate the service and run it.

3. *Services Publishing and Discovery*—UDDI provides the final level of abstraction. At this level, the service description is published in a UDDI registry, from which it can be dynamically located using the registry's search capabilities. At this level of abstraction the only information required is access to the UDDI registry and enough information to search for the service (for example, the service's name, or type of service to be performed).

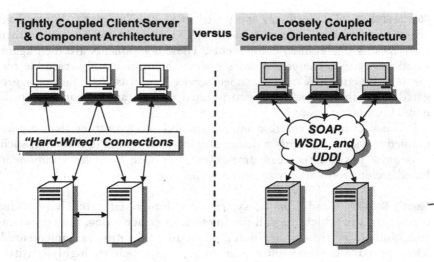

FIGURE 7.8   Loose coupling versus tight coupling.

The third level of abstraction, provided through service publishing and discovery capabilities, is discussed further in the following section.

Dynamically Discoverable In an SOA, services are published in a services registry. Services registries are central repositories, either within an organization or on the Web, which can be used to dynamically discover services. From a practical sense it is more than likely that business users will already know that the service they are looking for already exists, but the services registry provides an additional level of abstraction, allowing the service description to be dynamically retrieved when the service is run.

By publishing a new service description, an application or another service can download the updated description to determine if the service location or parameters have changed. For example, a service physically located on a server in San Francisco could be relocated to a server in London. As long as the published service description is updated with the new location, any applications using the service will be able to determine its new network location when they perform a look-up for the service.

THE FUTURE OF ENTERPRISE ARCHITECTURES

A well-implemented enterprise architecture can truly be a source of competitive advantage, where the architecture itself supports both the immediate needs of today as well as the execution of a long-term business strategy. The ability to achieve this objective has historically been challenged by the limitations of the then-available technologies and architectures. These limitations have made it virtually impossible to maintain an enterprise architecture that meets both near-term and long-term demands. But can the implementation of an SOA help make these goals more achievable?

Competitive Advantage

Creating an enterprise architecture using SOA principles perhaps for the first time delivers the flexibility and agility necessary to make the enterprise architecture a realistic and achievable goal. Enterprise architectures implemented using SOA principles promise to deliver:

- *Reuse*—An architecture that delivers on the long-promised ability to reuse software. In the service-oriented world, we will see reusable services as opposed to the reuse of code.
- *Flexibility and Agility*—An architecture that is less fragile and more adaptive to ever-changing business pressures, either tactical or strategic.

Reuse Software reuse has always been a key part of component-based software models, but it has been a utopian goal that was rarely practical or achievable. SOAs implemented using Web services will completely change this dynamic as follows:

- *Reuse from Legacy Systems*—Early services will be implemented by reusing existing functionality in legacy systems. As discussed in Chapter 3, "Web Services Adoption," the implementation of *virtual services* can be used as a basis for repackaging and repurposing legacy systems, greatly increasing their reach and longevity.
- *Reuse of Business Services*—Historically, reuse of components was especially challenging as they implemented fine-grained, low-level functions. An SOA implemented using Web services implements larger units of business logic as services, which if designed and implemented at an abstract level—specifically, not designed with a narrow, single-use perspective—will be used by multiple applications across the organization. For example, the user management service, introduced in Figure 7.4, could be reused as the basis for a user administration service used for all systems in an organization.

The ability to reuse services, either custom developed or repurposed from legacy systems, will have a profound impact on time-to-market considerations. For example, imagine a situation where time to market for a new product is critical, but the IT infrastructure is the primary bottleneck, even though 70% of the necessary functionality is already implemented in other systems. Without an SOA, the organization would likely need to design and develop new systems to support the product from scratch, leveraging existing components where possible. Unfortunately, this is not going to help with time-to-market considerations, as it will likely take many months of elapsed time and require many person years of development time to implement the new system. Conversely, in an environment where systems are implemented as a collection of services in an SOA, the organization could analyze requirements for the new systems, choose existing services to provide 70% of the requirements, and implement the remaining 30% as new services. By reducing the design and development requirements by as much as 70%, the new application can be implemented in a fraction of the time and cost otherwise required.

Flexibility and Agility Traditional architectures implement "hard-wired" point-to-point connections between systems. This "hard-wired" approach makes systems extremely fragile and limits the options available to reconfigure an application without the need to manually change the hard-wired connections to other systems. In a complex environment, changing a single application can require the modification of dozens of connected applications.

For example, many large organizations run multiple ERP systems, perhaps using a best-of-breed approach to implement required functionality. If an organization runs PeopleSoft for its Human Resources (HR) function, but runs Oracle Financials for its general ledger and payroll functions, then PeopleSoft and Oracle will need to regularly share the information required to ensure that the payroll information is aligned with HR records—for example, are pay raises or cuts to be applied, are bonus or commissions payable, and so on. To link these systems together, a programmer must develop a custom interface tailored specifically to the proprietary application interfaces available from PeopleSoft and Oracle. A change to the Peoplesoft or Oracle application at either end of the custom interface—for example, one of the applications is upgraded—will typically necessitate that the custom interface be retested and perhaps updated. The problem is that a custom interface is limited to providing a hard-wired point-to-point connection that is fixed and inflexible. As the number of systems and their associated point-to-point interfaces proliferate, the integration of systems becomes a nightmare to manage.

In an SOA, it is possible to remove point-to-point connections and replace them with dynamic references using services descriptions, maintained in a services registry. As hard-wired interfaces are progressively replaced with dynamic references, the enterprise architecture becomes more flexible, enabling the following:

- *Collaboration*—The SOA supports more flexible collaboration, both among an organization's own operating units and between the partner, supplier, and customer organizations. As illustrated in Figure 7.7, in-house systems, as well as partner, supplier, and customer systems, all operate via the services registry, from which all of the organization's services are accessible.

- *Outsource*—The SOA enables plug-and-play capabilities, making it much easier for organizations to outsource specific activities or processes when economically sound to do so. For example, as illustrated in Figure 7.7, by removing the hard-wired connections to the HR and Payroll systems, they can be easily and transparently outsourced, but continue to interoperate with in-house systems via the services registry.

Fundamentally, the value of the enterprise architecture, implemented using SOA capabilities, is in enabling reuse and greater flexibility and enterprise agility. Once an SOA is implemented the enterprise architecture

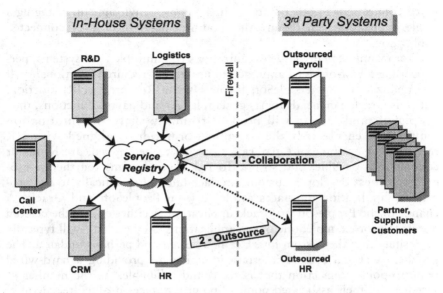

FIGURE 7.7   In-house or outsourced.

is no longer a "millstone" around an organization's neck, but instead becomes a true foundation for strategic and competitive advantage.

PLATFORM IMPLEMENTATION CONSIDERATIONS

When implementing an SOA it will be possible to reuse existing functionality from legacy systems, but inevitably it will be necessary to develop additional services that provide functionality that cannot be reused or support new business needs. When implementing new Web services there are two primary technological directions that can be taken—Java 2 Enterprise Edition (J2EE), or Microsoft .Net. This section reviews the J2EE and .Net options and explores the relative offerings and market positioning for each. Our goal is to help executives understand where and when they might want to use either, or perhaps even both.

As business leaders consider the merits of these competing implementation platforms, it is important to remember that "Web services are interoperable, but not portable."[5] That is to say that a Web service implemented using J2EE can seamlessly interoperate with a service implemented using .Net, but a .Net service cannot easily be ported to run on a J2EE platform, and vice versa. This means that when deciding to primarily focus on the implementation of J2EE or .Net Web services, the availability of skilled in-house resources is a critical consideration. For example, an organization focusing on the implementation of .Net, but with a significant base of Java programmers, will need to invest heavily in cross-training to .Net.

Given the lack of portability between Web services platforms, it is useful to consider the pool of skilled resources available to begin implementing Web services. Figure 7.8 illustrates the distribution of skill sets among the estimated 21.6 million developers worldwide as of 2000.

As illustrated, Java has fewer than 2 million developers while Visual Basic, C, C++, and COBOL, all of which can be used to implement .Net Web services, have many times more. Ultimately, it is likely that Chief Information Officers (CIOs) will leverage both pools of resources but will focus ongoing development of skills in a primary camp based on available skills.

J2EE versus .Net

One of the fundamental decisions executives will need to make is what platform to select for their initial forays into Web services. Fundamentally,

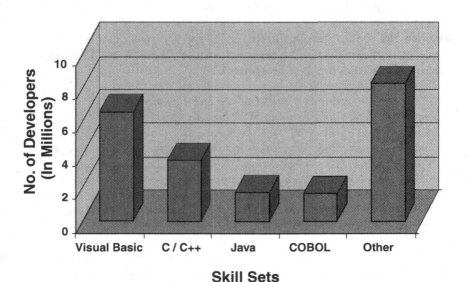

FIGURE 7.8 Software development skill sets.
Source: IDC, 2000, "IDC Developer Report 2000."

Microsoft .Net and J2EE tackle Web service and application implementation from two very different and very distinct perspectives:

- *Microsoft .Net*—The .Net approach to services and application implementation is *a multi-language, single-platform* approach. .Net services and applications can be implemented using more than twenty[6] distinct programming languages, but ultimately must be deployed in the Microsoft .Net Framework environment, running exclusively on Intel hardware.
- *Java 2 Enterprise Edition (J2EE)*—The J2EE approach to service and application implementation is a *single-language, multi-platform* approach. All J2EE applications are implemented using the Java language and its extensions, but can be developed and deployed using a multitude of development tools and applications from software vendors, including Sun Microsystems, IBM, BEA systems, IONA, Art Technology Group (ATG) and so on. Once developed, a J2EE service can be deployed to a variety of Operating Systems (OS) and hardware platforms.

The following sections discuss the J2EE and .Net platforms from the perspective of the tools available and how they facilitate the adoption of Web services within the business operations of an organization. The emphasis will not be on the technological merits, but on the big picture business impact of these two platforms and how they can help organizations progress in the adoption of Web services.

Microsoft .Net   Microsoft was early out of the gate with its positioning of the .Net Framework and MyServices (formerly known as "Hailstorm"). Microsoft describes the .Net Framework as:

> ". . . the programming model of the .NET environment for building, deploying, and running Web-based applications, smart client applications, and XML Web services. It manages much of the plumbing, enabling developers to focus on writing the business logic code for their applications." ". . . [.NET Framework] enables developers to build Web-based applications, smart client applications, and XML Web services applications which expose their functionality programmatically over a network using standard protocols such as SOAP and HTTP."[7]

Beyond the .Net Framework, Microsoft is positioning its Web services capabilities across a spectrum of product offerings, including the widely marketed MyServices and the Microsoft Office franchise. Microsoft's .Net platform will undoubtedly reach even further to encompass its mid-market enterprise offering, Great Plains Software, acquired by Microsoft on April 5, 2001, as well as its small business software services, Bcentral. This lineup is a tremendous arsenal with which to attack the emerging Web services market.

Let us take a closer look at the Microsoft .Net Framework, its market positioning for Web services, and the associated products and activities:

- *Market Position*—The .Net marketing strategy, which is the all-encompassing Web services theme Microsoft has established from the outset, beat almost every other player to the punch for Web services mind share.

- *Support of Open Standard*—Microsoft has positioned itself favorably in the Web services arena by publicly and aggressively participating in and supporting the standards efforts related to XML, SOAP, WSDL, UDDI, and others. This is a different Microsoft, far from the company that was outflanked on the Internet by Sun, IBM, and, of course, Netscape. In the Web services space Microsoft was early to market and continues to lead the charge into Web services with its comprehensive .Net Framework.

- *Development Environment*—Visual Studio .Net is Microsoft's Integrated Development Environment (IDE) for the .Net Framework. Visual Studio .Net provides a comprehensive application toolset for constructing Web services that support its Common-Language Runtime (CLR). CLR supports all of Microsoft's development languages including Visual Basic, Visual C++, and Jscript, as well as the new C# and J# (pronounced C Sharp and J Sharp, respectively).

- *Application Servers*—The BizTalk server is used for business integration, business process management, building and transforming XML schemas, establishing trading partner relationships, managing data and document exchange between trading partners, and even EDI and e-Commerce functionality.

- *Additional Servers*—Microsoft's .Net strategy is pervasive through all of Microsoft products, including Operating System platforms (Windows 2000 and Windows XP), SQLServer relational database, Web server (Internet Information Server, or IIS), and its messaging solution Microsoft Message Queue (MMQ). Add to this Exchange Mail Server as well as BizTalk, and suddenly there is a comprehensive product set repositioned to leverage the entire spectrum of Web services possibilities.

- *MyServices*—The most salient differentiation of Microsoft from the other turnkey platform providers has to do with Business to Consumer (B2C) Web services, namely .Net MyServices. Microsoft has long had its crosshairs aimed squarely on consumers with the MSN portal, its acquisition of Hotmail, and its Passport identity management platform

(.Net Profile). While other platform providers are only vocalizing their consumer strategy, Microsoft has been positioning for the consumer mass market. With this factor in mind, .Net MyServices offers many interesting features that would be attractive to increasingly mobile consumers who desire anywhere, anytime access to services such as e-mail (.Net Inbox), calendars (.Net Calendar), address books and contacts (.Net Contacts), and a host of others.

Java 2 Enterprise Edition (J2EE)   The Java approach to Web services is based on the use of J2EE. J2EE is a platform for the implementation and deployment of Java-based services and applications. Sun Microsystems, the inventors of Java, describe J2EE as:

> *"The Java™ 2 Platform, Enterprise Edition (J2EE) defines the standard for developing multi-tier enterprise applications. J2EE simplifies enterprise applications by basing them on standardized, modular components, by providing a complete set of services to those components, and by handling many details of application behavior automatically, without complex programming. . .,"*
> *". . . Java 2 Enterprise Edition adds full support for Enterprise JavaBeans™ components, Java Servlets API, JavaServer Pages™ and XML technology. The J2EE standard includes complete specifications and compliance tests to ensure portability of applications across the wide range of existing enterprise systems capable of supporting J2EE."*[8]

The vendor community supporting J2EE is substantial, including venerable platform vendors such as Sun Microsystems, IBM, Hewlett-Packard, Oracle, BEA, SilverStream, IONA, Art Technology Group (ATG), and a host of others. J2EE as an architectural approach simply seeks to avoid vendor lock-in to a single proprietary vendor, namely Microsoft. While .Net is a single platform strategy from Microsoft, the J2EE approach is a multi-vendor strategy that allows customers a wide variety of choices regarding the application server, the development tools, the integration server technology, and more. The development language will be Java, and the promise of J2EE, of course, is cross-platform portability of the applications developed. In the Microsoft case, what is developed in .Net will be targeted for a Microsoft environment on Intel processors. *Right now there are no other choices.*

The components of a J2EE architectural strategy revolve around the following elements:

■ *Market Position*—Industry-wide support from an army of Microsoft competitors, which guarantees that there will be a vibrant Java/J2EE marketplace for the foreseeable future. This situation ensures end-user choice and a level of technological maturity, reliability, and solution robustness that might not always be ensured with many of the new Microsoft .Net solutions.

- *Support of Open Standard*—Standards support driven by the leading platform and software vendors in the Web services space, such as IBM, Oracle, Sun Microsystems, BEA, WebMethods, and others.
- *Development Environment*—The development language is Java in a J2EE environment, which supports application portability across multiple application servers and runtime environments.
- *Application Servers*—Multiple vendors provide the application servers, implementation tools, development environment, and runtime environment for Java-based Web services. Noteworthy vendors include IBM WebSphere and BEA WebLogic, with Sun's iPlanet and Oracle's application server leading a pack of other smaller J2EE application servers and IDE vendors.
- *Additional Servers*—Integration servers from multiple vendors in the EAI space provide the connectivity to backend systems for J2EE Web services, as well as native support for a multitude of database servers.

J2EE provides many benefits to the Web services marketplace, the primary benefits revolving around vendor choice, solution maturity, and J2EE interoperability and portability. J2EE ensures the choice of components that will be used to ultimately build an SOA and develop Web services to run in it.

Both J2EE and .Net platforms support the ultimate objectives of Web services, and both can result in short- and long-term benefits. The fundamental difference between these two platforms is the question of vendor choice—specifically, the ability to use best-of-breed components as opposed to being locked in to Microsoft .Net.

Ultimately, the business decisions of an organization should be the litmus test as to whether to deploy .Net or J2EE architectures, not the religious zeal that development purists would like to use to make the decision. Organizations will need to juggle the demands of a heterogeneous architecture regardless of the overarching J2EE or .Net decision. Given this reality, the interoperability of a Web services strategy makes these decisions somewhat irrelevant, at least from the perspective of how services and applications work together to support the business objectives of the organization.

SUMMARY

In this chapter we sought to demonstrate that IT strategy and planning is a critical requirement for success in business today, and that the implementation of an enterprise architecture using SOA principles and Web services can be used as a competitive differentiator. To achieve this goal, we introduced enterprise architectures and examined the business realities and challenges that have made them so difficult to maintain. We introduced the SOA and examined how Web services can be used to enable implementation of an enterprise architecture using SOA principles. From a business perspective, we postulated that the resulting enterprise architecture could be used to enable competitive advantage and create business value for organizations. The business benefits of creating an enterprise architecture using SOA principles are many, but primarily fall into the categories of:

* Reduced IT complexity
* Lower IT costs
* Increased business flexibility and agility, and
* Improved time-to-market

Finally, we examined implementation considerations for a Web service-enabled SOA, looking at the two primary camps for their implementation: Java 2 Enterprise Edition (J2EE) and Microsoft .Net, reviewing their relative market positions from a business perspective.

In today's economy no business leader can dispute that organizational flexibility and agility are not just a desirable option, but are critical requirements for business survival. It is our hope that we have demonstrated the importance of enterprise architectures, SOAs, and Web services in creating a flexible and agile IT foundation for the future, upon which business value and competitive advantage can be built.

ENDNOTES

[1] www.arstechnica.com, Ars Technica, October 2002, "DNA Computing: A Primer" by Will Ryu.

[2] www.meta.com, Quote from Web site, By George Paras, META Group Vice President and Director of Enterprise Planning and Architecture Strategy.

[3] www.dmreview.com, DM Review, December 1999, "Enterprise Architecture: The Past and the Future" by John A. Zachman.

[4] Forrester Research, December 2001, "Reducing Integration's Cost" by Laura Koetzle.

[5] Forrester Research, June 2002, "Which Web Services Vendor?" p. 3, by David Truog.

[6] msdn.microsoft.com/netframework/productinfo/overview, Microsoft, "What Is Microsoft .NET?", accessed October 20, 2002.

[7] Ibid.

[8] java.sun.com/j2ee/overview.html, Sun Microsystems, "Java 2 Platform, Enterprise Edition (J2EE) Overview," accessed October 20, 2002.

CHAPTER 8

The Web Services Vendor Landscape

"The biggest gap in the world is the gap between the justice of a cause and the motives of the people pushing it."

John P. Grier

This chapter provides a high-level snapshot of vendors actively developing a presence in the burgeoning Web services market. Here we map categories of software and hardware vendors to a typical IT architecture and describe, at a high level, how vendors are positioning themselves to compete in the Web services market. It will become apparent that certain software categories, and associated vendors, are in an enviable position to influence the Web services market—given their current position in the IT value chain—while the emergence of Web services will likely imperil others.

VENDOR CATEGORIES

This section leverages a generic systems architecture as a foundation upon which to overlay categories of IT vendors. The resulting illustration, shown in Figure 8.1, demonstrates how a generic systems architecture, beginning with infrastructure at the bottom and ending with front-office and customer applications at the top, maps to the seven categories of tools and application vendors. Vendor categories are shown as horizontal bars that span multiple layers of the systems architecture stack, illustrating the overlap between vendor categories, as well as how each category maps to layers of the systems architecture.

Figure 8.1 illustrates the breadth of architecture coverage that each category of solution provider spans along the systems architecture. Clearly, the platform vendors and enterprise application vendors have tremendous

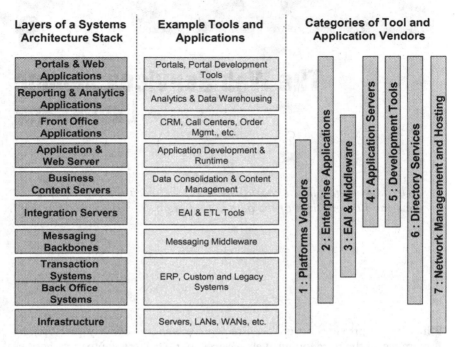

FIGURE 8.1   Web services solution provider categories.

influence across the systems architecture stack, as well as platform providers—such as IBM, Sun Microsystems, Hewlett-Packard, Microsoft, and Oracle. Beyond these two categories there are two others that will likely wield tremendous influence over the rapidly emerging Web services landscape: application server vendors (such as IBM, BEA, Oracle, Sun iPlanet) and Enterprise Application Integration (EAI) vendors (such as WebMethods, TIBCO, SeeBeyond, Vitria). Not surprisingly, there are many other vendors vying for control of critical elements of the Web services value chain. The ensuing battle will no doubt result in a Darwinian shakeout as the Web services standards and solutions evolve and mature over the next two to three years.

The systems architecture stack shows the most common elements of an organization's architecture and is not meant to be an exhaustive representation. The intent is to provide a framework within which to further discuss the Web services vendor landscape and provide a baseline for the following considerations:

* *Category Mapping*—What business and IT capabilities does each category enable? How are these capabilities impacted by the emergence of Web services?
* *Vendor Landscape*—Which vendors hold a dominant position within each category? How do these vendors intend to leverage the emergence of Web services? Which emerging vendors should be watched?
* *Category and Vendor Viability*—Are there viability issues that need to be considered for a category or its associated vendors?

The following sections explore these issues for each of the vendor categories below:

1. Platform Vendors
2. Enterprise Applications
3. EAI and Middleware
4. Application Servers
5. Development Tools
6. Directory Services
7. Network Management and Application Hosting

Based on the speed at which the Web services market is evolving, it is inevitable that by the time this book is released a number of vendors will have merged, been acquired, or even gone out of business. However, the majority of vendors discussed will still be in business and will be actively seeking to gain market share and mind share as Web services continue to gain momentum. Regardless of which vendors gain and which decline, the systems architecture and associated vendor mapping, provides a framework for evaluating current and future vendors in the Web services market.

Platform Vendors

The platform vendors, exemplified by the likes of IBM, Sun Microsystems, and Hewlett-Packard, typically provide a full range of hardware, operating systems, and infrastructure solutions to the enterprise computing market. Beyond the likes of IBM and Hewlett-Packard, Oracle and Microsoft could also be considered platform vendors—although from a predominantly software perspective—based on the broad reach of their extensive product sets. For this purpose Oracle and Microsoft are included in this category, as well as being considered in other categories.

The platform vendors have a strong market position and significant influence over the IT landscape. As the Web services market evolves, these vendors will undoubtedly be at the forefront. However, these organizations are somewhat mixed in how they are positioned to capitalize on the emergence of the Web services market. For example, consider the following:

- *IBM and Microsoft*—have been the leaders, followed by Oracle, in the charge for Web services market and mind share.
- *Sun Microsystems*—has been a laggard in its Web services support, both in product terms as well as its definition and support of Web services standards.
- *Hewlett-Packard*—has also been slow to adopt Web services standards, possibly due to the time and effort consumed by its acquisition of Compaq Computer.

Vendor Landscape   IBM, Microsoft, and Oracle are well positioned in the Web services landscape. They all command the high ground in the computing infrastructure and application portfolio of major organizations, as well as having significant professional services offerings to help their clients begin the adoption of Web services. The platform vendors in this category have three key strengths that they can leverage as the Web services market evolves:

1. *Trust*—The platform vendors have delivered complex IT computing infrastructure reliably over the years, and they have the market clout to continue doing so even without a compelling or leading edge Web services story. They are trusted by IT executives, and because of this the laggards in this category may have time to retool their products, services, and capabilities around Web services. They cannot afford to wait long however. Closing the gap on IBM, Microsoft, and Oracle will be no easy task.
2. *Market Share*—The platform vendors have significant market share in hardware and software, as well as control over significant IT budgets. They will not easily relinquish their incumbent status.
3. *Product Breadth*—The platform vendors have varying degrees of application strength, from IBM with its hardware, software, and services might to Sun Microsystems, relying on hardware, operating systems, and infrastructure solutions. Because these organizations control so much of the IT infrastructure and application portfolio, the platform vendors will likely command a leadership position in much of the emerging Web services market.

Conclusions   The industry presence of these IT titans should not be underestimated. While it is clear that IBM and Microsoft should be lauded for their early leadership in Web services, as well as Oracle (to be covered further under enterprise software), the slower and less focused efforts of Hewlett-Packard and Sun can not be discounted, as they have not yet lost the opportunity to influence the Web services market. Web services adoption is still in its early phases, and there is still time for Hewlett-Packard and Sun to refocus their efforts as the Web services market moves from the integration phase to the collaboration phase and beyond.

Enterprise Applications

Enterprise application vendors hold an interesting position with respect to Web services adoption. This category includes software vendors that fall in the following subgroups:

- *ERP Vendors*—such as SAP, Oracle, J.D. Edwards, and PeopleSoft.
- *CRM Vendors*—such as Siebel Software, SAP, Oracle, and Epicore, SalesLogix
- *Relational Database Vendors*—such as Oracle, IBM, Sybase, Microsoft, and Progress Software
- *Other Best-of-Breed Vendors*—serving vertical industries or departmental functions, such as supply chain planning and execution (i2 and Manugistics), claims software, and underwriting engines for insurance, HR software, and so on

The application vendors have multiple options for addressing Web services. Much as with the onslaught of client-server architectures in the early 1990s, many of these vendors may choose to rewrite their applications based on modular, service-oriented architectures, leveraging XML, SOAP, WSDL, and UDDI standards. This could be considered a big bang approach and would most likely only be used for specific modules or products that are outdated or acquired assets, and are therefore not architecturally similar to other related modules.

In the case of ERP vendors, their products are broad-based, multimodule applications that provide functionality spanning all operations and departments of an organization. The ERP players have multiple options, many of which are in progress already, including the following:

- *Rebuild*—the entire suite as a Web services architecture and recoup the cost by collecting subscription fees on smaller, componentized application modules (the existing modules provided without requiring the rest of the ERP suite).
- *Componentize*—portions of modules, or entire modules for high volume applications where more revenue can be collected from subscription fees.
- *Encapsulate*—collaboration components of the ERP suite where it makes sense. For example, where an ERP function, submodule, or module is used by many internal users, many external users via an extranet, or both.
- *Offer Integration Servers*—with EAI-like functionality to take control of integration challenges from within their own application suite,

which helps them maintain account and architectural control of their customer's IT portfolio.

The question is, "What are the business reasons for building Web services interfaces into ERP systems?" The answers are readily apparent, according to Kapil Apshankar in *Enterprise Resources Planning and Web Services*, "Ease of Integration and Reduction in Costs through the Hosted Application Model."[1] The enterprise application vendors control a large portion of the IT budget, especially the likes of SAP and Oracle with their broad ERP suites. As organizations move into the integration phase of the Web services adoption model, it is likely that the enterprise application vendors will be among the first to provide Web services-based interfaces for their applications.

Vendor Landscape A battle is looming between the enterprise software vendors and the enterprise application integration (EAI) vendors based on two broad forces. Firstly, the enterprise application vendors, realizing that they created the need for EAI solutions with their proprietary interfaces and complex software functionality, have begun offering their own application integration modules. Secondly, as Web services standards are embraced and incorporated into enterprise applications, organizations can refocus their own IT efforts on the more challenging requirement of Web service-enabling homegrown legacy systems.

SAP, PeopleSoft, Oracle, and Siebel are among the leading enterprise application vendors repositioning themselves for the Web services market:

- *SAP*—with its dominant market presence has made significant progress in opening up its architecture for Web services. It has adopted J2EE for development and scripting along with its proprietary ABAP language, and has also released a version of its own integration server in an attempt to ease the burden of connecting SAP to other business applications. The recent release of SAP's own Web Application Server also encroaches on the application server and EAI market.

- *PeopleSoft*—is offering its own integration broker called AppConnect with XML and SOAP support, providing open messaging, data transformation, and content-routing functions. This is clearly a downward move to add EAI-like functionality to its offering, and much like Oracle, SAP, Siebel, and others, they are clearly threatening the EAI market.

- *Oracle*—has entered the Web services market with Oracle Dynamic Services, J2EE tools, and an application server architecture that rivals the functionality of BEA WebLogic and IBM's WebSphere. Oracle has been actively participating in standards groups, and appears to be a serious player in the Web services space.

- *Siebel*—has announced its own Web services support with the introduction of their Universal Application Network, a hub-based architectural solution relying on XML and SOAP, as well as other core Web services standards.

Conclusions　What does all of this activity mean? The enterprise application vendors mean business and are positioning themselves in the Web services value chain in an effort to gain greater control of the enterprise technology footprint. Thus, they are beginning to offer their own integration solutions, leveraging Web services to create a standards-based, open integration platform, rather than having this imposed on them by the EAI competitors, the application server vendors, or the platform vendors such as Microsoft, IBM.

Additionally, the enterprise application vendors are already beginning exploratory forays with Web services to provide standards-based integration between the array of modules that they offer within their application portfolios. These integration solutions are as much a threat to the EAI community as the actual solutions that they will eventually roll out to the market.

The battle is just shaping up, and as Web services move beyond the integration phase into the collaboration phase, the enterprise application vendors are preparing Web services solutions that insulate their application footprint from encroachment by other vendors. These efforts will assure their continued relevance to the core business processes of large organizations. Furthermore, these future solutions will likely provide the connectivity and collaboration tools for development and execution of complex inter-enterprise business processes with customers, partners, and suppliers.

EAI and Middleware

At a high level the Enterprise Application Integration (EAI) and middleware category contains vendors whose primary focus is providing the tools used to coordinate disparate enterprise applications, enabling the rationalization and consolidation of information across an array of heterogeneous systems. With the emergence of Web services, these vendors are faced with a dilemma. On the one hand, they are forced to embrace Web services or be perceived as proprietary solutions. On the other hand, Web services by their very nature will diminish the need for EAI solutions. This really is a case of *"Damned if you do, damned if you don't!"*

Perhaps the real opportunity for EAI vendors is to be found in their deep understanding of back-end application integration environments. This deep understanding might be leveraged as a means to reposition themselves as Web services-enabled integration backbone providers, playing an important role in the initial phases of Web services adoption.

The EAI and middleware vendors are diverse ranging from middleware and messaging backbone providers, to EAI and integration server vendors, and finally to extraction, transformation, and load (ETL) tool vendors. The products provided by these vendors became especially important during the e-Business wave as it became clear that back-office and legacy systems needed to be integrated with corporate Web sites to enable Web-based customer support and real-time transaction processing (such as, order processing and inventory management). EAI tools were heavily utilized to integrate disparate back-end systems into a single integrated view of the enterprise, as well as to provide seamless access to multiple back-end data sources for real-time transaction support and data visibility.

The number of integration server vendors is staggering, and they are all vying for a position in the emerging Web services market. In positioning themselves for Web services, these vendors are starting from a similar point in the IT value chain: helping organizations integrate complex enterprise and legacy applications to support modern application solutions leveraging application servers and Web servers, such as portals and other Web-based applications. Generally, the integration vendors are addressing Web services by providing capabilities for:

- *XML-Based Enterprise Application Integration*—Continuing the enterprise integration focus but using XML as the integration method as opposed to proprietary data access and translation techniques
- *Encapsulating Legacy Systems*—Implementing Web services using existing legacy and enterprise applications to expose business functionality or create services leveraging existing system processes
- *Providing a Run-Time Environment*—Assembling and operating Web services once they have been composed, exposed, published, assembled, and bound

The challenge facing the EAI and middleware vendors will be the viability of the revenue model that they are pursuing. To date EAI vendors have provided expensive solutions, based on point-to-point system interface architectures. As Web services are leveraged to simplify internal integration needs, the value and viable price point for EAI solutions will be challenged, pushing license prices down and cutting into revenue streams.

Yet, EAI vendors have little choice but to provide the tools and adapters to facilitate back-end integration using Web services. In the short term, there will likely be a hectic scramble as EAI vendors seek to achieve some level of Web services compliance and support. Many vendors are already moving down this path. However, there will likely be a consolidation of EAI and integration server vendors as the usage of Web services grows and the associated need for integration software diminishes.

Vendor Landscape   Because Web services will initially be deployed as an internal integration solution, EAI and integration server vendors will initially experience growth associated with their forays into Web services.

This early growth, however, will likely wane as organizations realize that writing XML and SOAP interfaces is relatively simple, and that exposing legacy applications as Web services does not require expensive EAI licenses, costly development and maintenance costs, and dedicated IT integration staff. In the long term, EAI vendors will have to look for new sources of value in the IT value chain as integration ceases to be a primary factor facing IT executives in delivering information value to the business.

Business process management and workflow will be a looming battle between the application server vendors and the EAI/integration server vendors. This capability is an edge functionality that fits nicely in both domains, and in fact should rightfully cut across both. For this reason, business processes are likely to require information from legacy applications as well as more modern ERP and CRM applications, and therefore the vendors have as much information content contribution to the workflow of business processes as the front-end application server vendors.

Vendors to Watch   There are many EAI vendors to track as Web services adoption progresses, and as the standards evolve. The following is a list of the major vendors to watch (in alphabetical order):

- CrossWorlds (IBM)
- Mercator
- SeeBeyond
- TIBCO
- Vitria
- WebMethods— *see below for vendor spotlight*

As mentioned, WebMethods is a leading vendor in the EAI category, and as such is examined further below.

Vendor Spotlight: WebMethods   WebMethods is a heavyweight in the enterprise application integration market. WebMethods has strong market share, robust functionality in the integration server market, and a who's who customer list in many industry verticals. With the typical palette of EAI functionality, WebMethods provides a solid integration foundation for companies seeking solutions for back-end system integration, while looking ahead to Web services and maintaining their options to begin using them when they are ready. WebMethods functionality includes:

- *Web Services Support*—for XML, SOAP, and WSDL
- *Integration Server*—with standard adapters to multiple legacy and ERP platforms
- *Message Broker*—for synchronous and asynchronous messaging, providing transaction integrity across the diversity of back-end systems, hardware and OS platforms, and application solutions

▪ *Workflow Support*—to accommodate business rules and business process management on top of its integration server and messaging backbone

WebMethods provides a solid foundation for application integration as well as a starting point for Web services. Based on its support for the evolving Web services standards as well as its strong enterprise application integration functionality, WebMethods will continue to be a strong player in the Web services market.

Conclusions Broadly, the EAI vendors all support XML and have indicated their intent to support SOAP and WSDL. Suffice it to say that the leaders of the EAI movement will be aggressive in their Web services positioning. As we have mentioned, most initial forays into Web services will begin with internal integration projects, exposing legacy systems with XML and SOAP interfaces. The EAI vendors understand application integration, and they should be given strong consideration as organizations begin exploring their Web services options and their business objectives. One thing is clear: EAI solutions are not cheap, and as organizations gain Web services capabilities, simple integration challenges will be solved leveraging in-house skills, negating the need for expensive EAI solutions.

Application Servers

Application servers play a critical role in the systems architecture, separating the Graphical User Interface (GUI) and presentation services of business applications from the business logic and the database functions. The application server is frequently viewed as part of a generic three-tier application architecture consisting of a GUI, an application (business logic) server, and a database or data server. This three-tier application architecture can be further broken down into an n-tier distributed architecture, where performance at each of the tiers can be monitored and enhanced depending on peak system loads, transaction volumes, and other performance-related issues.

The application server market is replete with competitors that fall into two broad platform paradigms:

1. *Java 2 Enterprise Edition (J2EE)*—One camp is the J2EE camp, in which most of the existing application server vendors support J2EE development.
2. *Microsoft .Net*—The other camp is the .Net camp, which falls under the Microsoft umbrella.

Application servers are ideally positioned in the modern IT application architecture as they are the foundation for most modern application architectures deployed today. The application server market is one of the few technology areas projected to grow over the coming year. However, Web services are an influencer of this trend, not a driver.

Vendor Landscape Because of their central position in the application architecture of organizations, application servers are a critical hub of activity for Web services. Given the robust functionality of these products, they are a natural place to focus many of the services required of Web services applications. The application components and business logic of a Web services application will reside on the application servers, much like distributed applications of today. However, given the highly distributed nature of Web services, it is likely that applications will be assembled from Web services components residing in many different physical and logical locations, rather than being deployed in a single instance of an application server. This is a likely scenario based on projections of how Web services will be written and published to registries for distributed access. The implication of this is that future applications will be executed on virtual servers, comprised of a number of distributed application servers each involved in running the services that constitute an application.

Vendors to Watch The following are application server vendors to watch over the coming months and years as they reposition themselves for Web services. Some have the revenue streams and large customer bases to carry them until there is sufficient adoption of Web services. For the smaller vendors, however, they may find it rough going as the application server business consolidates to the few strongest players, namely IBM WebSphere and BEA WebLogic. Oracle is a new entrant to the application server business and may well be a contender in this category (in alphabetical order):

* BEA Systems—*see below for vendor spotlight*
* IBM—*see next page for vendor spotlight*
* IONA
* Microsoft
* Oracle
* SilverStream (acquired by Novell in mid-2002)
* Sun iPlanet

As previously mentioned, BEA and IBM are currently the market leaders for application servers, with WebSphere and WebLogic respectively. These two vendors bear closer scrutiny, and are examined further below.

Vendor Spotlight: BEA Systems BEA has been a pioneer of the application server market with its BEA WebLogic application server platform. BEA began with messaging middleware and rapidly moved up the application food chain with its WebLogic application server product. WebLogic is a fully featured J2EE application server and development environment. BEA not only ships the application server, but also provides an integration server, a portal solution, and a development environment for implementation of complex applications and business logic without needing to know the intricacies of Java's more complex features. The following is a summary of BEA's position:

- Full J2EE application server environment
- Operating system-neutral application server makes it popular with startups and other customers who prefer choice of hardware and OS platform
- WebLogic Workshop (formerly known by the codename "Cajun") shields developers from the complexities of Java development
- Business process management capabilities for workflow, integrating processes, systems, and human users
- Robust support for complex business transactions, which helps differentiate it from its typical application server competition

BEA is in a highly competitive market, with formidable competition from IBM, Microsoft, Oracle, and a host of other smaller application server vendors. In the coming year, BEA will likely find itself in a two-front battle: on one front against the large platform vendors and enterprise software vendors, and on the other front from the EAI competitors who are rapidly adding capabilities to their integration servers. Still, BEA is in a strong position to compete for control of the Web services value chain.

Vendor Spotlight: IBM WebSphere   The IBM WebSphere application server suite provides extensive capabilities, to which IBM continues to add functionality. Recent announcements include the addition of an integration module allowing content management and transformation, as well as EDI support allowing companies to manage partner interaction in an application server environment. WebSphere provides a rich set of tools and functionality that supports Web services development, publishing, and deployment on the WebSphere application server. The IBM WebSphere application server suite's capabilities include:

- Cross platform support covering the full range of IBM's mainframes and servers, including their mainframes, AS/400, RS6000 as well as Windows/Intel servers
- Deep development support for Java-based applications, having been a major driver and flag bearer of the J2EE movement

- Application development tools for Web site design, portal development, personalization support, content management and delivery
- Provides EAI-like capabilities for back-end integration and content transformation and delivery
- Allows the use of business rules and workflow management capabilities to support complex applications, user intervention processes, business process management
- Provides messaging and transaction management products to facilitate secure and reliable synchronous and asynchronous messaging across a business enterprise

In short, IBM has a formidable collection of capabilities within the WebSphere application server environment, as well as the surrounding IBM products for messaging, application development, and even a newly released Integrated Development Environment (IDE) called Eclipse, an open source tool for Web services development. IBM, next to Microsoft, has the deepest application server product depth, the strongest total application development and deployment capabilities, and the best supporting cast of complementary software products to help enterprises begin the transition to Web services using the WebSphere application server environment.

Conclusions The application server market is being challenged on two fronts. These vendors are stuck between the platform vendors and enterprise application vendors on one front, and the EAI vendors on the other. The move by enterprise application vendors such as Oracle and SAP into the application server space will inevitably challenge the dominant positions that IBM and BEA have historically maintained. Having said that, the application server vendors are in a strong position in the application architecture. As long as they continue to add support for Web services and strengthen their development tools, integration capabilities, and their transaction support, they will be in a position to compete for Web services market and mind share.

Development Tools

Web services development tool vendors are rapidly emerging. There is a mix of existing development tool vendors in this landscape, such as IBM, Bowstreet, Microsoft, SilverStream Software, and Sun Microsystems, as well as a number of newcomers. Web services development tools fall into two broad categories:

1. *Web Services Development*—Web services development vendors offer tools and visual development environments that allow software developers to create new Web services from scratch as well as create

Web services from existing applications. Typical vendor tools include Integrated Development Environments (IDE), application development toolkits, and runtime environments.

2. *Web Services Orchestration or Assembly*—These vendors provide the tools for assembling complex Web services from multiple sources into business workflows. Assembling Web services into a coherent business application requires system interfaces and data transformation capabilities to locate and bind a number of Web services into meaningful business processes. These tools are typically based on visual workflow tools and business rules engines, as well as data transformation and data mapping tools required to knit different Web services modules into more complex services. These vendors are leading edge in that they will rely on emerging Web services workflow standards, which are still very much in flux. The Web Services Flow Language (WSFL) and XLANG have recently been merged into the Business Process Execution Language for Web Services (BPEL4WS). The Web services orchestration vendors are ahead of the adoption curve and the standards for these complex capabilities, but nonetheless are forging onward in anticipation of the appropriate standards and security issues being resolved.

Vendor Landscape Given the cross-software category capabilities and momentum of large vendors, such as IBM, Microsoft, and Sun, the niche tool vendors have very little control of the Web services market. Furthermore, the Web services adoption model begins with the use of XML and SOAP for integration, and the leadership of those processes may well be driven by the EAI vendors, based on their existing knowledge of large enterprises and their deep knowledge of application integration. They are deeply entrenched, and already have the ability to expose back-end systems processes as Web services.

There will inevitably be considerable merger and acquisition (M&A) activity in the development tools arena as the platform vendors, enterprise application vendors, EAI and application server vendors all round out their portfolio of offerings by acquiring startups. Also, Microsoft with .NET and C#, as well as the massive J2EE movement headed up by IBM, BEA Systems, Oracle and Sun among others, will ensure that they are significant players in the Web services development tools environment.

Vendors to Watch The following are development tool vendors to watch over the coming months and years as they reposition themselves for Web services. This category falls into two distinct groups: large cross-category vendors and small niche players. Moreso than other categories, the smaller development vendors will increasingly struggle to compete against the likes of IBM, BEA, and Microsoft, resulting in consolidation of this category through both acquisitions and business failures. The following lists identify a number of the most visible players in both segments (in alphabetical order):

Large Cross-Category Vendors:

- BEA Systems
- IBM
- Microsoft
- Novell (with acquisition of SilverStream)
- Oracle
- Sun Microsystems

Smaller Niche Vendors:

- AltoWeb
- Avinon
- Blue Titan
- Bowstreet
- Cape Clear
- Cysive
- Killdara
- Systinet

Conclusions   As the collaboration phase of the Web services adoption model becomes a mainstream focus for organizations, the Web services development tools vendors may be able to exert more influence over the composition of complex, long-running Web services that span corporate firewalls and multiple organizations. But for now, in the big picture of the IT value chain and the Web services value chain, the large software vendors will most likely command the high ground of Web services development.

Directory Services

Remember calling the help desk for password resets? Remember filling out individual paper forms and sending them to various departments in order to gain access to corporate systems? Directory solutions, also referred to as registries, seek to overcome the challenges associated with proprietary management of identity and access control used by individual applications. Directories provide the ability to share identity information across application and business boundaries, allowing the creation of an organization-wide directory that can be used to more effectively maintain the following:

- Identity management
- User and resource provisioning
- Personalization and user profiling
- Authentication and security
- Reuse of identities across applications for customer satisfaction and cross-selling of products and services

The directory vendors represent a mix of platform vendors, development tools vendors, software infrastructure vendors, and others. While directory vendors are more infrastructure and platform-like than other elements of the Web services landscape, they are an important enabler for support of UDDI registries. For example, Novell Corporation has already released a UDDI-compliant version of its e-Directory product. Directory-based plays have interesting opportunities available to them based on the eventual use of UDDI in the Web services adoption model. Directory vendors such as Novell, Sun Microsystems (via iPlanet), Microsoft (Active Directory), IBM, and Netscape (also iPlanet) are actively promoting directories as part of their Web services positioning.

As directories are increasingly deployed as a key facet of IT architectures, organizations will begin to leverage these assets as publishing clearing houses for internal content other than identity information. As UDDI standards evolve, directories will be used as the publishing mechanism for internal Web services. Eventually, when UDDI is augmented with emerging security standards and related technologies for Web services, public directories will increasingly be used to search for, locate, and provide Web services across the Web.

Vendor Landscape From a Web services perspective, it is clear that UDDI registries are a sweet spot for directory vendors. Although we have discussed directory-centric strategies separate from the other vendor categories, they really are part of the platform vendor space and are increasingly being provided by application server vendors such as IBM, BEA, iPlanet, Oracle, and others. While the UDDI standards are not yet evolved enough to drive significant Web services adoption, this is a future play based on the evolution of the security standards and eventual maturation of UDDI. Novell, for example, will bundle its directory with the SilverStream Web services platform. IBM will add directory capabilities to its WebSphere platform, and Sun offers directory services as part of its iPlanet application server. Again, directories have been isolated here to highlight their importance relative to the evolution of UDDI registries, and should not be considered as totally distinct from the platform vendor category.

Vendors to Watch The following is a list of the major directory vendors to watch (in alphabetical order):

- IBM
- Microsoft
- Novell—*see below for vendor spotlight*
- Oracle
- Systinet
- Sun

Novell has been one of the early pioneers in development of directory-based solutions with its e-Directory product. Novell and the e-Directory product are discussed further below.

Vendor Spotlight: Novell e-Directory Novell has a long history of providing software infrastructure products, from its once market-leading NetWare Network Operating System (NOS) to more recent software products, most notably e-Directory. According to market research, Novell's e-Directory product is among the industry's best Lightweight Directory Access Protocol (LDAP) directory servers available today. Based on this market-leading directory presence, Novell has begun to aggressively position e-Directory as a UDDI registry. When combined with Novell's acquisition of SilverStream Software's Extend product, Novell now has the application server and development tools to be a serious contender for the emerging Web services market.

The SilverStream acquisition added the following software components to Novell's existing product portfolio:

- J2EE application server
- Visual IDE for rapid application development (or integrated services environment, ISE, as SilverStream called it), that exports a run-time application that will run on IBM's WebSphere application server or on BEA's WebLogic application server
- Light EAI module for tapping into back-end legacy environments and exposing them as Web services or as enterprise Java beans
- Application toolset for portal development, content management, data transformation, and integration to legacy systems

When these capabilities are added to Novell's directory strategy, as well as its metadirectory product, DirXML, Novell has to be considered as a serious player in the emerging Web services space. Only time will tell whether Novell has the staying power to leverage its directory product leadership as a competitive advantage in the Web services market. As Novell's historical NOS leadership continues to be eroded by Microsoft and Sun Microsystems, among others, Novell will have to rely more heavily on newer software products in its portfolio, including BorderManager, iChain, ZENworks, and products added through its silverstream acquisition.

Novell's ongoing viability will depend much on its ability to reposition itself for the Web services market. Conspicuously absent from many of the early Web services standards efforts, Novell recently submitted a specification for use of LDAP directories with the UDDI standard. Adoption of UDDI standards have been slow, giving Novell time to develop a strong Web services strategy to position itself in the UDDI registry space.

Conclusions From a strategic perspective, directories should be considered as part of a service-oriented architecture. Adding a directory server is an incremental approach toward centrally managing and identifying information for all enterprise applications, as opposed to maintaining silos of identity information within each individual application. Because a directory strategy provides the identity provisioning functionality for an organization's application and messaging systems, it is a natural extension to add UDDI registry functionality to directory solutions.

To date, UDDI registry adoption has been slow. The real need for Web services registries will not become apparent until organizations begin to develop a portfolio of Web services. As the number of available Web services increases, the complexity of services management will become overwhelming, spurring the rapid adoption of UDDI registries. This category will likely see tremendous growth once widespread adoption of Web services begins. However, we anticipate a lag during the next year and accelerated adoption moving into 2004.

Network Management and Application Hosting

The final group of vendors to be discussed is the network management and application-hosting vendors. These are a diverse set of vendors that provide an important function in the emerging Web services arena: They provide a secure and trusted runtime environment for operating Web services on behalf of the service requestors. The list of vendors is small but growing, and includes some venerable organizations as well as startups.

The fundamental requirement here is a secure virtual location to operate Web services built from multiple service providers, on behalf of service requestors, via service brokers—think back to the provider, requester, broker network introduced in Chapter 7.

Vendor Landscape The incumbents here include vendors such as GE Global Exchange Services, and EDI services bureaus that specialize in managing high volumes of transactions for large customers over secure, private networks. These vendors have trusted relationships with an extensive customer base, and have a proven track record of managing corporate data and transactions on behalf of their clients.

More recent entrants include Flamenco Networks, Grand Central Communications, Viacore, and Kenamea. These vendors provide hosted services that connect to their customer systems and provide hub-like exchange services based on Web services standards. These vendors provide Web services provisioning, security, and authentication, as well as more sophisticated functionality, such as data transformation and process workflow. As more complex Web services are assembled from multiple service brokers and service providers, again depending on the level of maturation of Web services standards, these vendors will become more powerful in the overall Web services value chain.

Conclusions While there are venerable companies in this category, the startups will have some advantage by not carrying forward legacy EDI infrastructure. On the other hand, the incumbents have deep experience in managing high volume transactions successfully for their large, Global 1000 clients. Positioning for the eventual Web services market is going to rely on development of many Web services standards, and some of these vendors may be in the mode of, *"If we build it, they will come."* If Web services do not mature in the ways these new hosting organizations expect, or if organizations are slow in adopting Web services in the volumes required to support all of these new ventures, then they will likely find that they do not have economically viable business models.

Remember the Application Services Providers (ASP)? Hosting is a challenging business if based on a rapidly emerging technology with volatile standards. The Web services adoption model suggests that until the collaboration phase is reached by a large number of early adopters, and the underlying Web services standards are in place, these vendors will have very low-volume businesses for the next few years.

Emerging Category

Beyond the seven core categories discussed in the previous sections, an eighth emerging category of "Web Services Backbones and Content Hubs" bears mention here. This category provides hybrid solutions that blend the functionality of EAI, content aggregation, transformation and distribution with directory-driven personalization, and multi-channel, multi-format distribution. These vendors fall outside the traditional EAI category as they specialize in hub-based content and transaction management rather than pure application integration. They seek to combine the best of a number of different categories in a single capability.

Vendors in this emerging category include Forum Systems, Kenamea, KnowNow, and StreamServe, among others. It is likely that additional vendors will appear in this category as organizations realize that the aggregation, transformation, and distribution of information to multi-channel receivers can be used to preserve the traditional business transaction channels of trading partners, regardless of their size and interface capabilities.

For example, StreamServe provides solutions built on XML-based transformation, bringing to its customers:

- *Connectivity*—to industry-leading ERP and back-end enterprise systems
- *Content Aggregation, Transformation, and Distribution*—based on a personalization engine (LDAP directory-based) that allows "recipient-driven personalization," or the receivers of content to determine the ways they want to receive it
- *Multi-Channel and Multi-Format Distribution*—using EDI, XML/SOAP, Email, SMS to mobile devices, HTTP, fax, and print
- *Business Rules Engine*—that allows complex processes to be modeled and orchestrated based on processing content transformations and distribution rules
- *Web Services Support*—for XML, SOAP, WSDL, as well as planned support for Web services workflow management with BPEL4WS

Conclusions This category represents a hybrid solution that uses an XML processing engine at the core of a hub and spoke-based architecture. Vendors in this category seek to deliver solutions that preserve the existing business transaction channels while providing leading edge Web services support. Although this emerging category will likely provide important capability for the transition from the integration phase to the collaboration phase of the Web services adoption, it is likely the EAI vendors will aggressively pursue capability in this category in an effort to further their Web services ambitions and position for growth beyond the integration phase.

SUMMARY

The vendors are numerous, and the standards and technology are shifting rapidly along with the multitude of Web services standards. In this chapter, we have tried to illustrate how the categories of tools and applications might fit into an organization's systems architecture and application portfolio. Based on the initial adoption phases identified in the Web services adoption model, the power positions in the Web services value chain will likely be held by four major vendor categories:

1. *Platform Vendors*—such as IBM, Microsoft, Oracle, Sun, and Hewlett-Packard
2. *Enterprise Software Vendors*—such as SAP, Oracle, PeopleSoft, and Siebel
3. *EAI Vendors*—such as WebMethods, TIBCO, Vitria, and SeeBeyond
4. *Application Server Vendors*—such as BEA, IBM, and Oracle

As discussed, the high-level analysis of the vendors in this chapter is not a definitive prediction of which categories and vendors will be the winners or losers in the battle for the Web services market and mind share. Rather, this chapter represents an attempt to place the major vendors into a business perspective and to facilitate the objective analysis of which vendors are most likely to gain leadership in the emerging Web services market. For now, anticipated Web services adoption favors the four categories of vendors we have highlighted, but as more companies move into the collaboration phase, new entrants may wrestle for control of the market.

For consumers of Web services technology, our advice is to maintain a business value and return on investment perspective of the various vendor categories and solutions. Do not buy into a vendor's product set because of where they say they are going. Rather, focus on short- to medium-term business payback, ideally with a one-year to 18-month horizon, while maintaining a clear focus on the compelling business problems you hope to tackle.

Considering the vendor categories discussed in this chapter, consider those vendors that can be trusted and have consistently delivered as opposed to those who have a questionable track record. Make partnering decisions based on primary platform partners, enterprise software partners, and augment these with specific technology solutions from the startups that really have a best-of-breed approach that the larger vendors have been slow to grasp. Anticipate where the power in the IT and Web services value chains will migrate based on the rapid evolution of the software products as well as the standards, and choose partners accordingly. Again, and this cannot be emphasized enough, make these decisions from a business perspective, and do not be tempted by technological "silver bullets." Experience has demonstrated that they do not exist.

ENDNOTE

[1] Web Services Architect, April 17 2002, *Enterprise Resources Planning and Web Services*, "Ease of Integration and Reduction in Costs through the Hosted Application Model" by Kapil Apshankar, p. 2.

CHAPTER 9

The End Is Only the Beginning

"This is not the end. It is not even the beginning of the end. But it is, perhaps, the end of the beginning."

Sir Winston Churchill, November 10, 1942

By now it should be clear that Web services are not hype, but they are also not a "silver bullet" for information technology. We believe that Web services *will* become a business reality based on the compelling business value that they can deliver and based on the industry-wide support they have garnered from major software and platform vendors such as IBM, Microsoft, HP-Compaq, Oracle, and BEA, to name a few. The specifics of how Web services will evolve and spread into our daily work and personal lives will unfold over the coming years as standards stabilize and corporations come to grips with Web services.

This book began with a simple goal: to explain Web services to the executive reader, presenting a balanced view of Web services to allow the reader to evaluate the potential value of Web services and initiate appropriate action within their organization. That challenge has not been an easy one. As this manuscript was prepared, standards came and went, acronyms changed and morphed, and the industry hype machine churned out the spin on Web services. Research on Web services has been a real-time experience as we watched new ideas emerge from industry factions, standards groups, and vendors, each promoting their own particular perspective and claims as to what Web services are and will become. We have sought to separate vendor and media hype from reality, explain what Web services are, and how they work, and help potential adopters evaluate, *from a business perspective*, how they may impact organizations. We have avoided brash predictions, and have not painted glorious visions of how

Web services will unfold. We have, however, tried to develop a consolidated view of how Web services might be adopted by organizations, both from a short-term, "What should I do today?" and a long-term, "What do I need to consider for the future?" perspective.

We began our journey with a dialog between a CEO and CIO. This dialog was meant to symbolize two things. First, we suggest that it is indeed possible for a CEO to team with a CIO in delivering business performance to an organization. The notion of IT and business users working together to create business value and competitive advantage, based on more effective use of information assets, processes, and capabilities, is not new. However, it could be argued that such an approach has been hampered by the failure to leverage IT as a strategic resource. Second, this dialog was intended to emphasize this book's intent to take a business-oriented perspective on Web services, not purely a technology-based perspective. We believe the adoption of Web services will be better achieved through the demonstration of businesses' benefit, not based on the technological elegance of Web services.

We then introduced the Web services adoption model to describe the phases in which Web services are likely to be adopted by organizations into their business operations. The Web services adoption model represents our perspective of how Web services will be deployed in organizations over the next several years—based on current adoption patterns and vendor capabilities. The specifics of how each step in the adoption model will eventually play out will likely differ in specific details, but the broad steps in the path toward Web services adoption are clear.

- *Phase 1: Integration*—Why is integration the first phase? It provides low-hanging fruit, but also mainly because it is an on-going challenge for many organizations today. Using Web services to tackle integration issues can save money and enable improved business performance. For these reasons, integration is a natural starting point for Web services adoption.
- *Phase 2: Collaboration*—Collaboration has been a talking point for many years, but has not delivered on its promise due to the immaturity of tools, as well as a lack of supporting standards. Web services remove many of the remaining barriers to the mainstream use of collaboration between organizations.
- *Phase 3: Innovation*—The innovation phase represents a level of capability, an accumulation of skills, as organizations explore how Web services can deliver business benefit both as an integration strategy and as a collaboration platform. The innovation phase will spark tremendous growth in Web services adoption as new business processes are created, and as new business models are devised. A new business landscape will emerge as organizations identify creative

applications for Web services, and new ways of conducting business. This phase is significant as it represents a maturation of Web services in their practical, everyday usage by organizations.

■ *Phase 4: Domination*—Finally, the domination phase is where organizations will establish themselves as market leaders through their ability to leverage Web services into new forms of a competitive advantage. The domination stage will be characterized by the separation of the leaders from the pack of competitors. This phase of Web services adoption will be based on high levels of accumulated skills and experience with Web services in driving the business models of the winners.

As we learned in Chapter 2, Web services standards are evolving and emerging at a rapid pace. The Web services standards framework breaks down the relevant standards into three levels—enabling, evolving, and emerging. The enabling standards are the classical Internet standards augmented by XML as a meta language. The evolving level includes the SOAP, WSDL, and UDDI standards, which have gained widespread support and are progressively being refined. The emerging level contains those remaining standards that are yet to gain widespread industry adoption.

The rate of Web services adoption will be determined somewhat by how evolving and emerging standards develop over time. If the technology and standards do not enable businesses to operate more effectively, then they will become a gating factor for Web services adoption. Assuming that standards continue to evolve rapidly, and reach maturity, then we will witness tremendous adoption of Web services through the integration, collaboration, innovation, and domination phases.

Web services will be increasingly used to enable business processes that drive the use of information-based business models. A real challenge for many organizations will be determining what business problems to attack first. We have devised a number of frameworks to help organizations target their first Web services projects, as well as help them determine where to expand their Web services efforts following their first successful pilot program.

We have considered Web services from a business strategy perspective, creating a high-level view of how business models can be modified or enhanced using Web services. This strategic view of Web services again reinforces our fundamental premise of business value driving Web services adoption, not technological sophistication. Web services will enable new business models to be crafted, as well as driving greater performance from existing business models.

We have used value chain analysis in our view of Web services. We feel that Web services possess real opportunities for organizations to take costs out of processes through the widespread use of Web services across the full spectrum of operations. Value chain analysis is one way to understand the ways in which Web services may shift the value equation for corporations, fundamentally altering the makeup of the core business processes, as well as the ways that participants in industry-value chains interoperate in industry-wide processes and intercompany processes.

The strategic view of Web services shows how corporate strategy and the resultant business model can leverage Web services in innovative ways. Once corporate strategy and the business model have been infused with Web services, the organization and structures of the firm can be injected with Web services to enable the business model. Breaking down of the company's value chain and the IT value chain will determine how costs can be reduced, how customers can be reached in new and innovative ways, and how suppliers can be tied into the organization to add new value.

Value chains have been around for a long time, but they have not been rigorously applied to the processes of information technology or to the processes that deliver information value to the business operations of a organization. This is a new application of value-chain analysis, and viewing Web services in this fashion provides a helpful lens in ascertaining the potential impact of Web services on the business and IT operations of an organization. This is especially important because many of the processes for creating and deploying Web services will be new for organizations. Therefore, the use of value chains may help shed some light on how the normal processes of information delivery will change.

We also have articulated a vertical market of how Web services may be adopted. Chapter 5 discusses how to begin analyzing the opportunities for using Web services to improve business processes. Based on the industry an organization competes in, as well as the company structure, a firm can leverage Web services in ways that enhance its ability to participate in an industry through its interaction with suppliers, customers, and other trading partners. In addition, this chapter examines the structure of the organization, which has bearing on its ability to compete within an industry. These forces of business have a definite impact on business processes that may benefit from the use of Web services.

Once the strategic and value chain and vertical market perspectives are understood, only then can organizations really begin the detailed planning for their first Web services project. Chapter 6 explores how a business can determine where to begin with Web services. Separating the hype from the reality of Web services is critical for realistically evaluating the organization's ability to implement Web services in useful and beneficial ways. Clearly, evaluating an emerging technology must be done only after the appropriate due diligence has been performed.

In Chapter 7, we discuss the enterprise architecture and the case for implementation of an enterprise architecture using Service-Oriented

Architecture (SOA) principles. Having the necessary infrastructure and an appropriate hardware, software, and application architecture are critical for beginning the transition to Web services. Beyond the enterprise architecture discussion, Chapter 7 compares the virtues of Microsoft's .NET versus the J2EE paradigm which will become increasingly irrelevant as the capabilities of Web services expand beyond internal integration and into true inter-enterprise collaboration, and then on to the remaining phases of Web services adoption. In the end, the programming methods used will be of lower importance if the standards assuring interoperability are adhered to and embraced.

Chapter 8 presents a vendor survey representing various categories of vendors and their respective approaches to Web services. In many respects, we are witnessing a turf war for Web services mind share, which is, of course, far ahead of the market's readiness for Web services. There are early adopters exploring Web services and kicking the tires on emerging standards and technology, which we clearly encourage. However, in a tight economy and with discretionary spending constrained as it is, most organizations are not straying too far from their trusted vendors of choice—the platform providers and enterprise software vendors. This chapter represents a point-in-time, high-level overview of software vendors, and highlights the current vendor categories with account control of the corporate IT budgets—enterprise software vendors, platform providers, application server vendors, and the enterprise application integration vendors.

There is a battle looming with Web services as the prize, and how these vendors are positioning for battle is important for companies seeking to invest in Web services as early adopters. Of course, as with any emerging market space, there is the usual gaggle of new entrants and start-ups with hopes of making their own mark on the computing world, or at least with hopes of being acquired by the 800-pound gorillas. These new entrants fill the smaller gaps in the solutions offered by the existing established vendors, and in that way they are rapidly shaping the world of Web services, creating new categories of software, and providing new functions to facilitate the use of Web services.

Naturally, Darwinian selection will ensure that the fittest organizations survive—those that have compelling feature sets and unique value propositions will last, and those that are simply hoping to be acquired will not. This much is true: These niche vendors are providing a tremendous service in expanding the current capabilities of the existing software giants while ensuring that Web services remain vibrant and free from the inertia of those whose interests Web services may harm. The defense of their markets and control of corporate IT budgets will be the motivating force that drives legacy technology providers, and the new entrants will seek to dethrone them or be bought.

We now come to a set of recommendations for potential buyers and users of Web services. These are simple, concise thoughts to bear in mind as firms dive into the Web services fray:

- Embrace the idea of Web services and what they promise, yet maintain a healthy skepticism of vendor claims and industry hype.
- Always ask yourself, "What will Web services do for my business?"
- Then ask yourself, "How will Web services help me serve my customers?"
- Seek business value and ROI in Web services, but realize that in the fast-moving early stages of adoption, there may not be a clear payback in hard dollars, but there may be a hard payback (or cost avoidance) in the lessons learned.
- Put on a CEO and CIO hat for a moment, and ask yourself, how would you justify a Web services project to yourself? Is there business value to be found? Is there a business reason for the investment?
- Map out your organization's value chain, and examine the areas where Web services can alter the way in which you deliver value to customers. Map out your IT value chain, and define how IT can provide better value to the business. This will ensure that a business perspective will be the foundation for your Web services activities.
- Watch the vendor community from a number of perspectives. Remember that the platform vendors and enterprise software vendors have motives that are different from the new entrants in the Web services market space. Some seek to change the balance of power in the IT industry, while some seek to maintain their control over the hearts and minds of IT executives. Anticipate how vendors will respond to Web services, and use this motive-based evaluation to decide who your partners will be for support of your Web services strategy and technology decisions.
- Maintain as many strategic and architectural degrees of freedom as possible. Avoid lock-in scenarios into which some vendors will try to box you. Web services are about interoperability and breaking down barriers to communication between applications within an enterprise, as well as across enterprise boundaries and corporate firewalls.
- Finally, get started with your Web services strategy and do not wait. This is the time to plan and experiment, and a bunker mentality now will cause negative consequences in the future. Experiment and learn about Web services as soon as possible to help ensure that a basic competency level exists within your organization. Finally, it will be critical to ensure that both business and IT leaders partner with each other to ensure that Web services are used to unlock and fully enable the business potential of your organization.

EPILOGUE (ONE YEAR LATER)

It is Friday. In the CEO's office, Bob Dunston is pleased following a hectic, yet exhilarating week. He had just come from a board meeting, and he was pleased with their reaffirmation of his strategy and direction for the firm. The good news is that the quarterly results reflected these decisions. Earnings were up 12 percent over the same quarter last year, and revenue grew an astounding 15 percent despite the difficult economy and the integration of an acquisition Dunston's firm made earlier in the year.

"Nobody thought we could do it," he chuckled to himself. "Wait until next quarter."

With that, he punched up Bill Sedgewick on the speakerphone while he unwrapped a Snickers mini and opened a bottled water.

After one ring, Sedgewick's voice boomed over the speakerphone. "Hi, Bob. What's up?" Dunston could hear Sedgewick tapping away on his computer keyboard, his chair squeaking as he leaned into the speakerphone to talk.

"Bill, do you have a couple of minutes? I wanted to recap a few things from the week and prep for next week's staff meeting."

"Sure, Bob, be right there." The phone line goes dead, and Dunston clicks over to voicemail while he waits for Sedgewick to walk across the building. As he scans his messages, he recalls the year the firm has had. First, there was the acquisition of the number-three competitor in their industry, which had worried many investors and analysts because of the timing and the industry downturn. Then there was the series of business initiatives that Sedgewick's team supported with Web services. Between the inventory management portal, the customer and supplier self-service initiatives, and the M&A integration project, the IT organization had not only responded to a huge project load, but had excelled in engaging the business leaders and users in the dialog. What's more, these projects were completed more or less on time, which was not the norm for this firm in the pre-Sedgewick days.

"The guy is worth his weight in gold," Dunston thinks to himself. "Hmmm, I'll have to do something special, a nice bonus or something." Then he caught himself, amazed at the changes that IT had been able to achieve in this company in such a short time. It hadn't been that long since the previous VP of IT was vilified by the business leadership for his failure to deliver on any of the promises IT made to the business. In those not-so-distant days, IT was the scourge of the firm, and the standard jokes of IT ineptitude were the theme of many a conversation in the company cafeteria. Those days were long gone, however, and the new IT organization had established an early track record of success with the business leaders and user community unmatched in the firm's history.

A knock on Dunston's door brings him out of his reverie, and Sedgewick saunters into Bob's office and slides into a chair at the conference room table. His sinewy arm snaked across the table toward the candy jar, plucking a Baby Ruth from the mix and unwrapping it with considerable skill.

"So, Bob, when did you switch from Snickers to Baby Ruths?" Sedgewick's inquiry is delivered with a wry grin and a chuckle. "These are good. Keep up the good work." They both laugh at this, while Dunston sat down at the smaller, round conference table in the corner of his office.

Their relationship had warmed considerably over the last two years, and especially so during the year in which so much of the company's success had been attributed to their close partnership in making business and technology decisions together, and enlisting the complete and unwavering support of the entire corporation in their pursuit of the new company strategy.

Dunston put on a serious face. "Bill, we've had quite a year here haven't we? I keep thinking back to our conversation about Web services over a year ago, and to me that signaled a change for our company in how we were going to drive our business. I don't know if you've recognized it, but I certainly have, as have the other members of the management team, and especially the board."

Sedgewick's assault on the candy jar stops now, and he settles into a thoughtful expression as he intently listens to his boss and good friend.

"Just taking care of business, Boss," Sedgewick allowed, looking down briefly before re-engaging eye contact with Dunston. Sedgewick is too experienced to let one good year of success paint a career for him. However, he does feel his team has had a great year in delivering the business initiatives and results that were expected of him. He is indeed pleased.

Dunston continues. "I think you underestimate the impact you and your team have had on the company, and I want you to know that it is recognized by everyone. The quarterly results, as well as the business performance for the whole year, have a lot to do with the business activities your team has supported with the IT organization.

"The work your team did in educating the executive staff on Web services was great. That got the team thinking about our business in new ways, and in ways that leveraged IT to drive our business performance to new levels. The strategy for M&A that you devised was instrumental to absorbing the acquisition of TransTech, and Web services was key to driving that integration strategy. There's no way we could have done that without your leadership and vision. Web services are a great example of that because we were clearly early adopters. I had no idea that an emerging technology, applied in a business sense, could drive such tremendous business impact for any organization, much less ours."

Sedgewick, clearly uncomfortable with such high praise, shifts in his chair.

"Bob, first of all, it was clearly a team effort, not only the IT team but the combined forces of business and IT. That is the most important critical success factor here, the melding of the business and IT leadership into a cohesive organization seeking new ways to drive business results. Web services have been an enabler, not a magic potion. But as I have always maintained, the right technology, when applied to a business scenario and measured by business value, will lead to positive business results, period. That lesson has yet to be learned by many executives, but we've got a leg up on our competition and certainly on many other corporations in any industry."

Dunston nodded his head, agreeing with everything Sedgewick said. "But Bill, I want you to take more credit than you have been. You helped make it happen by providing the vision and leadership we needed. There's no way we would have listened to this strategy had it come from the previous VP of IT. You engaged the business, and delivered the business results with the leadership and support of IT. We all know it."

"Jeez, Bob, does this mean I get a bonus this year?" Sedgewick laughed as he said this.

Bob stood up, assuming a sober business-like expression. "Bill, I think you already know the answer to that question. Congratulations on a great year, and I'm looking forward to many more with you at the helm of the IT and business team. By the way, have you ever considered being a CEO someday?"

The color drained from Sedgewick's face as he absorbed this question. "You're not serious, are you?" he stammerd, his eyes wide with disbelief.

Dunston replies, laughingly clapping Sedgewick on the shoulder. "Yes, I am, but not just yet. I'm just getting started here, but I think you should think about that possibility and let's slot some time to discuss getting you groomed for an operations role soon."

With that, Sedgewick stood and reached for the candy jar once more as he walked out the door.

Dunston shook his head, chuckling to himself. "Yes, he will make a great CEO one day, and he certainly helped make me one. Yes, a nice bonus and a promotion are in store for Bill."

index